COMMENTARY ON THE NEW LECTIONARY

Revised Edition
VOLUME 1

COMMENTARY ON
THE NEW LECTIONARY

A scriptural and liturgical guide
to the two-year cycle of readings
for Holy Communion on Sundays
and Holy Days

Revised Edition

VOLUME 1
Ninth Sunday before Christmas to
Easter Day

JOHN GUNSTONE

London SPCK

First published in 1973
Revised edition 1979
to accord with the
Alternative Calendar and Lectionary

SPCK
Holy Trinity Church
Marylebone Road
London NW1 4DU

Printed and bound in Great Britain at
The Camelot Press Ltd, Southampton

ISBN 0 281 03738 8

Did we not feel our hearts on fire
as he talked with us on the road and
explained the scriptures to us?

CONTENTS OF VOLUME 1

ACKNOWLEDGEMENTS

Acknowledgements are due to the Faith Press Ltd, Leighton Buzzard, for permission to use material from two of my books, *The Feast of Pentecost* and *Christmas and Epiphany*, published in 1967, and to the Church Literature Association, 199 Uxbridge Road, London W.12, for permission to use material from two booklets, *Lent* and *Holy Week and Easter*, published by them in 1969.

Quotations from the New English Bible 2nd Edition © 1970 are made by permission of the Oxford and Cambridge University Presses.

INTRODUCTION

This book is a scriptural and liturgical guide to the *Alternative Calendar and Lectionary* now in use in the Church of England.[1] The scheme of lessons was originally published by the Joint Liturgical Group in Britain as *The Calendar and Lectionary*, edited by R. C. D. Jasper (Oxford 1967), which has been used in various denominations throughout the world as well as in Britain. The scheme of lessons is, then, an ecumenical project of considerable significance. When the Churches read and expound the same passages of scripture on Sundays and Festivals across the world, they are demonstrating a unity in the proclamation of the gospel of Jesus Christ which offers many opportunities for united teaching and evangelism.

The Group drew up the lectionary on a two-year cycle with an Old Testament lesson, an epistle, and a gospel for each Sunday and Holy Day. In selecting the readings, they worked on the principle of letting one of the lessons guide them in the choice of the other two. This reading is called 'the controlling lesson', and is distinguished in this commentary by an asterisk placed to the left of the reference at the heading of the passage to be commented on. During the pre-Christmas period (nine weeks) the OT lesson is the controlling one, from Christmas to Whitsunday it is the gospel, and for the rest of the year it is the reading from the Acts or the epistles. With this structure in mind, they composed a lectionary trying to keep in balance the Church's traditions and present-day needs. In adapting this lectionary for the Church of England the Liturgical Commission has made some modifications after a period of experimentation that began in 1968 but without disturbing the general principles behind the work of the Joint Liturgical Group.

The ministry of the word of God has its own long tradition in Christian worship which cannot be ignored if we are to hear what the Spirit is saying to the churches in our day. The reading and exposition of scripture is intimately linked with the evolution of the Christian year, so this book begins with a brief survey of how the calendar and lessons developed, especially with reference to the eucharistic liturgy. This should give preachers and readers something of the 'feel' of the days and the seasons. Over the centuries time has been sanctified by the way in which the

---

[1] The new readings are authorized alternatives to those of the Book of Common Prayer, which retain full legal authority. In its complete form, the Alternative Lectionary contains, besides the provisions for Holy Communion covered in this commentary, lessons for Morning and Evening Prayer both on Sundays and on weekdays.

Church has been led to reflect on different aspects of the work of our redemption through the year. Though tradition must never be a burden, yet respect for it as a living heritage can give us a glimpse of that vision which the author of the Letter to the Hebrews had when he spoke of 'all these witnesses to faith around us like a cloud'. A particular passage was read on a certain day because it spoke to our forefathers in the faith on that occasion. On that same day it may well speak to us also. Our past is part of ourselves, and tradition is still one of the ways in which the Holy Spirit guides us as we move forward on our pilgrimage to 'the city which is to come'. The first section of this book, The Christian Year and the Lectionary, may help us to assess the value of the past in this respect.

Each passage of scripture is then given a short commentary. I should stress that these commentaries are not intended to be sermons. Rather, I hope that they will do something that biblical commentaries are intended to do when a sermon is being prepared. At this point I must say that I owe an enormous debt of gratitude to those scholars whose understanding of scripture is far deeper than mine can ever be; their books have supplied so much of what is in this volume. It has been impossible to acknowledge in footnotes where each explanation or suggestion about a word or a passage originated, much as I would have liked to do this.

I have used the New English Bible as the basic text, though where it seemed helpful I have referred to the Revised Standard Version and the Jerusalem Bible. The quotations from the passage commented on are printed in heavy type. Other quotations are between inverted commas. Where only the chapter and/or the verse numbers are given, it means that they refer to the book of the Old or New Testament from which the passage has been taken.

This book will not, I imagine, ever be read from cover to cover in a short space of time. It is more likely to be picked up for reference week by week. I have therefore tried to make each set of commentaries for a particular day self-explanatory, with some repetition and occasional references to other parts of the book. The length of the commentary depends on what a lesson contains and what I felt might be useful to make notes on.

The new lectionary is part of that great movement to enable the people of God in the latter part of the twentieth century to respond to God in worship and living. We can no longer rely solely on the past. It is true that through liturgical scholarship we have recovered the simplicity and directness of the early Church's worship—which is why a knowledge of the past is as important in the revision of a lectionary as it is for, say, a eucharistic prayer—but in applying what we have learnt to the needs of today and the possibilities for tomorrow, we require the creativity and inspiration of the Holy Spirit. Only then will Christian congregations worship in spirit and in truth.

It is helpful to remember that every act of worship is essentially an assembly of the people of God to hear the word of God and to respond to him by participation in the Christian cultus, and in their daily lives. The presentation of the word of God is based on the reading of select passages of scripture. These can be expounded in the normal manner through a sermon or a discussion (if the congregation is a small one in a house group) and their meaning demonstrated with the use of further non-scriptural readings, visual aids, dramatic and musical presentations, and so on. But all additional material should be presented in such a way that it enables the congregation to 'hear' the word of God in Isaiah's sense of 'hearing'.

But it is equally important to exercise care and sensitivity in the choice of other material with which congregations can articulate their response to that word. The receiving of Holy Communion is, of course, the climax of that response, and its implications are worked out in the course of ordinary living during the days following the act of worship; but the people must be given words to say or to sing so that they can lift up their hearts and minds to God in praise for what he has done, is doing, and is going to do. For what we hear in the scripture readings are the words of eternal life, and our response to those readings in worship is powerfully effective in building up our faith. The clergy and those who plan worship are the servants of God and of his people in this respect as well—they must be led by the Holy Spirit, not only to write the sermon, but also to select the right psalm, canticle, or hymn which will enable the congregation to respond to God for what they hear in the ministry of the word. And this is especially vital in those gatherings for worship where there is no opportunity for any spontaneous response.

At the beginning of the service, therefore, the congregation must be helped to prepare to receive the word of God. The purpose of the first hymn is not to give the congregation something to do while the choir, the minister, and his assistants enter the church; it is to create in them a feeling of expectancy and an assurance of acceptance by God and by each other. New rites like the Alternative Service Book provide seasonal sentences as overtures to the main theme of the day. There is no reason why another key phrase or sentence from the readings should not be used for this purpose. A rubric in the Roman Catholic mass suggests that the celebrant or some other suitable person should briefly introduce the subject of the readings so that the congregation may listen or follow the lessons in their Bibles more intelligently. A pause after each reading encourages the members of the congregation to reflect upon what they have heard. The hymn, canticle, or psalm between the readings (if there is one: it is not always necessary, even at sung services), provides the congregation with words with which to meditate further on what has been read. The new lectionary suggests psalms and canticles for the different readings. If they cannot be sung without distracting the congregation from the meaning of their words, then it is better to say them, chorally or antiphonally, sitting. Nothing should be allowed to hinder the Holy Spirit as he stirs in those listening to the word of God.

The Second Vatican Council declared that 'like the Christian religion itself, all the preaching of the Church must be nourished and ruled by the scriptures'. Every preacher who uses this book should, I believe, remember this declaration each time he begins to write his notes for a sermon. He will want to comment on one or more of the readings to draw the congregation's attention to those verses or events to which the Holy Spirit has led him as he prayed and prepared for his part in the ministry of the word. The things that Jesus said and did, as revealed in the gospel for the day, will be especially precious to him, and the manner in which he speaks of Christ will stir within the hearts of his hearers a deep love for the Saviour. He will also discuss the mysteries of God with a reverence and humility that convey the awe of the believer in the presence of the Most High. It may be right from time to time not only to expound and comment on the readings, but also to explain why they have been read on a certain day or during a particular season for centuries. That may give the congregation a sense of their oneness with the Body of Christ across the ages. I hope this book will help the preacher to fulfil that aspect of the ministry of the word. The application of scripture to a group or congregation can only be done by the man on the spot, since he knows the attitudes, the backgrounds, and the problems of those he is addressing.

After the sermon the people's response to the word of God still continues. The theme of the readings can be recalled at appropriate points in the service, even in the final hymn. Thoughts and words from the lessons can be included in those parts of the intercessions which have to be composed locally or said spontaneously. The Roman mass has a whole series of proper prefaces which link the readings to the eucharistic prayer. Where it is permitted, as in some of the eucharistic prayers of the Episcopal Church of America, home-made proper prefaces can be written based

4

on the ministry of the word. If silence is kept after communion or at a later part of the service, then it is sometimes effective if the key phrases and sentences of the lessons are read out meditatively for the congregation. This develops the purpose for which material is provided in the seasonal sentences after the communion in the Alternative Service Book.

The ministry of the word, then, is very much more than writing a sermon based on the readings of the day. It is the exercise of those gifts of the Holy Spirit which enable an individual and a team to prepare for and to lead an act of worship in such a way that God's word can be 'alive and active', sifting 'the purposes and thoughts of the heart' among those who assemble for it. It is a ministry through which the Church of Jesus Christ is built up in the Spirit as each congregation recognizes corporately and as individuals that they may 'boldly approach the throne of our gracious God, where we may receive mercy and in his grace find timely help'. For the response of the people is nothing if it is not the response of the Holy Spirit within them, drawing them through the word of God into the presence of God. Then, equipped as 'a chosen race, a royal priesthood, a dedicated nation, and a people claimed by God for his own', they are enabled so to live that they 'proclaim the triumphs of him who has called you out of darkness into his marvellous light'.

THE CHRISTIAN YEAR AND
THE LECTIONARY

Certain passages of scripture are traditionally associated with particular days or seasons in the Christian year. To understand why this is so, it is necessary for us to review briefly the evolution of the calendar as it affected the Church in the West. The readings set for the Sundays and Holy Days in the old missal of the Roman Catholic Church were the basis for the epistles and gospels in the Book of Common Prayer—the variations being due partly to differences in the lectionaries in use in western Europe in medieval times, and partly to some amendments by sixteenth- and seventeenth-century revisers in the Church of England. We can therefore assume for the purposes of this essay that the Book of Common Prayer and all the Prayer Books which have descended from it share in the lectionary of western Christendom, and that is why we have to pay attention to the development of certain liturgical traditions in Rome when that lectionary was in the process of formation. The period during which this formation took place was roughly the fourth to the eighth century.

The most important development was the emergence of Easter as the Christian Passover. This set the pattern for the rest of the liturgical year. We shall therefore discuss first the appearance and significance of the Easter cycle of feasts—Easter Day itself, Holy Week, Lent, and the great Fifty Days, in that order. Then we shall turn to the origins of Christmas and Epiphany and see why they came to be observed in our calendar. Finally we shall deal more briefly with a few of the other Holy Days and special occasions which have lessons assigned to them in the new lectionary.

THE EASTER CYCLE OF FEASTS

Until about the middle of the fourth century, the Christian calendar was a very simple affair. It was marked by a weekly assembly for the Eucharist, and a christianized version of the Jewish Passover; and that was all.

If the absence of festivals in the calendar appears somewhat puritanical to us today, we have to remember that the first generations of Christians associated feast days with the pagan practices of the people among whom they lived. It is calculated that by the beginning of the third century, about one hundred and seventy-five festivals were held every year in Rome.

Many of them had a religious significance, and they were occasions for savage games in the circuses, immoral plays in the theatre, and excesses of various kinds. The Church had no inclination to copy these! That is why Paul warned the Galatians about 'special days and months and seasons and years'. Observances such as these belonged to the time when they were 'slaves to "gods" which in reality do not exist' (4.8, NEB footnote).

The weekly assembly for the Eucharist can be traced back to the New Testament. It took place on 'the first day of the week'. In Jewish society the sabbath was the only free day, so Jewish Christians probably began observing the day of resurrection with a Eucharist by prolonging the sabbath into the night of Saturday-Sunday. By custom a day began at sundown the previous evening. What we would reckon as the end of the sabbath, Saturday night, was in New Testament times the beginning of the next day, the first day of the week. The incident at Troas, when Paul addressed a gathering until well past midnight and then broke bread, suggests something like this. The author of the Book of Revelation refers to 'the Lord's Day', and by the second century its observance was a well-known feature of Church life.

'On the day which is called the Sun's Day', wrote Justin (d. 165), 'there is an assembly of all who live in towns or in the country . . . because it is the first day, on which God put to flight darkness and chaos and made the world; and on the same day Jesus our Saviour rose from the dead.'

EASTER DAY

The origins of Easter are more obscure. It was hardly possible for Christians to ignore the significance of the Passover when it arrived in the spring of each year; the redeeming work of God is focused on this festival, and paschal themes are interwoven within the context of the Church's teaching and devotion. Paul wrote, 'Our Passover has begun; the sacrifice is offered—Christ himself' (he was probably referring to the paschal nature of the eucharistic assembly, not to the celebration of the feast in the year he was writing his letter to the church in Corinth), and the author of the fourth Gospel drew his picture of the mission of the Word made flesh within the framework of three successive Passover festivals. The first Christians, being Jews, must have brought the observance into the new Israel with them.

Be that as it may, the first real evidence for the Church's observance of Easter comes from the middle of the second century, when a controversy arose about the day on which it was to be kept. The churches in Asia observed it on the same day as many Jewish communities, the fourteenth

7

Nisan (March–April), whether this fell on a Sunday or a weekday. Elsewhere Christians kept the feast on the Sunday following the fourteenth Nisan. The details of the controversy need not concern us here, but we notice that from this time references to the *Pascha* begin to appear in Christian letters, treatises, homilies, and liturgical material.

Because of its roots in a Jewish observance, the celebration of Easter has always been a Saturday-night-and-Sunday-morning affair. It was during the night that the paschal mysteries of the Old Testament had taken place (the escape from Egypt and the crossing of the Red Sea) and it was during the night of the first day of the week that the Lord had risen from the dead. Christians kept the Passover, therefore, with a vigil which began at sunset on the Saturday and ended with a Eucharist in the early hours of Sunday morning. During the vigil the catechumens were baptized. It was felt that the sacrament of participation in Christ's death and resurrection was most fittingly administered during the paschal night, and this association with Christian initiation gave the formularies for the vigil, especially the readings, their baptismal theme.

Yet Easter in the early Church was not just a commemorative occasion. The Christian Passover celebrated the Lord's death and resurrection as a here-and-now reality. It was effective in the lives of those who repented and turned to him. The vigil, the baptisms, and the Eucharist represented, in one paschal mystery, the totality of God's saving work in Jesus Christ through the Holy Spirit; and that salvation was offered to the individual on the paschal night. The commemoration of Christ's Passover as a series of historical events was a later development in the Church's life.

In fact, the attitude of early Christians to the vigil and the feast was eschatological rather than historical. They kept Easter expecting the Lord to appear. In the parable of the wise and foolish virgins, the bridegroom came at midnight: the paschal vigil seemed to be the most likely moment in the year when this promise would be fulfilled. So the Church watched for the second coming of Christ on this night and, when the Bridegroom did not appear in his glorious *parousia*, her members met him in the paschal Eucharist instead.

Many different passages of scripture were provided for use during the Easter vigil in the early lectionaries—the story of creation in Genesis 1, the cleansing of Jerusalem in Isaiah 4 (leading into chapter 5, 'I will sing for my beloved a love-song about his vineyard', used as a canticle) and Moses' charge to the people about the book of the covenant, Deuteronomy 31. These passages were chosen because they unfolded the meaning of the baptismal rites which were performed later in the night. But two readings had a special significance. One was Exodus 14, the crossing of the Red Sea—the culmination of the original Passover when God saved his people from the Egyptians. The other was 1 Cor. 5 quoted above, 'Our Passover has begun; the sacrifice is offered—Christ himself'. The former reading is set among the lessons for Easter Day in the new lectionary. The Eucharist at the end of the vigil had as its gospel the Matthean account of the resurrection. When the observance of the vigil was brought forward to Holy Saturday, another Eucharist was provided with either the Marcan or the Johannine account of the resurrection as its gospel. These three accounts are also set for Easter Day in the new lectionary. Other readings, Isa. 12, 1 Cor. 15.12–20, and Rev. 1.12–18, preserve the eschatological character of the feast and remind us that the resurrection of Christ points us forward to the second coming, the last judgement, and the resurrection of Christians.

HOLY WEEK

The controversy about the observance of Easter in the second century also provides us with evidence that the Church prepared for the festival by keeping a fast. Irenaeus, Bishop of Lyons (d. 200), mentioned it in a letter which he wrote to Victor, Bishop of Rome, remonstrating with him for the harsh way he had treated the Asian Quartodecimans: 'Some think they ought to fast one day, some for two, others for still more; some make their "day" last forty hours. . . . In spite of that, they all lived in peace with one another, and so do we: the divergency in the fast emphasizes the unanimity of our faith.'

By the following century the fast had been lengthened to include the week before Easter. The Syrian *Didascalia Apostolorum*, which was supposed to contain the teaching of the twelve apostles, directed that a moderate fast should be kept from the Monday to the Thursday until the ninth hour (3 p.m.) by taking only bread, salt, and water, and that a stricter fast should be kept on the Friday and the Saturday immediately before the paschal vigil. In a letter to Basilides, Bishop of the Churches in Cyrenaica, Bishop Dionysius of Alexandria (d. 264) complained about those who did not keep the six days' fast with equal rigour. Unlike Irenaeus, he evidently did not appreciate the ecumenical principle that unity does not necessarily entail uniformity!

Since the Easter vigil became the major—if not the only—occasion when baptism was normally administered, the catechumens prepared for their initiation by keeping a fast during the days immediately before it.

By pious custom, their sponsors and some of the congregation used to keep the fast with them. This gave the week before Easter the tradition of a corporate fast. Besides this, a weekly fast was kept on Wednesdays and Fridays in some parts of the Church (another inheritance from sectarian Judaism), so a pre-paschal fast would seem only like an annual extension of it.

It was not in any sense commemorative. It was simply a period of preparation for the greatest festival in the year. Yet as early as the third century there was in the *Didascalia Apostolorum* an attempt to explain the significance of the six days' fast observed in Syria in terms of the Passion events: you fasted on Monday because of Judas' betrayal, on Tuesday because of the arrest after the last supper, on Wednesday because of the detention in the house of Caiaphas, on Thursday because of the examination before Pilate, on Friday because of the crucifixion, and on Saturday because of the burial in the sepulchre. Already Christian devotion was beginning to assign historical happenings to particular days; and in the following century this process crystallized.

The historicization of the liturgical year began in Jerusalem because of the circumstances in which the Christians of that city found themselves after the peace of the Church. The emperor Constantine (d. 337) visited the Holy Land and sponsored an ambitious scheme to build churches over the sacred sites associated with the life, death, and resurrection of Jesus Christ. As a result of this scheme, the Church in Jerusalem possessed at the end of the fourth century a number of magnificent basilicas which were the object of wonder and devotion among Christians throughout the empire.

The most important of these churches was a building—or rather a complex of buildings—over the sites of the hill of crucifixion and the sepulchre. From the main street of the city, which roughly coincided with the north-south section of the present Via Dolorosa, the visitor entered a richly furnished basilica known as 'the Place of Witness', the *Martyrium*. Beyond this church at its westward end he passed through doorways into a courtyard containing a baptistry and an outcrop of rock believed to be the original Golgotha. The courtyard then merged into a splendid rotunda called 'the Resurrection', the *Anastasis*, built over the cave where the body of Jesus was supposed to have rested. All that remains of the Martyrium-Anastasis is the Church of the Holy Sepulchre which incorporates a later version of the rotunda; but present-day pilgrims are usually taken to the back of a sweetshop in the Via Dolorosa to see one of the ancient columns which once formed part of the entrance to the

Martyrium. The adjoining Russian Excavations also contain certain remains.

Other basilicas were built on the site of the house with the upper room, the church of the Apostles or *Sion*, in the Garden of Gethsemane where Jesus taught the disciples, the *Eleona*, and on the summit of the mount of Olives, the Church of the Ascension or the *Imbomon*. A church was also constructed at Bethlehem—but we shall notice its importance when we come to discuss the Christmas cycle of feasts.

As people began to make pilgrimages to the Holy Land to visit the sacred sites and the churches, the bishop and the clergy in Jerusalem organized themselves with commendable ingenuity to cater for the spiritual needs of the pilgrims. In the manner of modern tourist agents, they set about providing devotional treats for the travellers with services in the different churches at which passages of scripture were read and prayers offered uniting the worshippers with the saving events associated with that particular place. These services took on a historical and dramatic character during the days before and after the celebration of Easter, and there were special commemorations of the entry of Christ into Jerusalem, the Last Supper, the agony in the garden, the trial and crucifixion, and the burial.

One of these pilgrims at the end of the fourth century was a nun from Spain called Egeria. She remained in Jerusalem throughout Lent and Eastertide and afterwards wrote an account of what she had seen and done for the benefit of her sisters in religion at home. Much of her journal has survived and from it, together with some other material, it is possible to discover in some detail how Jerusalem observed 'the paschal week'. 'Here', said Egeria, 'they call it "the Great Week".'

On the eve of Palm Sunday there was held in Bethany a service commemorating the supper in the house of Simon the leper. Then on Palm Sunday afternoon the people assembled in the church on the mount of Olives for longer devotions. Towards evening there was read to them the gospel of Christ's entry into Jerusalem and a procession moved off towards the city. 'All the children in the neighbourhood, even those who are too young to walk, are carried by their parents on their shoulders', wrote Egeria, 'all of them bearing branches, some of palms and some of olives, and thus the bishop is escorted in the same manner as the Lord was of old.' In later years the role of the bishop was made even more like that of Christ: he rode into the city seated upon a donkey!

During the following weekdays services of readings, hymns, psalms, and prayers were held in the Anastasis. The last office, which began about

4 p.m., included the lighting of candles from a lamp burning before the sepulchre, blessings, and prayers. On Maundy Thursday there was a Eucharist in the late afternoon in the Martyrium at which the account of the last supper was read as the gospel, and then the congregation went out to keep an all night vigil on the mount of Olives, with readings and prayers to commemorate the agony in the garden of Gethsemane, which lies at the foot of the hill.

On the morning of Good Friday the congregation returned to the Martyrium-Anastasis for a special service during which a relic of the Cross—found, it was said, by Constantine's mother Helena, when the Anastasis was being built—was produced in a silver casket for veneration. Egeria described the cremony: 'When it (the relic) has been put on the table, the bishop, as he sits, holds the ends of the sacred wood firmly in his hands, while the deacons who stand around guard it. It is guarded in this way because the custom is that the people, both the faithful and the catechumens, come one by one, and bowing down kiss the sacred wood and pass by. And because, I know not when, someone is said to have bitten off and stolen a piece of the holy wood, it is guarded in this way.' At midday the people assembled round Calvary for a three hours' vigil, ending at 3 p.m. with the reading of the death of Christ from the fourth Gospel.

On the eve of Easter a vigil was kept in the Anastasis; it included the reading of Matt. 27.62–66, the Jews' request to have Christ's tomb sealed (still read on this Saturday in the new lectionary), and the singing of Psalm 88.4, 'I am counted as one of them that go down into the pit', which was interpreted as Christ's prayer as he descended into hell. Then the congregation moved into the Martyrium for the keeping of the paschal vigil, during which the bishop, his clergy, the catechumens, and their sponsors went into the baptistry for the rites of initiation. Finally the Eucharist was celebrated.

Behind these ceremonies and readings, of course, was the intention of re-enacting and sharing in the events of the passion from the entry into Jerusalem to the resurrection, on the day and at the hour when they originally happened; and when the clergy and the pilgrims returned to their own homes, there was an irresistible urge to repeat the services for the benefit of those who could not make the long journey to the Holy Land. Out of this the universal observance of Holy Week grew. In Spain and in Gaul the pattern of the Jerusalem ritual was copied in elaborate detail, and a harmony of the gospels was compiled so that the story of the passion could be read in its fullest dramatic extent.

But the Church in Rome was more conservative. Some ceremonies, such as the Palm Sunday procession, were not introduced until the middle ages. The older tradition in Rome was to point the congregation to the whole mystery of the passion during the week, not to the events narrated in a quasi-chronological order. Leo the Great preached on the passion on Palm Sunday, Wednesday, Good Friday and Easter Day. The reading of the passion according to Matthew on Palm Sunday and that according to John on Good Friday is attested in the first lectionaries.

The Church in Rome achieved a dramatic effect another way. When a passion narrative was read, other lessons were selected to provide a kind of script for the *dramatis personae* involved. The first readings assigned to the Tuesday in Holy Week in the old lectionaries are a good example of this:

I had been like a sheep led obedient to the slaughter; I did not know that they were hatching plots against me and saying, 'Let us cut down the tree while the sap is in it; let us destroy him out of the living, so that his very name shall be forgotten' (from Jer. 11.18–20)

'Let us lay a trap for the just man. . . . He knows God, so he says; he styles himself "servant of the Lord". . . . He boasts that God is his father. . . . Let us test the truth of his words, let us see what will happen in the end; for if the just man is God's son, God will stretch out a hand to him and save him from the clutches of his enemies. . . . Let us condemn him to a shameful death, for on his own showing he will have a protector' (from Wisd. 2.12–22)

Jesus knew that his hour had come and he must leave this world and
-go to the Father. . . (from John 13.1–32).

The special character of Good Friday and Holy Saturday as a two days' intensive fast in preparation for the paschal vigil was recognized from early times. Augustine, Bishop of Hippo (d. 430), called the three days the *sacratissimum triduum crucifixi, sepulti, suscitati*. But Maundy Thursday at first did not have any particular importance. The pope used it as an opportunity for blessing the oils for the rites of initiation to be performed during the paschal vigil; he also absolved those who had been doing penance during Lent to enable them to take their full part in the ceremonies of the next three days. The formularies for these services have survived in the older Roman sacramentaries. In time, the service for the reconciliation of penitents was performed in the stational churches which specialized in penitential discipline, and the pope added to his duties an evening mass in commemoration of the last supper. Eventually this Eucharist also spread to the stational churches in the city and then to all churches where the Roman rite was followed. Maundy Thursday was the last day in Holy Week to receive its distinctive commemoration; and when it did, the gospel of the feet-washing and the accompanying discourse (John 13.1–15) was transferred from the Tuesday to this day. The passion according to Mark was read on Tuesday instead.

There were no Eucharists on weekdays in the Roman Church until the sixth century. The liturgy of the day consisted simply of readings, a homily, and prayers. This ancient liturgy was retained in the Roman rite on Good Friday. The climax of the lessons is the passion according to John and the so-called 'solemn prayers' are the primitive form of offering intercessions to God. The ceremony of the adoration of the cross and the chanting of the Reproaches were imported from the East and added to this ancient liturgy about the seventh century. The custom of receiving communion from the reserved sacrament was also an importation from the East. The Church of England practice of keeping Good Friday with the service of Antecommunion, therefore, is true to the oldest traditions of the western Church.

When we turn to the Alternative Calendar and Lectionary we find that in general these traditions of Holy Week have been preserved. Palm Sunday has the familiar account of the entry into Jerusalem, Matt. 21.1–13, as an extra gospel, to be used as an integral part of the ceremonies of a Palm Sunday procession if required, together with the passion according to Mark. The passion according to Matthew is read as a *lectio continua* during the Monday, Tuesday and Wednesday of Holy Week in Year 1, that according to Luke in Year 2. The songs of the suffering servant of God from Isaiah are read on Palm Sunday, Monday, Tuesday, and Wednesday, and in the epistles we share in the thoughts of Paul and the authors of Hebrews and 1 Peter as they meditated on the significance of the cross. Maundy Thursday commemorates the last supper with the account of the institution of the Passover from Exodus 12 as its Old Testament lesson, 1 Cor. 11.23–29, Paul's account of the last supper, as its epistle, and the narrative of the feet-washing, John 13.1–15, as its gospel. The passion according to John is still in its customary place on Good Friday.

Passiontide has not survived in the modern calendars but something of the spirit of Passion Sunday remains in the Alternative Lectionary's readings for Lent 5.

LENT

While the pre-paschal fast was evolving into Holy Week, its effect was also stretching back to the sixth and seventh weeks before Easter. This, too, influenced what passages of scripture were appointed for these weeks. Much work has been done by liturgists in recent decades to reconstruct the evolution of the Lenten lectionary in Rome in the period from the fourth to the eighth century. Early lists of readings in codices of scripture (*capitula*), epistle books and gospel books, and complete lectionaries have been important sources for the investigation. The oldest list of epistles for the Roman rite comes from a Fulda codex containing the Pauline letters, written between 540 and 546 for Victor, Bishop of Capua. In England the *Lindisfarne Gospels* are an important source. According to G. Morin its annotations reveal the readings of the ancient liturgy of the Church in Naples.

Five elements influenced the choice of readings during Lent.

1 THE CATECHUMENS The first element was the preparation of the catechumens for their baptism at Easter. Even when the number of adult baptisms declined and the baptism of infants became normal, the ancient rites were still performed, though in a truncated form. The most important of these were the 'scrutinies'—services during which the evil powers which, it was believed, possessed all neophytes, were exorcized and the Creed and the Lord's Prayer were formally 'handed over'. In the latter half of the fourth century there were probably three such scrutinies in Rome. Each service was associated with a passage from the fourth Gospel —the Samaritan woman at the well (John 4.5–42), the man born blind (John 9.1–38), and the raising of Lazarus (John 11.1–45). These pericopes taught the meaning of baptism in terms of the water of life, an enlightenment, and a death-and-resurrection respectively. A continuous reading of the fourth Gospel from Christmas to Easter was a feature of the early Roman lectionary,[1] and it is possible that the three passages formed part of this sequence and were used on or near the Sundays of a three-week Lenten fast which was observed in Rome in the fourth century.[2]

---

[1] Traces of this continuous reading of the fourth Gospel can still be seen in the choice of the pericopes for Christmas Day, Christmas 2, Epiphany 2, Lent 4, Passion Sunday, Good Friday, Easter Day, and Easter 1 in the Prayer Book. These readings were, of course, taken from the Sarum missal.

[2] It is believed that the three passages were read on the fourth, fifth, and sixth Sundays in Lent before they were moved to the Wednesdays and Fridays of the fourth and

By the end of the fourth century the Lenten fast had been stretched to six weeks, making forty days from Lent 1 to what is now Maundy Thursday, then the day before the *sacratissimum triduum* of Good Friday, Holy Saturday, and Easter Day. Leo the Great (d. 461) regarded the forty days' Lent as a venerable institution—'the greatest and most sacred of the fasts' —so it must have been well established by the beginning of his pontificate in 440. More scrutinies were added to the pre-baptismal ceremonies. A pericope about the casting out of the dumb demon (Luke 11.14–26) was one of the readings associated with these, perhaps when salt was placed on the lips of the candidates. The feeding of the five thousand (John 6.1–14) may also have come into the lectionary of Lent at about this time, to teach the significance of the Eucharist. The healing of Naaman (2 Kings 5.1–14) was among other passages chosen to demonstrate to the catechumens the healing power of baptismal water.

2 THE FORTY DAYS' FAST The second element to influence the choice of readings was the desire to emulate the forty days' fast of Jesus Christ in the wilderness. The Pauline passage, 'Now is the acceptable time' (1 Cor. 6.1–10), and the story of the temptations in the wilderness (Matt. 4.1–12) were being read at the beginning of Lent during Leo's pontificate. During the Wednesday and the Friday of the week following Lent 1, the accounts of Moses' forty days on mount Sinai, Elijah's forty days' fasting journey to mount Horeb, and the forty days' fast of the people of Nineveh, were included in the lectionary to emphasize the symbolic meaning of the number of the days. Then on Lent 2 the gospel of the transfiguration (Matt. 17.1–9) brought together with Jesus Christ the figures of the two men referred to in the previous week's readings, Moses and Elijah; purified by the fast, they were able to share with Christ the glory of God. This was the goal which the ministry of the word set before Christian congregations at the commencement of the fast.

Certain trends began to lengthen the pre-paschal season. Sundays are not fast days in liturgical tradition, so that a six-weeks' Lent contained only thirty-six days on which a fast could be kept (six weeks minus the Sundays but including Good Friday and Holy Saturday). Gregory the Great (d. 604) was content to teach his people to offer this tithe of the year to God; but shortly afterwards four days were added to provide forty fasting days before Easter, so that Lent was now reckoned from the

fifth weeks in Lent, where they are to be found in the old Roman lectionary. They have been restored to the third, fourth, and fifth Sundays in Lent in the new Roman lectionary, Cycle A.

Wednesday of the seventh week before the festival. Christ's instructions about fasting and almsgiving (Matt. 6.16–21) have been read as the gospel for the first day of Lent, Ash Wednesday, from the time that this particular day appeared in the lectionaries.

In the east ascetical zeal lengthened the pre-paschal fast to fifty, sixty and even seventy days, and the Sundays within this longer season acquired the names of 'the Sunday in the Fifty Days, . . . in the Sixty Days, . . . in the Seventy Days' (*Dominica in Quinquagesima*, . . . *in Sexagesima*, . . . *in Septuagesima*). The practice was never adopted in Rome, but the names attached themselves to the three Sundays before Ash Wednesday, giving them a quasi-Lenten character. Paul's exhortation to asceticism ('Every athlete goes into strict training'—1 Cor. 9.24–27) has always been read on Septuagesima Sunday. In planning a pre-Easter season of nine weeks, therefore, the Joint Liturgical Group brought this development to its logical conclusion, although the new Church of England calendar has abandoned the Latin names.

3 THE PENITENTS The third element to influence the selection of lessons for Lent was the practice of imposing penances on those who were separated from the community because of some grave sin, and who wished to be readmitted to communion at Easter. Once a sinner had confessed his fault to the bishop or to the priest-penitentiary appointed for the purpose, he was enrolled in the ranks of the penitents at the beginning of Lent. At first, this was a simple service during which the bishop laid hands on him and the congregation prayed for him. Later it was elaborated with additional ceremonies such as the sprinkling of ashes and the imposition of a sackcloth. In the old Roman missal the gospels for the Monday and the Tuesday of the first week in Lent (the beginning of the penitential season when it was only six weeks in length) seem to have been chosen to teach the penitents and the people the effect of sin and the intention behind the Church's disciplinary action: one was the separation of the sheep from the goats (Matt. 25.31–46), the other was the cleansing of the temple (Matt. 21.10–17). The penances undertaken by the sinners included fasting and almsgiving, mentioned in the readings at the beginning of Lent.

As in the case of the catechumens, congregations tended to identify themselves with the penitence of the sinners and to use the forty days as a season of general confession and sorrow for sin. This strengthened the penitential character of the pre-paschal fast. Later, when the ceremony of the ashes came into use for all worshippers, it was as if the whole Church enrolled herself corporately into the ranks of the penitents.

4 THE PASSION The fourth element to affect the choice of readings was the stress on the passion of Christ as the cost and means of redemption. This element is associated with the evolution of Holy Week, which we have already outlined, but we notice here that by the middle ages the last two weeks of Lent acquired the name of 'Passiontide', probably because in the chronological pattern of the Lenten season these two weeks were near the climax of the sufferings of our Lord. The fifth Sunday in Lent was given a pericope from the epistle to the Hebrews on the sacrificial nature of Christ's obedience (Heb. 9.11–15) and a reading from the fourth Gospel describing how the Jews attempted to stone Christ because he said, 'In very truth I tell you, before Abraham was born, I am' (John 8.12–20). 'Types' of the passion in the songs of the Suffering Servant of Yahweh and the story of Daniel also came into the lectionary for these two weeks. Passiontide has been suppressed in the latest Roman calendar, although its character has been retained in the Church of England's readings for this day.

5 THE STATIONAL CHURCHES The stational churches in Rome were a fifth element in the choice of the Lenten readings. During the pre-paschal season the pope visited the different churches in the city each day to demonstrate the unity of the Christian community, and the old Roman missal still carries notices of these stations. On days when a large congregation was expected, the great basilicas were used, such as St John Lateran, which has been the stational church for Lent 1 since the time of Anastasius I (d. 401). On other days the pope went to the smaller churches.

The Thursdays in Lent, the last to be given their own synaxes, received readings chosen because they could be linked with the stational church in which the pope celebrated mass that day. For example, the station for the Thursday of the third week in Lent was SS. Cosmas and Damian, a church founded by Felix IV (d. 530) in a hall which once housed the city archives. Cosmas and Damian were two early Syrian medicos or wonder-workers, whose cultus developed in the fifth century and who were invoked as the patron saints of the medical profession. They were known as 'the holy money-less ones' because it was believed that they practised medicine without charging fees. For the Lenten mass in this stational church, therefore, the story of the healing of Peter's mother-in-law and of the sick in Capernaum was set as the gospel (Luke 4.38–44).

The Joint Liturgical Group drew up the new lectionary for the period between Christmas and Whitsunday so as to trace through the gospel readings Jesus Christ's ministry from his nativity to the sending of the Holy Spirit. But the traditions associated with Lent were so powerful that the chronological order of the events in the synoptic Gospels was not followed completely. The temptation in the wilderness, a reading of great significance for the penitential season as we have seen, had to be included at the beginning of Lent even though the lesson would then be read five or six weeks after the gospel of the baptism of Christ (itself traditionally associated with Epiphany, for reasons which we shall discuss shortly). The Joint Liturgical Group, therefore, chose the gospels round the general theme of 'The King and the Kingdom', recalling some of the most significant events in our Lord's ministry. This enabled the Group to include in the lectionary some of the readings traditionally associated with Lent.

So we find that after passages depicting Christ as teacher, healer, and worker of miracles on the three Sundays before Lent, Ash Wednesday has retained its old gospel, Matt. 6.16–21, 'When you fast . . .', with a parable about true repentance, Luke 18.9–14, the Pharisee and the tax-gatherer, as an alternative. The temptation in the wilderness is still the gospel for Lent 1, Matt. 4.1–17 in Year 1, Luke 4.1–13 in Year 2. (The lectionary takes advantage on a number of Sundays of the two-year cycle by setting the parallel account from a synoptic Gospel for the same Sunday the following year.) The ancient scrutiny lesson, Matt. 12.22–32, the casting out of the dumb demon, is provided for Lent 2 Year 2. In Year 1 Luke 19.41–48, the prophecy over Jerusalem, is appropriately read. The lesson containing the confession of Peter at Caesarea Philippi, the first prediction of the passion and the resurrection, and the 'take up his cross' saying, Luke 9.18–27 and Matt. 16.13–28, listed for Lent 3 Years 1 and 2 respectively, is not a Lenten reading in the old Roman missal (the first half of this pericope is the gospel for the feast of SS Peter and Paul, June 29), but it fits in well with the themes of the pre-Easter season we have been examining. The story of the transfiguration is read on Lent 4, Luke 9.28–36 in Year 1, Matt. 17.1–13 in Year 2. On Lent 5 our thoughts are turned towards the victory of the cross by reading John 12.20–32, the sayings of Christ about 'the grain of wheat' and 'when I am lifted up', in Year 1 and Mark 10.32–45, a prediction of the passion, the reference to the crucifixion as 'the baptism I am baptized with', and 'the Son of Man did not come to be served but to serve, and to surrender his life as a ransom for many', in Year 2.

Before we leave the pre-Easter season, it is perhaps worth mentioning that some other ancient Lenten readings are included in the new lectionary. Moses' encounter with God on mount Sinai is read on Lent 4. The healing of Naaman, 2 Kings 5.1–14, is the Old Testament lesson for the Eighth Sunday before Easter, Year 2. 1 Cor. 9.24–27, the old epistle for Septuagesima, is now read on Ash Wednesday Year 1. The Passion Sunday epistle on the sacrificial nature of Christ's obedience, Heb. 9.11–15, is still in its traditional place in Year 2. Some of the other old Lenten lessons have been moved to different parts of the calendar. The parable of the sheep and the goats, Matt. 25.31–46, which once impressed on sinners the implications of their penances, is now fixed for Advent Sunday Year 2. The cleansing of the temple, Matt. 21.12–16, which was read on the Tuesday of the first week in Lent to warn penitents of the possible consequences of their sins, is now the gospel for the Festival of the Dedication or Consecration of a Church!

THE GREAT FIFTY DAYS

The early Christian Passover—the fast, the vigil, the baptisms, and the Easter Eucharist—ushered in a glorious season of fifty days when penitential acts such as fasting were suspended and praise to the risen Lord in acclamations like the *Alleluia* dominated the Church's worship. The Bridegroom had not come at midnight during the Easter vigil, but Christians were still able to meet him sacramentally in the Eucharist, joining the newly-baptized in their first communion. And then for seven weeks they rejoiced in their union with God through the risen Christ. Turning back to the early Church we find the spirit of this great festive season in the words of Tertullian (d. 220):

It is the time when the Lord's resurrection was made widely known among the disciples, when the gift of the Holy Spirit was inaugurated, and when the hope of the Lord's second coming was revealed. It is the time when, after his ascension into heaven, the angels told the apostles that he would return as he had gone up into heaven, that is, at Pentecost. And when Jeremiah said, 'I will gather them together from the farthest parts of the earth on a feast day', he meant by that the Pasch and Pentecost, which is truly a festal day.

Tertullian called it the *laetissimum spatium*, 'the most joyful season'. Nowadays we know it as Eastertide. But at least until the beginning of the fourth century the period was given the title of 'Pentecost'—the Greek word being used in Christian circles to refer to the whole of the fifty days rather than the last day of the season, our Whitsunday.

From its scriptural background as a 'week of weeks'—the ritual season of the Jewish grain harvest—the great Fifty Days symbolized the fulfilment of all that God had promised through Jesus Christ, 'the first fruits of the harvest of the dead'. Later, the unity of this festive season was broken up as individual days were kept as commemorations of the ascension of Christ and the sending of the Holy Spirit; but in its primitive form Pentecost represented in the cycle of the year what the Lord's Day represented in the seven-day cycle of the week. Athanasius (d. 373) called the season (in the Latin version of his letters) the *magna dominica*, 'the great Sunday'. It was when Lent and Holy Week took on a more commemorative character, that the great Fifty Days began to lose their unity. Certain days within them acquired an importance of their own.

1   The Easter octave was established. In Rome the newly-baptized were expected to attend church each day for the week after their initiation for further instruction. This was made possible because in the christianized Roman Empire Holy Week and Easter Week were made public holidays. The neophytes wore their white baptismal robes until the first Sunday after Easter, which became known as the *Dominica in albis deponendis*, 'the Sunday for the laying aside of white robes'. The themes of the resurrection and baptism dominated the choice of the readings on these days with pericopes from the fourth Gospel and from the sermons in the Acts of the Apostles. On the octave day, Easter 1, the gospel was John 20.19–31, which included the appropriate words, 'A week later his disciples were again in the room. . . .'

2   In the process of elaborating the ceremonies in Jerusalem, special services were arranged to commemorate the ascension of Christ in the church of the Imbomon and the gift of the Holy Spirit in the church at Sion. The chronology of Acts 1 and 2 set the pattern: the fortieth day after Easter became Ascension Day and the fiftieth day after Easter, the last day of the ancient season of Pentecost, now became the Sunday of Pentecost. Whitsunday thus came to be regarded as a feast day in its own right and was given an octave.

3   The Rogations were instituted in the fifth century and when the prac-

tice of observing them spread in the west they interrupted the continuity of the great Fifty Days.

Yet the unity of the great Fifty Days has survived. We still call it Eastertide. We still sing 'Alleluia' more frequently during these weeks than at other times of the year. And the lectionary still recalls the triumphant character of the season with readings from the fourth Gospel, Acts, and Revelation.

The unanimity with which the different liturgical traditions selected their Eastertide lessons from these three books is remarkable. Not only in the Roman rite but also in the Milanese, Spanish, and Byzantine rites, the fourth Gospel, Acts and Revelation are all used during the great Fifty Days. We can understand the choice when we remember what the ancient Pentecost stood for: these three books more than any others in the New Testament see through the veil to what lay within the incarnate life of our Lord, and they herald the fulfilment of what God has done in Jesus Christ through the power of the Holy Spirit. John shows us that from the moment of his baptism Jesus was the paschal Lamb and that his work would be completed by 'the Advocate, the Holy Spirit whom the Father will send in my name'. Acts portrays the apostolic Church advancing in the triumph of the paschal proclamation and in the dynamic of the Spirit from Jerusalem to Rome. And the Apocalypse unfolds for us the secret plan of God which will become a reality on earth because 'this is the hour of victory for our God, the hour of his sovereignty and power, when his Christ comes to his rightful rule'. It was in response to such readings that the early Church kept 'the most joyful season'.

Much of this Eastertide joy echoes in the lessons for the great fifty days in the new lectionary. Many of the gospels are taken from the fourth Gospel, those for Easter 1 Year 1 and Easter 2 Year 2 and Easter 5 Year 1 being in the places they occupied in the past. There are readings from Revelation on Easter 2 Year 1 and Easter 4 Year 1. But the opportunities offered by a two-year cycle have been taken to give the first four Sundays after Easter different overall themes on alternative years. In Year 1 the gospels are accounts of the resurrection appearances, giving Eastertide a rather more historical flavour than it had before when it was regarded more as a season of joy; the epistles in Year 1 point to the triumphant eschatological consummation of Christ's resurrection victory. In Year 2, following the lead of the Prayer Book gospel for Easter 2, a series of four 'I am' passages from the fourth Gospel point to the eternal Christ and his abiding reality to the Christian and to the Church. The remaining Sundays retain their main themes, though Easter 6, the Sunday after

Ascension Day, seeks to bring home the truths of the ascension more adequately for the benefit of Sunday worshippers. The season ends with the feast of Pentecost, which is also used in the new lectionary to open up the next section of the Church's year.

THE CHRISTMAS CYCLE OF FEASTS

When we come to discuss the Christmas cycle of feasts we leave the Christian inheritance from Judaism with its Passover and Pentecost celebrations and move into the pagan Hellenistic world within which the members of the early Church lived. In that society men and women worshipped many kinds of deities and believed that their destinies were governed by the powers whose mysterious will they could trace in the sun, moon, and stars. The sun especially fascinated their imagination and even roused their devotion:

> Glory of the earth and sky,
>   The sun is the same for all.
> Glory of light and darkness,
>   The sun is the beginning and end.

The ancient hymn tells us something of this devotion to the blazing orb of the heavens. So much depended on its light and warmth. People's lives were caught up in the annual rhythm of sowing and harvesting, and a bad year meant starvation for thousands. No wonder that the day when the sun began its journey back into the northern hemisphere—the winter solstice—was one of great rejoicing!

In the early Christian era the inhabitants of the Roman empire worshipped not so much the sun itself as the god or gods that they believed it manifested. To the devotees of Apollo or Mithras, Dionysus or Aion, the winter solstice was a sign of divine birth or rebirth, an advent or coming of the deity to dwell among his followers. Signs of this were eagerly awaited. Folk were spiritually hungry. When Paul and Barnabas healed the cripple in Lystra, the people of the town thought it was a sign that the gods had come among them, and the priest of Jupiter brought out the dedicated oxen and prepared to offer a sacrifice. It was only with difficulty that the apostles convinced them that 'we are only human beings, no less mortal than you' (Acts 14.15). For everyone, therefore, the winter solstice was a day of profound significance. All over the empire ceremonies and legends were connected with the occasion. In Rome they lit bonfires and listened to the mysteries unfolded by wise men from the east. In Alexandria they processed round the temple of Koré and at midnight celebrated the virgin birth of her son, Aion. In the Nile and in other rivers there were ritual washings and blessings of the water for purification and fertility. In Cilicia and at Jerash rumours went round of wells and springs flowing with wine as a sign of future richness and joy (Epiphanius, a fourth-century Bishop of Salamis in Cyprus, claimed that he had tasted some!).

Since the sun was the focus of so much devotion and superstition, it served to draw men of different faiths together in a kind of ecumenical celebration on the day of the winter solstice. The authorities saw advantages in encouraging this. In A.D. 274 the emperor Aurelian proclaimed the day as a public holiday and erected a temple to the sun-god, *Sol*, in Rome. It was a shrewd political move. By it the emperor united the many races and religions under his rule in a universal festival and proclaimed himself patron of all his peoples' deities. The day was immensely popular, with all-night dancing and junketing as the joyful crowd watched for the dawn that heralded a new birth of light and life.

There was, however, one complication. In the western part of the empire they calculated the day by the Julian calendar, and according to that the winter solstice fell on 25 December; but in the eastern part of the empire they used the venerable calendar of Amenemhet I of Thebes (*c.* 1996 B.C.), and according to that it fell on 6 January. The long-term effect, as far as we are concerned, is that when the Church took over the pagan festival and baptized it for her own purposes, she found herself celebrating two days instead of one.

To say that the Church took over the pagan festival is perhaps misleading. It was not a conscious movement. In the first centuries the Church's preachers and writers assimilated and used Hellenistic ideas and words to proclaim and expound the Gospel—we see the process beginning within the New Testament itself (a few instances are noted in the commentary). The same kind of thing happened in Christian devotion. The gospel was the news of salvation to men who looked for light in a world darkened with sin, pain, and death. When the Christian saw his pagan neighbour looking to the shining light of *Sol* as a symbol of joy, peace, and eternity, he told him that as a Christian he worshipped another and greater sun—the one foretold by the prophet, 'the sun of righteous . . . with healing in his wings' (Malachi 4.2). He told him of Jesus Christ, whom Zechariah had heralded as 'the morning sun from heaven' (Luke 1.78) and whom the evangelist had proclaimed as 'the real light which enlightens every man' (John 1.9). What their pagan neighbours celebrated on 25 December and 6 January, therefore, the members of the Church believed that they could also celebrate—but more hopefully and joyfully, for in Jesus Christ what all men looked for had been fulfilled.

This is one reason why the two dates came to be linked with the coming of Jesus Christ into the world. But there was also another reason. In those same centuries the Church's theologians were struggling to maintain against various heresies the truth of the incarnation, and a day celebrating the manifestation of God in Jesus Christ, when the Word became flesh, offered a wonderful opportunity of proclaiming the basic doctrine of the Christian faith. Phrases were added to the creed to underline the divinity of Christ:

> God from God, Light from Light,
> begotten, not made,
> one in Being with the Father.

The Church urged men to cast aside the pale shadows which they followed in vain and to turn to the one true God,

> who was manifested in the body
> > vindicated in the spirit,
> > > seen by angels;
> who was proclaimed among the nations,
> > believed in throughout the world,
> > > glorified in high heaven. (1 Tim. 3.16)

Originally the Church celebrated on 25 December and 6 January the early events in the gospel narratives through which Jesus Christ revealed his true nature to men, from the birth at Bethlehem to the miracle at the wedding in Cana. The earliest title of the feast was the *Apparitio Domini*, 'the appearance of the Lord'. It was only gradually that 25 December came to be associated exclusively with the birth of Jesus and the adoration of the shepherds, and was called the feast of the Nativity. 'Christmas' is an English title: 'Christ's mass'.

This link between the birth of Christ and 25 December was possible because no one knew on what day of the year the Saviour was born. A few have wondered if 'the sixth month' in which, as Luke recorded, Mary miraculously conceived the Son of God, could have been the sixth month of the Jewish year, *Elul*, August–September, thus fixing the nativity in May–June, but most commentators have taken the phrase to refer to the sixth month of Elizabeth's pregnancy. And there have been many other

25

suggestions based on a mixture of scriptural guesswork and allegorical arithmetic. Clement, Bishop of Alexandria (d. *c.* 215), wrote that some believed 20 May to have been the day, but that his own calculations led him to favour 18 November. Hippolytus (d. *c.* 236) thought that Christ must have been born on the day of the week on which God made the sun —the fourth day, a Wednesday—and *De pascha computus*, written in north Africa about 243 argued that, as the first day of creation must have coincided with the vernal equinox, 25 March, our Lord's birthday must be the fourth day after that, 28 March.

But by the beginning of the fourth century the dates of the winter solstice were accepted as Christian festivals of the appearing of Jesus Christ; in the second quarter of that century a list of Roman martyrs was composed at the top of which were the words *VIII Kal. Ianu. natus Christus in Bethleem Iudaea*, 'on the eighth day of the Calends of January, Christ born in Bethlehem of Judaea'. The Julian calendar retained the custom of numbering the days according to the lunar month. As the Calends of January were those days in December which follow the new moon, the eighth day was 25 December. This is the earliest evidence we have for the observance of Christmas.

The years from which this list originated—the 330s—also witnessed the end of the emperor Constantine's reign, and this inevitably raises the question whether the emperor himself was responsible for promoting the Christian celebration on 25 December. We know that he promulgated a decree concerning 'the venerable day of the sun' and made it possible for Christians to worship on the weekly Lord's Day. And we know that with his mother, Helena, he was interested in the circumstances of the Saviour's birth, for he arranged for a basilica to be constructed over the grotto of the nativity at Bethlehem. Furthermore, the fact that 25 December was kept as a religious festival by almost every subject in the western empire may well have prompted him to encourage its observance by the Church.

We have already seen how important a source for liturgical studies is Egeria's diary. From her we learn that on 6 January the birth of Christ was celebrated at midnight in the church at Bethlehem. Then, as dawn broke, the bishop and the congregation processed to Jerusalem, singing psalms. 'In Bethlehem throughout the entire eight days', she wrote, 'the feast is celebrated in festal array and joyfulness by the priests and all the clerics there and the monks who are stationed in that place.' At about the same time the pope had instituted a mass in Rome on Christmas morning—a radical move, this, for weekday celebrations were unheard-of in those days. Soon a midnight mass was added and, a little later, another mass at dawn for the Byzantine court officials in the church of St Anastasia near their spacious homes on the Aventine. This is how the three masses for 25 December came to appear in the Roman missal.

In the eastern half of the empire Christians kept 6 January as 'the Birthday' or 'the Theophany' or—more commonly—'the Epiphany'. The word means 'the showing forth' or 'the manifestation' of God in Jesus Christ and not, as the seventeenth-century Anglican revisers of the Prayer Book thought, the manifestation of Christ to the Gentiles. In their reading and teaching they included not only the birth at Bethlehem but also those first events in the Gospels which demonstrated that God was revealing himself in Jesus Christ. Perhaps the pagan customs and legends which the Church found in contemporary society had something to do with it. She wanted to answer what was false with what was true. Wise men had brought their cults from the east: magi had come to Christ, too. There were ritual washings and blessings in rivers: Christ, too, had been baptized by John in the Jordan, when the voice of the Father had been heard from heaven and the Spirit had descended as a dove upon him. There were legends of water changed miraculously into wine: Christ, too, had once changed water into wine at Cana.

When in the west the Church began to keep 6 January as well as 25 December as a festival, and when in the east Christians began to observe 25 December as well as 6 January, the saving events were divided between the two days. 25 December became the celebration of Christ's birth, 6 January became the commemoration of the magi, the baptism, and the miracle at Cana. The antiphon for the Magnificat at vespers on the feast of Epiphany sums up its intention: 'We keep this day holy in honour of three miracles: this day a star led the wise men to the manger; this day water was turned into wine at the marriage feast; this day Christ chose to be baptized by John in the Jordan, for our salvation. Alleluia.' So did Christopher Wordsworth in this hymn:

> Manifested by the star
>   to the sages from afar. . . .
> Manifest at Jordan's stream,
>   Prophet, Priest, and King supreme;
> And at Cana wedding-guest
>   In thy Godhead manifest. . . .
>
> (English Hymnal 47, A. & M. Revised 81)

The Alternative Lectionary preserves the traditional scripture readings for this cycle of feasts and allocates them to the Sundays as well as the feast days themselves (which, since they generally fall on weekdays, are less likely to be observed by many people). Isa. 9.2–7, 'The people who walked in darkness have seen a great light', which supplied the verses for the propers in the old Christmas rite, is the Old Testament lesson for Christmas Day, together with the epistle and gospel from the Roman midnight mass—Titus 2.11–14, 'The grace of God has dawned upon the world', and Luke 2.1–10, the adoration of the shepherds. Luke 2.22–40, the presentation in the temple, is also the gospel for Christmas 1 Year 2 as well as that for the festival of 1 January, and it is followed on Christmas 2 Year 1 by the story of the boy Jesus sitting with the teachers in the temple. The visit of the magi, Matt. 2.1–12, is read on Christmas 2 Year 2 as well as on the feast of the Epiphany. The baptism of Christ now has a right-fully prominent place in the lectionary as the gospel for both Year 1 and Year 2 on Epiphany 1 (one of the advantages of a two-year lectionary is shown here in that the Matthean account is read on Year 1 and the Johannine on Year 2). The wedding at Cana, John 2.1–11, another ancient Epiphany theme, is the gospel for Epiphany 3 Year 1. On other Sundays after Epiphany we read of the early events in the ministry of Jesus—the call of the first disciples and the signs of future glory. The feasts of 1 January and 2 February are among the Table 2 Festivals, and both are clearly focused on Jesus Christ, not on the Virgin Mary: the Circumcision is given 'The Naming of Jesus' as its main title, and the Purification is given back its old designation, 'The Presentation of Christ in the Temple'. This latter festival used to be known in the East as *Hypapante*, 'the Meeting'—the Christ-child brought to the temple to meet the saints of the Old Israel, Simeon and Anna. The use of candles on this day, Candlemass, goes back to some Roman pagan ceremony.

ADVENT

Advent is an entirely western institution. It does not appear in the calendars of the Orthodox Churches. In Rome it seems to have developed from the December fast of Embertide, and in Gaul it served as a second Lent when catechumens were preparing for their baptism on the feast of the Epiphany. The name was taken from the old title of the Christmas period, *De Adventu Domini*, 'Of the Coming of the Lord'. The great figures of Advent are Isaiah, John the Baptist, and the Virgin Mary—those who prepared for and co-operated with the incarnation of the Son of God. Their words and activities have been the subject of the readings in Advent since the time when the season began to appear in the Roman lectionary about the sixth century.

But in the early middle ages another note began to sound during Advent, that of Christ's Second Coming. The last weeks in the year reminded the Church of the end of all things. The famous 'O antiphons' of the Magnificat both look back to Christ's earthly coming and forward to the parousia:

O Day-spring, Brightness of Light Everlasting, and Sun of Righteousness: Come and enlighten him that sitteth in darkness and in the shadow of death.

But in the Church of England other themes were introduced into Advent through the collects and epistles. Advent 2 happened to have Rom. 15.4–13, 'All the ancient scriptures were written for our instruction', as its epistle, and this gave it the character of a 'Bible Sunday'. Advent 3 happened to have 1 Cor. 4.1–5, 'Stewards of the secrets of God', as its epistle, and since this Sunday is near the time when the Advent ordinations are usually held, it has become an occasion for preaching and praying about the Church's ordained ministry.

The Joint Liturgical Group boldly extended the pre-Christmas season to nine weeks (there is precedent, for those who want to look for it, in the longer Advents of the Gallican calendars) and, using the Old Testament lesson as the controlling readings, traced the story of God's work from the creation to the incarnation—creation, the fall, Noah, Abraham, Moses—and then merged this with the traditional themes of the season— the Advent hope, the word of God in the Old Testament, the Forerunner and the annunciation. The Church of England has retained this scheme, the liturgical year now beginning on the Ninth Sunday before Christmas.

SUNDAYS AFTER PENTECOST AND HOLY DAYS

SUNDAYS AFTER PENTECOST

The title of 'Trinity Sunday' became attached to the first Sunday after Pentecost in northern Europe in the middle ages. Its special popularity in England was due to its association with the ordination of Thomas of Canterbury. In the Alternative calendar the older custom of numbering the Sundays after Pentecost has been restored. Before the days of set lectionaries the choice of scriptures was left to the bishop presiding over the Eucharist. Sometimes a book of the Bible was read through more or less continuously. The epistles and gospels in the old Roman missal and in the Prayer Book seem to have come from a collection of passages which by the seventh century had been attached more or less haphazardly to certain Sundays. This series existed in two forms containing substantially the same passages in nearly the same order but assigned to different weeks. One came from northern Europe, the other from Rome. The differences account for the divergences which used to be found between the readings in the Prayer Book and the Roman Missal. For the new lectionary a completely fresh selection has been made. This has been drawn up with the epistle as the controlling lesson. The story is told of the continuing life of the pilgrim Church after Pentecost in the experience of the living Spirit of Christ. Four lessons from Acts in Year 2 describe the life of the apostolic community in Jerusalem following the gift of the Spirit, Acts 2.37–47, Peter before the Sanhedrin, Acts 4.5–12, the Ethiopian eunuch, Acts 8.26–38, and the Gentile Pentecost, Acts 11.4–18. In Year 1 are key passages teaching the significance of union with the risen Christ by the Spirit, Eph. 1.3–14 ('every spiritual blessing'), 1 Pet. 2.1–10 ('a chosen race'), Rom. 6.3–11 ('alive to God'), and Gal. 3.23—4.7 ('You are sons').

ROGATION DAYS

The Rogation Days, *Litaniae minores*, were instituted by Mamertus (d. *c.* 475), Bishop of Vienne in Gaul, when his diocese was stricken by volcanic eruptions. He led his congregation in penitential processions in the open air. The practice was copied by neighbouring churches in Gaul and by the sixth century there were canons passed by councils ordering their observance throughout the country. They appeared in service books in the seventh and eighth centuries. Two of the lessons provided in the new lectionary, Matt. 6.1–15, teaching on prayer and Luke 11.5–13, the friend at midnight, reflect the character of Rogationtide as a period of intense prayer. Intercessions for a fruitful harvest and processions in the fields led to 'beating the bounds' to establish parish boundaries.

EMBER DAYS

The Ember Days are early fasts attached to certain Wednesdays, Fridays, and Saturdays of four weeks in the different seasons of the year. They were devoted to prayer to implore God's blessing on the new season. They also became occasions for ordinations, held during the Saturday-Sunday vigil at the end of each Embertide. The readings for these days in the new lectionary concentrate on the ordained ministry. The gospel for the

Advent Ember Days, Luke 12.35–43, 'Be like men who wait for their master's return', is one of the gospels for the ordination service.

SAINTS' DAYS AND COMMEMORATIONS

The practice of commemorating the saints on certain days of the year arose out of the cult of the martyrs. These who suffered for their faith were highly esteemed in Judaism from the time of the Maccabees, and when the Church began to acquire its own list of martyrs, beginning in New Testament times with Stephen and James in Jerusalem and Peter and Paul in Rome, their memory was honoured in that they had suffered like their Lord as a witness (the meaning of 'martyr') to the gospel. The cult began in the east and in Gaul with the records of the sufferings (the 'passions') of Pothinus and his companions at Lyons, Perpetua and her circle at Carthage, and Polycarp at Smyrna. In the letter reporting Polycarp's death in *c.* 155 it was said that the Church carefully preserved his relics 'in a fitting place' and celebrated the anniversary of his death joyfully. The first mention in the west of a register of martyrs being kept occurs in the correspondence of Cyprian, Bishop of Carthage (d. 258). He instructed his clergy to bury the remains of a confessor of the faith carefully and to note the day of his death. It was out of such lists as these that the martyrologies developed. The practice of commemorating local saints within the eucharistic prayer is an early feature of the Roman and other liturgies.

It was, however, in connection with the dedication of churches in honour of saints and the reinterment of the relics of the martyrs that other dates became attached to the calendar to make the *Sanctorale*. The cult of Peter and Paul began in Rome in the second century (the memorial over the supposed grave of the apostle under St Peter's is dated from about 150) and developed in the third, for their relics were taken to the catacomb of St Sebastian for safety during the Valerian persecution of 258. 29 June may have been connected with this event or, more probably, with the transfer of their relics to the great basilicas built and dedicated in their honour in the fourth century. The Blessed Virgin Mary was honoured in Rome in the following century when Sixtus III (432–40) rebuilt the old basilica of Pope Liberius and inscribed on its walls, 'Virgin Mary, it is to thee that I, Sixtus, have dedicated this new temple. . . .' These words can still be seen in St Mary Major. That church was dedicated on 5 August. Some dates, such as the Annunciation, 25 March, and the Birth of John the Baptist, 24 June, were calculated from Christmas Day. The new lectionary provides readings for Festivals which are substantially the same as the Red Letter list of the Prayer Book, together with the feasts of the Visitation of the Blessed Virgin Mary, St Mary Magdalen, and the Transfiguration of our Lord. The feast of the Circumcision has been changed to the Naming of Jesus. St Joseph of Nazareth has been added on 19 March, St Matthias moved to 14 May, and St Thomas to 3 July. Local commemorations are encouraged and provisions are made for Martyrs, Doctors, etc., in Table 3. The Roman requiem mass had its origins in the ancient practice of celebrating the Eucharist at the tombs of dead members of a family. The readings for the Commemoration of the Faithful Departed can be used at a Eucharist before a funeral or on the anniversary of a Christian's death. The Thanksgiving for the Institution of Holy Communion does what the medieval feast of Corpus Christi was intended to do—namely, to provide an opportunity to focus the Church's teaching and devotion on this sacrament without its being caught up in the observance of Holy Week. Many of the readings in the new lectionary are traditional for these days.

This, then, is the background to the development of the lectionary which now takes form in the two-year cycle of readings based on the proposals of the Joint Liturgical Group. We begin to prepare for Christmas nine Sundays before the feast with the story of God's creation of the world and the establishment of his covenant with Abraham and Moses. As a Christian community we are conscious of our ancestry in the old Israel at this time of the year, so it is appropriate that on Advent 3 we should be led to meditate on the word of God in the Old Testament. But the promise of the Second Coming of Christ, born out of the hope that Judaism had for its vindication by God in the last days, breaks into these themes on Advent Sunday, and until Christmas we hold together faith in the parousia with faith that Christ came in flesh; and before us on the two Sundays preceding Christmas we have the example of those who were full of God's grace, John the Baptist and the Virgin Mary.

The rich content of the Christmas cycle of feasts is now spread over the Sundays at the beginning of the new year. Excessive concentration on the Bethlehem story could obscure the fact that what we are celebrating is the epiphany of God in man. Christmas and Epiphany are festivals of God's new creation, the consequences of which are to be seen by those who have the eyes of faith in events such as the visit of the magi, the presentation in the temple, the baptism of Christ, the wedding at Cana, and the call of the first disciples. At this time of the year, therefore, the ministry of the word expounds the initiative of God in revealing himself to men.

The three Sundays before Lent dwell on various aspects of Christ's ministry before we begin, through the liturgy, to make our spiritual pilgrimage to Jerusalem with Christ in the season of Lent. The proclamation of the Kingdom of God and the opposition that it roused in Jerusalem causes us to reflect on our own disobedience. These are weeks of penitence, of self-denial, of recalling all that baptism means and all that God has done in Christ to make regeneration possible for us sinners. The sufferings which we experience in this life are brought to the suffering Servant as he treads the road to Calvary. But it is a glorious and a victorious road. The temptations and the conflicts in the gospels for the first three Sundays in Lent lead to the glory of the transfiguration and the victory of the cross in the gospels of the fourth and fifth Sundays. And so we are brought to the great and holy week in which we participate in the entry to Jerusalem, the last supper, the garden of Gethsemane, the interrogations before the Sanhedrin and Pilate, the horror of the Via Dolorosa and the death on the cross, and the rest in the tomb. The whole content of the passion from the gospels, together with the prophecies and the types from the Old Testament and the reflections and the teachings from Acts and the epistles, lay before us the cost of our redemption, what the Passover of Christians has meant for the Lamb of God.

Then comes the triumph and joy of Easter Day and the great Fifty Days, the ancient Pentecost, in which we rejoice in the accomplishment of God's purposes in Christ and that foretaste of their fulfilment which is ours through the Spirit. Eastertide closes with the glorious celebration of Christ's ascension as King to heaven and the outpouring of the Holy Spirit. This is, perhaps, more than any other time of the year the occasion for the Church to proclaim to the world the mighty work of God in Jesus Christ and the power of the Holy Spirit, when the fruitfulness of creation (in the northern hemisphere) is a sign of the fruitfulness of God's love for his people.

In the weeks after Pentecost the emphasis shifts to our fellowship. We reflect on the Church as the temple of the Holy Spirit and ourselves as members of a prophetic, priestly, and royal race to minister in the name of Jesus Christ in God's world. The lessons teach us the many aspects of Christian duty and service. The initiative is still from God, but now we learn more of what God is doing through the Body of Christ and what he is calling us to do. And so, looking to the future, we once more approach the Sundays before Christmas and Advent, and the yearly cycle of readings begins again.

This is the outline of God's saving and sanctifying purposes to which the scriptures point us as they are read in the new lectionary. And it is the task of the preacher and those who assist in the ministry of the word to help us to understand that word, to apply its message to our lives, and to respond as members of Christ to its demands and encouragements as we live, love, hope, doubt, and believe in today's world. Their ministry is to say what Paul said to the Colossians, 'Since Jesus was delivered to you as Christ and Lord, live your lives in union with him. Be rooted in him; be built in him; be consolidated in the faith you were taught; let your hearts overflow with thankfulness.'

TABLE OF SUNDAY THEMES

The Sunday themes are to be understood as guides for those who wish to follow them.

9th Sunday before Christmas
The Creation

8th Sunday before Christmas
The Fall

7th Sunday before Christmas
The Election of God's People: Abraham

6th Sunday before Christmas
The Promise of Redemption: Moses

5th Sunday before Christmas
The Remnant of Israel

1st Sunday in Advent
The Advent Hope

2nd Sunday in Advent
The Word of God in the Old Testament

3rd Sunday in Advent
The Forerunner

4th Sunday in Advent
The Annunciation

1st Sunday after Christmas
The Incarnation

2nd Sunday after Christmas
The Holy Family

1st Sunday after the Epiphany
Revelation: The Baptism of Jesus

2nd Sunday after the Epiphany
Revelation: The First Disciples

3rd Sunday after the Epiphany
Revelation: Signs of Glory

4th Sunday after the Epiphany
Revelation: The New Temple

5th Sunday after the Epiphany
Revelation: The Wisdom of God

6th Sunday after the Epiphany
Revelation: Parables

9th Sunday before Easter
Christ the Teacher

8th Sunday before Easter
Christ the Healer

7th Sunday before Easter
Christ the Friend of Sinners

1st Sunday in Lent
The King and the Kingdom: Temptation

2nd Sunday in Lent
The King and the Kingdom: Conflict

3rd Sunday in Lent
The King and the Kingdom: Suffering

4th Sunday in Lent
The King and the Kingdom: Transfiguration

5th Sunday in Lent
The King and the Kingdom: The Victory of the Cross

Palm Sunday
The Way of the Cross

Easter Day

1st Sunday after Easter
YEAR 1 *The Upper Room*
YEAR 2 *The Bread of Life*

2nd Sunday after Easter
YEAR 1 *The Emmaus Road*
YEAR 2 *The Good Shepherd*

3rd Sunday after Easter
YEAR 1 *The Lakeside*
YEAR 2 *The Resurrection and the Life*

4th Sunday after Easter
YEAR 1 *The Charge to Peter*
YEAR 2 *The Way, the Truth, and the Life*

5th Sunday after Easter
Going to the Father

Sunday after Ascension Day
The Ascension of Christ

Pentecost

35

Trinity Sunday
(1st Sunday after Pentecost)

2nd Sunday after Pentecost
(Trinity 1)
    YEAR 1 *The People of God*
    YEAR 2 *The Church's Unity and Fellowship*

3rd Sunday after Pentecost
(Trinity 2)
    YEAR 1 *The Life of the Baptized*
    YEAR 2 *The Church's Confidence in Christ*

4th Sunday after Pentecost
(Trinity 3)
    YEAR 1 *The Freedom of the Sons of God*
    YEAR 2 *The Church's Mission to the Individual*

5th Sunday after Pentecost
(Trinity 4)
    YEAR 1 *The New Law*
    YEAR 2 *The Church's Mission to All Men*

6th Sunday after Pentecost
(Trinity 5)
  The New Man

7th Sunday after Pentecost
(Trinity 6)
  The More Excellent Way

8th Sunday after Pentecost
(Trinity 7)
  The Fruit of the Spirit

9th Sunday after Pentecost
(Trinity 8)
  The Whole Armour of God

10th Sunday after Pentecost
(Trinity 9)
  The Mind of Christ

11th Sunday after Pentecost
(Trinity 10)
  The Serving Community

12th Sunday after Pentecost
(Trinity 11)
  The Witnessing Community

13th Sunday after Pentecost
(Trinity 12)
  The Suffering Community

14th Sunday after Pentecost
(Trinity 13)
  The Family

15th Sunday after Pentecost
(Trinity 14)
  Those in Authority

16th Sunday after Pentecost
(Trinity 15)
  The Neighbour

17th Sunday after Pentecost
(Trinity 16)
  The Proof of Faith

18th Sunday after Pentecost
(Trinity 17)
  The Offering of Life

19th Sunday after Pentecost
(Trinity 18)
  The Life of Faith

20th Sunday after Pentecost
(Trinity 19)
  Endurance

21st Sunday after Pentecost
(Trinity 20)
  The Christian Hope

22nd Sunday after Pentecost
(Trinity 21)
  The Two Ways

Last Sunday after Pentecost
(Trinity 22)
  Citizens of Heaven

COMMENTARY
Ninth Sunday before Christmas to Easter Day

NINTH SUNDAY BEFORE CHRISTMAS
Fifth Sunday before Advent

* Genesis 1. 1–3, 24–31a

The shortened version of this passage screens for us the highlights of
God's creation of the world as seen by the Priestly source of the Pentateuch, the first five books of the OT. Out of darkness and formlessness
and stormy seas, God brought light and order and goodness. The mythological concept of creation as a conquest of primordial chaos was inherited
by Israel from Mesopotamian cultures. Into this mythological picture
Judaism placed in a supreme position the figure of the one transcendent
God who existed before the world he created, moving over it with his
3, spirit and calling all things into existence by the power of his word: **God**
etc. **said . . . There was** or **So it was.** *Ruach*, Heb., and *pneuma*, Gk, are
7, used for 'wind', 'breath', and 'spirit'. The association of God with the
etc. power of his word and the effect of his spirit was interpreted by the early
Christian Fathers as a revelation of the Trinity. The plural pronoun,
26 **Let us,** reflects the use of *Elohim*, a common Hebrew name for God which
is in plural form.

Man is given the primary place in God's creation not only because he
has authority under God over all created beings but also because God
26 made him in his own **image and likeness:** that is to say, he was created
with a personal intelligence, will, and authority that set him nearer to
God than any other creature. One consequence of this likeness is that
the relationship between God as Creator and man as creature is such
that it was possible in the course of time for God to reveal himself within
the limitations of one human life. Another consequence is that man is
able by grace to share in God's divine nature.

The last verses give us an idyllic scene of man and animals enjoying
God's blessings and abundance and living at peace with one another,
31 each provided with their own food. All that God had made **was very
good**—the goodness that is the essence of creation unspoilt by sin.

Colossians 1. 15–20

This passage may have been a primitive Christian hymn, adapted by the
apostle for this letter in which one of his purposes was to refute the false
notion that Jesus Christ himself was God's creature (a notion which gave

* An asterisk denotes the 'controlling lesson' (see p. 1).

38

rise to various heresies). He did this by developing the OT idea that God had Wisdom at his side in his work of creation. Wisdom, already personified in later Judaism, was manifest in Jesus Christ, who was with God
15 from the beginning and who was the image (*eikon*), of the invisible God.
19 In him the complete being (*pleroma*) of God, by God's own choice, came to dwell. The NEB translation emphasizes the totality of Christ's divinity and preserves the evocative verb 'to dwell', which recalls the tabernacling of God with his people (also echoed in today's gospel). The JB, however, translates this sentence in the light of the biblical vision of the entire cosmos filled with the creative presence of God: 'God wanted all perfection to be found in him.'

Christ has the position of honour in creation, **the primacy over all**
15 **created things.** The NEB footnote, **Born before all created things,** must not be taken in the temporal sense of 'born first', but in the relative sense of being the first who brought into existence the many. Christ's primacy extends in spiritual as well as material realms and, since he is
17 God's agent in creation, what God made through him, is **held together in him.** Wisdom writers pictured divine Wisdom as 'the flawless mirror of the active power of God', 'a pure effluence from the glory of the Almighty' (Wisd. 7.26, 25); Paul saw Christ as the divine Wisdom who is the active power of God in maintaining the unity of the universe.
18   Christ is also **the head of the body, the church.** Through the work of reconciliation sealed by his sacrifice on the cross, it has become possible for the whole created order to be brought back into a right relationship with its Creator. Jesus is the agent of the redemption of the world as well as the agent of its creation. The apostle here outlines a vast and mysterious prophecy that in God's saving work it is not only human beings who are
18 involved. In his resurrection Christ was **the first to return from the dead,** and thus he is head of the new creation as he is head of the natural universe.

John 1. 1–14   See Christmas Day.

NINTH SUNDAY BEFORE CHRISTMAS
Fifth Sunday before Advent

* **Genesis 2. 4b–9, 15–end**

The Priestly source of the book of Genesis saw the creation of the universe as a demonstration of the divine fiat (OT reading Year 1). The Jahwist source set man and his destiny in these passages against a primitive conception of the world's origins in a waterless desert. God is depicted
7 shaping man from the dust of the ground (Adam = Heb. *adamah*, 'ground', NEB footnote) as a potter might shape a vessel out of clay, and then breathing into the figure to make a living soul. 'The first man was made "of the dust of the earth"', wrote Paul, comparing Adam with the 'second man' who was 'from heaven' (1 Cor. 15.47).

The two trees are symbols, one for immortality, the other for the ability to decide what is good and what is evil. In the garden (*paradeisos*, LXX)
17 God placed the man with the commandment not to eat of the tree of the knowledge of good and evil: to be aware of the ability of choice is death. Behind the myth is the Jahwist's concern for the theological truth that man is created as a being free in the will of God to obey or to disobey.

As in the Priestly narrative, man is in a position of lordship over other creatures, formed like himself out of the dust of the desert. The status was given him by God, who presented him with other creatures to name them. The act of naming signifies man's lordship, for to know the name of a person or a thing is to know its nature and purpose and to have power over it. But none of the creatures was capable of that intimate relationship which man required to remove his loneliness, so God created woman out of his body, the rib being a primitive explanation for the physical attrac-
23 tion of the sexes. The poem, **This shall be called woman**, plays on the Hebrew words *ish*, 'man', and *ishshah*, 'woman' (NEB footnote).

Revelation 4

After the letters to the seven churches, this passage begins the descriptions of John's visions. Like a true prophet, he was taken in a Spirit-inspired trance to the door of the heavenly court or council to learn God's will and purpose. ('Which of them has stood at the council of the Lord, seen him and heard his word?' Jeremiah challenged the false prophets,

* An asterisk denotes the 'controlling lesson' (see p. 1).

23.18). And John's vision opens with an affirmation of the divine sovereignty. The central figure, that of God himself, is not described—understandably—but the glory of his throne is compared with precious stones. John saw the crowd of worshippers and the canopy of the rainbow, the symbol of divine mercy from the days of the Flood. Thunder and lightning are theophanic music, and the spirits of God glow mysteriously before the throne.

Commentators have guessed that the twenty-four elders represent the twelve patriarchs of the old covenant and the twelve apostles of the new, but their precise significance matters little. They form the company of God's redeemed or servants who worship him together with the living creatures, supporting the throne (figures from Isa. 6.2). The sea of glass is not part of heaven; it is the sea of evil out of which the monster is to arise later in the scenario (13.1), and is the barrier over which the redeemed must pass before they can enter the promised land. In this new heaven—which in the vision is not the final one—and new earth there is no more sea (21.1). The water is the celestial counterpart of the Jordan; perhaps it is also an image of Christian baptism in its fullest sense as that by which a man shares, through his sufferings in this life, in the baptismal death and resurrection of Jesus Christ.

The *Trisagion* hymn is from Isa. 6.3, adoring God in his holiness. The last verse of the reading continues the act of worship, blessing (thanking) God for his creative work—an element which is included in many new eucharistic prayers.

John 3. 1–8

Wonderful though the creation of man is, it is not through the created order that he enters the Kingdom of God. A re-creation or new creation is necessary. He must be born over again. This is what Jesus told Nicodemus, a member of the Sanhedrin, a Pharisee and a rabbi. The statement
3 is prefaced by, In truth, in very truth I tell you—a phrase used in this Gospel to introduce a saying of the utmost importance.

Nicodemus represents the old dispensation, which thought that created man could achieve the Kingdom by obeying the law. The fact that he came to Jesus by night could be an indication that he was being discreet; it could also mean that he came with his understanding darkened. He recognized Jesus as a teacher like himself and as one who manifested the
2 presence of God: No one could perform these signs of yours unless God were with him. His visit was an opportunity for the evangelist to

present the main thrust of the gospel in its impact upon man as a creature —that those who accept Jesus as Christ are not born 'by fleshly desire' but 'of God himself', as he had put it in his prologue (1.13). They are 5 re-born **from water and spirit.**

The concept of a new birth, echoed in the mystery religions of the first centuries of the Christian era, expresses the need for an essential change 6 in the whole of a man's personality. **Flesh can give birth only to flesh:** in the psychology of the time this meant that the human personality in its natural state is untouched by God. A man's spirit is that essential part of himself which is capable of responding to God and which is brought to life when the Spirit of God touches it—'Like begets like' as an old philosophical saying put it. This is why the capital S in the JB version of verse 6 is helpful: 'What is born of the Spirit is spirit.' Physical birth is but a parable of the spiritual birth which a man must undergo before he can enter the Kingdom. To be born a Jew does not exempt a man from this.

The agent in this act of re-creation is the Holy Spirit; the sacramental sign is water. John the Baptist had prophesied that the one coming after him would 'baptize in Holy Spirit' (1.33). Before Nicodemus stood the new Baptizer. Both the Spirit and water have their place in the creation epics of Genesis, the former as the life-giving power of God, the latter as the symbol of the chaos and evil which the act of creation arrested until man chose to sin. In the new creation it is the same Spirit who gives life to redeem man; but now water is a sign of a new birth, a death to sin, and a rising to life in Christ. Like the wind (the same word in Greek, *pneuma*), which indicates the way it is blowing but whose source and destination are mysterious, the Spirit moves among men for this re-creative 7 purpose. By baptism man is **born over again**—or 'born from above': the Greek can mean either, and the second translation suggests that baptism has eternal consequences, introducing a man to the divine world above. Baptism is also called 'rebirth' in Titus 3.5.

The style of Jesus' teaching is different in John from that in the other Gospels. His words are cast in the form of literary monologues and dialogues, a feature of the Gospel which has led many commentators to conclude that the evangelist is not reporting the actual words Jesus spoke. But this does not necessarily make a sharp division between this Gospel's narrative and that of the others. All the evangelists adopt their own methods of presenting the sayings of Jesus. It is improbable that he delivered the sermon on the mount in the form in which Matthew has written it. It may well be that in John we come closer to the essential meaning of what Christ taught than in any other part of the NT.

EIGHTH SUNDAY BEFORE CHRISTMAS
Fourth Sunday before Advent

* Genesis 4. 1-10

Behind the Jahwist source for this passage there seems to be the story of two different communities, one pastoral, the other agricultural, each possessing some form of religious institution for the offering of sacrifices.

2 Abel was a shepherd, Cain a farmer. Perhaps there is also behind it the memory of some ancient feud stemming from the success of one and the failure of the other. This would account for the different responses to the (fertility?) sacrifices. Whatever the source, however, the Jahwist uses the story to demonstrate that the result of rebellion against God—the first sin recounted in Gen. 3 (see Trinity 24 Year 2)—produces not only a breach between man and God but also between man and man, resulting in anger, violence, and murder. It is against these interrelated consequences that the summary of the Law is directed: ' "Love the Lord your God with all your heart, with all your soul, with all your mind." That is the greatest commandment. It comes first. The second is like it: "Love your neighbour as yourself." Everything in the Law and the prophets hangs on these two commandments.' (Matt. 22.37-40.)

Why God should have accepted Abel's oblation and not Cain's is a mystery. It is sufficient for the OT that the ultimate choice remains in the sovereignty of God's will: 'I will be gracious to whom I will be gracious, and I will have compassion on whom I will have compassion' (Exod. 33.19). Is it possible that behind the source there is some primitive belief that an offering of blood is more acceptable to a deity? In the narrative it is no more than an occasion for a fit of temper. God warns Cain about this anger, which distorts his features, and appeals to his better nature:

7 If you do well, you hold your head up (NEB footnote). Sin is personified as a beast of prey, prowling about seeking whom he may devour.

9 God's question, Where is your brother Abel? has social implications. Responsibility before God is responsibility for one's brother. Love binds man to man as well as God to man. Graphically the narrative pictures the blood appealing to God. Spilled blood cannot be hid, it can cry to the Lord of life. When a man commits murder, he attacks God's very own right of possession—life itself.

1 John 3. 9-18

9 Not a warning but an affirmation. Because the divine seed has been

43

implanted in the Christian—and 'seed' here may mean either the principle of the new life which is implanted when a man is born again into the family of God, or the seed which is the word of God as in the parable of the sower (Mark 4.14): the exact meaning does not matter, for the result is the same—he is prevented from sinning. God's child does not sin. The finality of this statement is startling. We are aware of our failings 10 (or some of them!) Does their existence mean that we are the children of the devil? No, for John was not a perfectionist. He recognized the occurrence of sin within the Christian fellowship, for in 1.9 he wrote, 'If we confess our sins, he is just and may be trusted to forgive our sins and cleanse us from every kind of wrong.' What he meant was that there is in the heart and mind and will of the child of God a continuous renunciation of sin which began when he was baptized. This renunciation is so radical that the intention of sinning is never accepted; and sin, when it occurs, is immediately repented, confessed, and rejected as utterly alien to the Christian life.

Verse 10b leads into a consequence of this renunciation of sin. Just 10 as the one who does not do right is not God's child, neither is anyone who does not love his brother. We cannot be neutral in our attitude to others. Love is the opposite of hate. Not to love is to hate and is to make one a murderer. Cain is cited as a figure or 'type' of the world (in the Johannine sense of 'the world' in its rebellion against God and the Church). The quality of Christian love was demonstrated by Jesus Christ himself, who laid down his life for us, his brothers. In the context within which 1 John was written, this may have sometimes entailed a death in martyrdom for the Christian on behalf of his brothers; within the context of modern society it always entails other kinds of 'deaths'— 17 death to self and death to the things of this world. That love for God (an important NEB footnote) shows itself in those forms of compassionate concern which reverse the effects of the world's sin. The epistle is repeating the terms of the new commandment given by Jesus in John 13.34: 'I give you a new commandment: love one another; as I have loved you, so you are to love one another. If there is this love among you, then all will know that you are my disciples.'

Mark 7. 14–22

The passage commences with a 'parable' in the Marcan sense of a brief enigmatic saying which can be fully understood only by those who have a deeper perception of Christ's words. Jesus addressed the people authoritatively, as Moses did when he spoke the commandments of God.

15 Listen to me is the equivalent of saying, 'Listen, O Israel, to the statutes
and the laws which I proclaim in your hearing today' (Deut. 5.1). In the
next few words Jesus appears to sweep away much of the OT law about
the ritual uncleanness of certain foods. Explaining the parable to his
disciples later, Jesus pointed out that there is nothing unclean about
food, which is only supplied for a man's bodily wellbeing. It is from
within the heart of a man, not from his stomach, that the thoughts emerge
which lead to evil.

The interpretation of the parable seems to be more appropriate to a
mixed community of Jews and non-Jews than to Jews in Palestine. More-
over, the list of evil deeds and vices is more typical of the conventional
language of Hellenistic ethics than of the teaching of Jesus. The principle
given here was certainly accepted by the Church by the time the Gospel
was written, but there is plenty of evidence in the NT that the problem
of table-fellowship with Gentile Christians was acutely difficult for those
of Jewish upbringing (Peter's vision before going to the house of Cornelius,
Acts 10.9–16; Paul's conclusion that the law was a temporary arrange-
19 ment pending the arrival of something better, Gal. 3.19–24, etc.). **Thus he
declared all foods clean** is an editorial comment by Mark, reflecting
the position on this matter that the Church had reached by this time.
Could it be that the interpretation of the parable was one given to it in
mixed Jewish-Gentile Christian circles? Was the original saying a
profounder reflection on the mainspring of evil in man?

EIGHTH SUNDAY BEFORE CHRISTMAS
Fourth Sunday before Advent

* Genesis 3. 1–15
Ancient mythologies lurk behind the symbol of the serpent as representative of all that is evil. They lie, too, behind the idea that God might be
jealous of man's admission to sacred secrets. But such mythological
associations are transcended by the theology of the Jahwist, who tells
us that man knowingly departed from God's ways in an act of deliberate
disobedience and that this is the beginning of evil in a universe once
created good. The serpent was identified with the devil in the book of

Wisdom and in the NT, and so the symbol passed into Christian tradition.

In this passage the serpent contradicts the word of God—a typical device of the devil—and leads the woman to desire the fruit of the 6 forbidden tree, **pleasing to the eye and tempting to contemplate.** Desire leads to sinful act, another is tempted and involved—the familiar chain-reaction of evil in all its forms.

8   The picture of God **walking** like a lord **in the garden at the time of the evening breeze** may be crudely primitive, but the psychology of Adam and Eve's guilt has profound insights. The realization of their nakedness stripped them of their innocence. And Adam defended himself 12 in the way of fallen man: **The woman you gave me for a companion, she gave me fruit from the tree and I ate it.** He blamed others—and implied that ultimately God was responsible for his sin.

Later in the chapter ancient myths about the pain of childbirth and the difficulties of agriculture are brought into the curse of God, together with the rejection of Adam and Eve from the garden; but the words addressed by God to the serpent in verse 15 contain the first hints (to the Christian reader, not to the Jahwist) that the enmity between the serpent and the woman's offspring will result ultimately in man's victory. The Latin translation of this verse reads, 'She shall strike at your head'; it echoes the early Church's meditation on the office of Mary, the mother of Jesus, in the work of our redemption.

Romans 7. 7–13

The question at the beginning of the passage presupposes the discussion in the previous verses contrasting the new life of grace which is offered to us through the work of Jesus Christ with the old life which was formed on obedience to the law of Moses. Since the effect of this law had been 7 to make man aware of his sinfulness (the phrase **to become acquainted with sin** means to experience evil in its power and degradation), the problem had been raised: Does this mean that the law is the same as sin? Paul negatives the suggestion firmly. The law is God's word, a gift to his chosen people. But, he conceded, there is a connection between law and sin in that a man's inclination to rebel against God becomes evident when God's law is revealed to him. The apostle quotes the tenth commandment in a shortened form from Exod. 20.17 to show that law can rouse the desire in man to set himself over against God. The law makes clear the difference between God as Creator and man as creature, and presents man with the possibility of disobeying God. (Although Paul, as a Jew, is thinking primarily of the law of Moses, he is not forgetting the 'law' imposed by a conscience enlightened to the knowledge of good and evil in any age or race.) In this sense, then, law can be said to 'produce' sin.

9   In saying, **There was a time when, in the absence of law, I was fully alive,** Paul may have been referring to his own childish innocence until the time came for him to learn the law of Moses, as a boy brought up in a strict Jewish household; but it is more likely that he is describing in personal terms the tendency in every man to rebel against God's law

9   when faced with it. **Sin sprang to life and I died:** the commandment which should have led to life led to death. Man's original sin was exposed. Gen. 3 may have been at the back of the apostle's mind when he wrote this passage. Covetousness led to the first sin, when the serpent put into the woman's mind the temptation to disobey God: 'Of course you will not die. God knows that as soon as you eat it, your eyes will be opened and you will be like gods knowing both good and evil' (Gen 3.4–5).

10– The woman might have said with Paul, **The commandment which**
11 **should have led to life proved in my experience to lead to death, because sin found its opportunity in the commandment, seduced me, and through the commandment killed me.**

John 3. 13–21

Part of the discourse arising out of the conversation with Nicodemus (see Ninth Sunday before Christmas Year 2), now becoming a soliloquy as the evangelist meditates on the office of Christ in the re-creation of man. Central to this Gospel is the concept of eternal life—life in communion with God through Christ, life with a quality of heavenly blessedness about it. Given by Christ to those who follow him, it replaces the dying life of sinful man; it is enjoyed in its fulness only in heaven, but man has a fore-taste of it here and now—an experience of paradise restored, as it might have been, before the fall. In describing the office of Christ, John uses the

13 title which appears in the other Gospels: **the Son of Man.** The title comes from Daniel 7 where the son of man makes his triumphal appear-ance at the last judgement, and in the other Gospels it is used in sayings foretelling Christ's passion. John's version of these sayings is the prophecy

14 that **the Son of Man must be lifted up.** Lifted up on the cross? Lifted up to heaven? Both are implied, but the evangelist explains his meaning by referring to the serpent that Moses raised for the healing of those bitten by snakes: 'Moses made a bronze serpent and erected it as a standard, so that when a snake had bitten a man, he could look at the bronze serpent and recover' (Num. 21.9). According to Jewish tradition, the serpent became a 'symbol of salvation' for the people (Wis. 16.6). So

man, bitten by evil (the snake image from Gen. 3), could look to the crucified and ascended Jesus and be saved; 'salvation' has the sense of being restored to health as well as being saved. Those who have this faith
15 in Christ possess eternal life.
16   God's love for the world he had created ('world' being used here for God's creation rather than in the usual Johannine sense of evil within the world setting itself against God) was such that he gave his Son that the faithful might have this eternal life. God's primary purpose, then, was not to judge the world but to save it: to find what had been lost; 'The Son of man has come to seek and save what is lost' (Luke 19.10). Yet judgement is inevitable where Jesus is, for Christ is the embodiment of that new commandment of love which reveals by its presence the sin of man. He is the light of the world which reveals its evil. And just as in Christ men can have a foretaste of eternal life, so in Christ's presence they have a foretaste of the last judgement when Christ comes a second time. But the believer does not come under judgement. 'There is no condemnation for those who are united with Christ Jesus, because in Christ Jesus the life-giving law of the Spirit has set you free from the law of sin and death.' (Rom. 8.1.)

John's picture of Christ as the light coming into the world to reveal the sinfulness of man is what Paul meant by saying that the law brought man under judgement. We think of Adam and Eve hiding from God in the shadow of the garden, ashamed of their nakedness because it was a sign of their disobedience. But the light of Christ is more positive than the law of Moses: the law condemns, the light shines on believers and brings them to eternal life.

SEVENTH SUNDAY BEFORE CHRISTMAS
Third Sunday before Advent

* **Genesis 12. 1–9**
The beginning of the saga of Abraham, son of Terah, from southern Mesopotamia. It is a saga which was important to the Jews, but it was

even more important to the Christian Church, as we shall see when we examine today's epistle.

Although Abraham is probably a historical figure—his character comes over strongly in the stories about him—it is difficult to fit him in with the ancient history of Babylon. Probably he was one of those who revolted against contemporary polytheism and sought a new home where he could worship his God in peace. The main feature of Abraham's life is that he was willing to answer God's call and to believe in God's promise 5 about the future, and to set out with his childless wife, Sarah, and **all the dependants they had acquired in Harran,** together with Lot, for the unknown land. It was this act of faith which led to the raising up by God of a people of faith, the nation of God's choice through Abraham.

'Abram' and 'Abraham' were two forms of the same name, the difference being due to varying dialects. The name meant 'High Father' or 'He is great because of his noble descent'. But because of its similarity with the Heb. *ab haman*, it was interpreted as 'Father of a multitude' or 'Father of a host of nations' (Gen. 17.5 NEB footnote).

3   The formula, **All the families on earth will pray to be blessed as you are blessed,** is repeated four times in the book of Genesis and in the NT. Another translation is, 'The nations shall say to each other: may you be blessed as Abraham was', but in the LXX and NT this becomes, 'In you all the nations shall be blessed'.

Two background features are worthy of note. The first is that to leave home and to break ancestral bonds was to expect of ancient men almost the impossible. The attachment to one's family district in a largely static society was exceptionally strong, and one moved only in drastic circumstances, such as famine or warfare. The second is that although the story tells an actual fact about Israel's beginnings, it is doubtful whether the narrator's interest here and in what follows is solely in the representation of past events. In this call Israel saw not only an event in her earliest history, but also a basic characteristic of her life under God. Taken from the community of nations and never really rooted in Canaan (she considered herself even there a stranger, Lev. 25.23, Ps. 39.12), Israel saw herself being led on a special road whose plan and goal were in the Lord's hand. God's people are always a pilgrim people.

Romans 4. 13–end

The concluding part of Paul's examination of the way Abraham became

a friend of God. Later Jewish writings made Abraham's loyalty and
bravery an example of a man's being justified—placed in a status of acceptance by God—through the works which he accomplished. (E.g. 'Did not
Abraham prove steadfast under trial, and so gain credit as a righteous
man?' 1 Macc. 2.52.) But Paul shows that Abraham's justification came
through his faith in God, and his works were an expression of that faith.
Faith is the total commitment of a person to God, and it was because
Abraham had this that God promised that he should have a son and that
his descendants would be like the stars of heaven. Abraham's true descendants, the apostle argued, are not those who enjoy a physical descent
from the patriarch (though under the old covenant Israel enjoyed a special
place in God's purposes as his chosen people), but those who also commit
themselves to God in the way Abraham did. What justified Abraham was
his unshakeable faith that God had the power to do what he said he would
do. And the promise that God made was not in the nature of a legal
transaction (the Jewish law took the attitude that obedience was man's
side of the 'bargain') but a gift of God's grace. It is in this way that
17 scripture was fulfilled in Abraham as **father of us all**; here Paul was
speaking of Christians.

Paul strengthened this last assertion by referring to the way the patriarch
18 was willing to believe that God would give him an heir and become **father
of many nations** in spite of the fact that both he and his wife were long
past the age of having children. The way God honoured his promise to
Abraham is, for the Christian, a type of resurrection: the miraculous
birth of a son to aged parents was a resurrection from a grave. Abraham's
22 faith in God's ability to do this was **counted to him as righteousness**
(quoted from Gen. 15.6). So, also, if we believe that **the God who makes**
17, **the dead live and summons things that are not yet in existence**
24 **as if they already were** . . . **raised Jesus our Lord from the dead**,
then this too will be 'counted to us as righteousness', justifying us in the
sight of God (see page 392).

John 8. 51–end

51 **In very truth** is a Johannine phrase introducing an important statement
by Jesus. Those who obey Christ's teaching will **never know what it is
to die**. Life comes to the Christian by cleaving to the words of Christ.
The statement is made at the climax of Jesus' controversy with the Jews
in the fourth Gospel. 'Death' and 'life' had a special meaning in the
vocabulary Christ used in John, but the Jews missed the point and asked

53 if he knew what he was claiming. **Are you greater than our father Abraham, who is dead? ... What do you claim to be?** They began to believe, as they had suspected all along, that he was possessed by a devil.

Hitherto Jesus had (in this Gospel) avoided a direct answer to this question. Now he was going to make a positive claim. But before doing so he tried to deflect attention from himself to the Father in heaven. Whatever answer he made must be understood as giving glory to the Father, not to himself. Any glory Jesus manifested was of the Father, not of himself. And he warned the Jews that their most serious error was not that they did not recognize him for what he was; their error was
54 that they did **not know** God ('knowledge' being an expression of intimate relationship with a person, not merely an intellectual understanding).
56   After these preliminaries, Jesus made his claim. **Your father Abraham was overjoyed to see my day,** he began. According to rabbinic tradition, Abraham was allowed by God to see into the future history of Israel, including the dawn of the messianic age: 'To him (Abraham) alone, secretly, at dead of night, you (Lord) showed how the world would end' (2 Esdras 3.14). Again the Jews misunderstood him. How could Abraham have known Jesus when he was obviously less than fifty years of age? The figure does not mean 'just under fifty': it is a more general term than that. Luke's evidence is that Jesus was about thirty. The idea was ridiculous in the normal way, but in the Johannine picture of the work of Christ their question unwittingly embraced the truth. Jesus *was* alive at the time of Abraham, for 'When all things began, the Word already
58 was' (1.1). Then Jesus said, **Before Abraham was born, I am.** The **I am** is nothing less than the title given to God. It is the name revealed by God when Moses asked who was sending him to the Israelites: 'I am; that is who I am' (Exod. 3.14). Appropriating this title for himself, Jesus revealed his divinity—and incidentally vindicated the faith of Abraham.

SEVENTH SUNDAY BEFORE CHRISTMAS
Third Sunday before Advent

* **Genesis 22. 1–18**

The story of the testing of Abraham's faith is told from two levels: from the level of heaven, where God decides to put Abraham to the test to see if he is worthy of his promise, and from the level of earth, where the narrator unfolds the step-by-step response of Abraham to God's command, with an attention to detail which is striking and moving: e.g., Abraham himself carried the fire and the knife, objects with which a boy might injure himself, and permitted his son to carry the wood for the sacrifice. The testing shows the lengths to which a man is called to go in obeying God. The patriarch had already taken the drastic step of leaving his ancestral home. Now he is summoned to offer in sacrifice his only son, born in extreme old age, his one hope of being the father of descendants as numerous as the sands upon the sea-shore, as God had promised him. Abraham had cut himself off from the whole of his past; he must apparently be tested to prove whether his faith in God was such that he was willing to give up the whole of his future. It was as if God was saying to Abraham as he was later to say in Christ to Peter, 'Do you love me more than these?'

2 It is not known where **the land of Moriah** was. A Syriac version has 'the land of the Amorites'; the LXX has something different. The variations probably indicate that at an early period in the handing down of the story, different sanctuaries competed for the honour of being the traditional place for this event. Nor is the name Jehovah-jireh, 'the Lord will provide' (verse 14), identifiable with any known mountain. We notice that at one place in the narrative God addressed Abraham directly whilst in other places he used an angel: the differences reflect later stages in ideas about the divine transcendence, when it was believed that God would use messengers in communicating with humans.

Behind the passage is the practice of redeeming the first-born of Israel. This expressed itself ritually in the offerings made for the first-born son of a family, such as Joseph and Mary made after the birth of Jesus (Luke 2.22ff). All firstfruits belonged to God, including the first son; but, unlike other firstfruits (animals, etc.), children were not to be offered in sacrifice but were 'redeemed' and an oblation of animals or birds was made in their place (Exod. 13.11). The Fathers of the Church saw in the story a prophecy of the cross. Abraham handed over his son to death in obedience to God and received him back alive; God the Father handed over his only-begotten Son to death for the sins of the world and raised him back to life. The words of Abraham, 'God will provide himself the lamb for a burnt offering' (verse 8 RSV) reveal the sacrifice of Isaac as a type of the sacrifice of Christ.

James 2. 14–24 (or to end)

James' teaching on faith is contrasted with that of Paul (see epistle of 23 Year 2), though both quoted the same scripture, **Abraham put his faith in God, and that faith was counted to him as righteousness** (Gen. 15.6, Rom. 4.3). The verse may have been one of the Christian *testimonia* used for catechetical purposes. Paul taught that it was Abraham's faith which made him righteous in the eyes of God; James that it was Abraham's actions (works) through which he was justified.

But in fact both authors are saying the same thing in a different way. Paul wanted to rule out the idea, which faithfulness to the law seemed to promote, that a person can earn salvation by the performance of good deeds without having faith in Jesus Christ. Such a view contradicted the truth that man is sinful and in need of redemption; it also suggested that faith in Jesus Christ was unnecessary. Yet Paul did not deny that the Christian who has been saved by grace must demonstrate his new status as a son of God by his actions: 'The only thing that counts is faith active in love' (Gal. 5.6).

James, on the other hand, was refuting those who say that only faith 17 of an orthodox and intellectual kind is necessary. **If it does not lead to action, (faith) is in itself a lifeless thing.** To feed the hungry with nothing but good wishes is a mockery of the Christian religion. The epistle takes two examples from the OT. The first is Abraham, whose willingness to offer his son Isaac as a sacrifice was proof of his faith. Abraham was justified by his actions inasmuch as they were tangible proofs of his faith and of the extent to which he trusted God. The other example is that of Rahab, who assisted the two spies sent by Joshua into Jericho. (The use of a character whose profession was highly dishonourable as an illustration of faith is another way in which the Bible underlines the unexpected element in God's dealings with men.) Rahab, by giving assistance to the spies, demonstrated her faith in God through his people. These actions are not such as, according to the law, would justify a man in themselves, they are 'works' which reveal the quality of a person's faith in God.

Luke 20. 9–17

The parable of the vineyard uses a familiar image: 'Thou didst bring a vine out of Egypt; thou didst drive out nations and plant it' (Ps. 80.8). 'I will sing for my beloved my love-song about his vineyard' (Isa. 5.1–7). The image of Israel as the vineyard of the Lord of hosts is a recurrent one in Judaism.

The way Jesus used it in the parable, however, turned it almost into an allegory of his Father's mission to Israel. The servants are the prophets, who were unheeded or ill-treated, as Jeremiah was by the people. The
13 last to be sent was the owner of the vineyard's **own dear son**—a phrase which recalls the words of God at the baptism of Christ (Mark 1.11; Matt. 3.17; Luke 3.22). The fate of the son is a prophecy of Christ's passion and death outside the walls of Jerusalem. But perhaps to his hearers Jesus' parable came as a warning to the hierarchy of the Jews. They had defied every representative sent to them from God and now they were so far removed from God that they no longer were able to hear his appeal, even through his Son. The vineyard would be let to others: God's people would be fathered from other nations, leaving the Jewish leaders to their fate.

SIXTH SUNDAY BEFORE CHRISTMAS
Second Sunday before Advent

* Exodus 3. 7–15

Moses, given his apostolic mission by God (see Lent 4 Year 2) began to
11 find difficulties with it. He made two objections: (1) **Who am I that I should go to Pharaoh, and that I should bring the Israelites out of Egypt**? This is one of genuine humility at the presence of God. In reply, God assured him of divine assistance in fulfilling his mission and announced a prophetic sign: when the people had been rescued from Egypt, they would worship on that very spot and God would reveal himself and
13 thus vindicate what he had done through Moses. (2) **If I go to the Israelites and tell them that the God of their forefathers has sent**

54

me to them, and they ask me his name, what shall I say? This
information was essential, for knowledge of the divine name guaranteed
14 the authenticity of his mission. The Name, God told him, is **I am**: in its
various forms (**I will be what I will be**, NEB footnote) it expresses God's
unlimited existence as contrasted with the nothingness of other gods; it
also denotes God as 'the God who acts'. Another tradition behind the
text reveals the Name as Yahweh (Hebrew YHWH), often pronounced
15 'Jehovah'. The eternal nature of God is affirmed in the last sentence, **This
is my name for ever; this is my title in every generation.**

Hebrews 3. 1–6

Moses was a forerunner of Jesus Christ or a 'type' of the Messiah. The
preceding section of this letter ends with a description of Jesus as a
merciful and faithful High Priest; chapter 3 opens with an explanation
about the way in which Jesus can be called faithful.

1   Addressed to fellow-Christians, **brothers in the family of God,
who share a heavenly calling,** the writer of the letter reminded them
that Christ is both **Apostle and High Priest.** 'Apostle', meaning 'one
who is sent', indicates Jesus' status as one sent by God to mankind;
'High Priest' indicates Jesus' function as one who represents mankind
before God, in the manner of the high priests of the Jewish cult. It is at
this point that the writer brought in the figure of Moses. In his day the
patriarch also combined apostolic and priestly offices—he was sent by
God and he was the representative of the people before God. The care
of God's household was entrusted to Moses as to a steward (a familiar
job in the extended well-to-do family groupings of the New Testament
era), and in this vocation he was faithful to God and fulfilled his task.
Stewardship of this same household was also entrusted to Jesus Christ,
3 but Jesus is **worthy of greater honour than Moses, as the founder
of a house enjoys more honour than his household,** for he is Son of
the Founder.

The term 'household', or 'family of God', would be meaningful in
apostolic times, for the contemporary household, like that of Cornelius,
included relatives, servants, and other dependents as well as the family
gathered round its head. It was around such households that the local
congregations gathered in the early Church for their life together and
worship. The household of God, to which Christians belong, is seen as
the continuation of the old Israel.

John 6. 27-35

Part of the bread of life discourse which followed the feeding of the five thousand by the Sea of Galilee. The fourth Gospel tells us that Jesus was speaking at Passover time, and many of the features in the discourse —bread, manna, heavenly provision—figured in the ritual of the feast. The crowds had been searching for Jesus after the miracle, perhaps supposing he would do something else for them; they had failed to grasp the meaning of the 'sign', the Johannine name for that by which Jesus revealed his glory (2.11). To turn their minds away from only material benefits, Jesus told them to look for those spiritual blessings which would

27 bring them past the judgement on the last day, **the food of eternal life.** These spiritual blessings would be given by the Son of Man—Jesus applied to himself the title of the mysterious figure of Daniel 7 associated

27 with the judgement of God. The meaning of **He it is upon whom God the Father has set the seal of his authority** is debatable: the crowd would have taken it to refer to the Son of Man in Daniel 7; Christians interpret the saying as a reference to Jesus himself on whom God 'set his seal', e.g. at Christ's baptism.

28 The concept of **work** was important in the Jewish religion: a man worked to fulfil the law of Moses, he applied himself to the observance of God's commandments. Asked about this, Jesus replied that the only

29 'work' required of them was faith **in the one whom God has sent.** The question and reply are virtually the same as in Mark 10.17, 'What must I do to win eternal life? . . . Follow me.' The Jews retorted that they must have a sign from Christ to justify their belief in him. They had not seen that Jesus had already, since the wedding at Cana in the fourth Gospel, been working signs pointing to himself as *the* Sign, the manifestation of God in flesh. They hinted that further miracles of feeding with bread such as the Israelites were given by Moses in the desert would be acceptable. (In suggesting this, they unknowingly presented Jesus with the temptation he faced in the desert, when the devil suggested he win popular support by turning stones into food.) Manna was believed to be one of the marks of the messianic age.

Again Jesus had to point out errors in their suggestion. First, it was not Moses who gave bread in the desert but God. Second, the sign they

33 demanded of bread from heaven had already been given them—**he who comes down from heaven** (NEB footnote). This is food for eternity.

34 Their next request, **Sir, give us this bread now and always,** echoes the petition in the Lord's Prayer. Jesus then revealed that he himself is

35 **the bread of life** in one of the **I am** sayings of the fourth Gospel which

56

point to the Name of God (see p. 51). What Jesus was offering was not satisfaction for physical needs only but the fulfilment of all human desires into eternity.

The questions and answers resemble those with the woman at the well (see Epiphany 4 Year 2), and the two discourses stand together: Jesus is the living water and the heavenly bread. The bread of the Eucharist is related to what is said, though John looks beyond the sacrament to that which it signifies. We note that those who enjoy the blessings of Christ's gifts are those who believe *in* him.

SIXTH SUNDAY BEFORE CHRISTMAS
Second Sunday before Advent

* Exodus 6. 2–8

A fresh call and encouragement to Moses, following the dispute with the 2 foremen and Moses' uncertainty (5.6–23). **I am the Lord** is another form of the 'I am who I am' saying, containing the revelation of God as pure being. The oracle begins and ends with these words, indicating that God is speaking in terms of himself, not in terms of one of his attributes. He identifies himself with the God of Abraham, Isaac, and Jacob, and 3 repeats the divine name, **Jehovah (see p. 55)**.

The oracle contains a summary of Israel's faith in God through his action in revealing himself to the patriarchs; making a covenant concerning the land of Canaan, recognizing Israel's captivity, recalling his promise to release them, adopting them as his people, and leading them into the land of promise.

Hebrews 11. 17–31

It is faith that is the keynote of this reading, summoning up a roll-call of the great heroes of the faith of Israel's past from Abel to the Maccabeans. These were men and women who lived by the conviction that the things they saw and the things that happened were not God's last word; that out of disasters, even death itself, God would vindicate his own. 'Faith gives substance (assurance, NEB footnote) to our hopes, and makes us certain of realities we do not see' (11.1; see p. 373). The list of names, of which this passage is a selection, forms a fitting summary to the themes of the readings for the last few Sundays.

17   The roll-call begins with **Abraham**, who was prepared to offer up **his only son** at the word of God, thus demonstrating the quality of his faith; he believed that God was capable of raising the dead if necessary to vindicate God's promise to him. Isaac's faith is exemplified in the blessing he gave his sons, showing his belief in God's promise to Abraham (though the author's memory is playing tricks with him, since it was only Jacob who was blessed. What Isaac said of Esau could hardly be called a blessing! Gen. 27). Jacob handed on the blessing to his grandchildren in faith (Gen. 48.16–20). Joseph's faith was even more remarkable in that, before there was any oppression of the Israelites in Egypt, he foresaw the Exodus and made arrangements for his mummified body to be taken to the land of promise (Gen. 50.24–25).

But most important in this roll-call for our readings today is what was said of Moses. The author drew on five incidents in Moses' experiences as illustrations of faith. First, his parents by faith defied the king's edict by hiding the child to save him from being drowned. Secondly, Moses himself refused recognition as the son of Pharaoh's daughter and rejected
25   high office under the Pharaoh; **sin** in this connection seems to be the sin of apostasy involved in serving the Egyptians, though it could also mean the immoral pleasures associated with the life of Pharaoh's court. Moses
26   preferred to identify himself with the people of Israel, **God's Anointed** collectively (Ps. 89.50). The author saw that Moses believed God would recompense them for their ill-treatment, as he later vindicated Jesus,
27   his Christ ('Anointed One'). Thirdly, Moses **left Egypt** at the Exodus (rather than after the killing of the Egyptian, when it is said that 'Moses was alarmed' Exod. 2.14—unless it is perhaps another occasion when the
28   author forgot the detail of the OT narrative). Fourthly, **he celebrated the Passover** and put the blood of the paschal lamb on the lintel and two sideposts of the Israelites' houses as a sign for God to deny access to the destroying angel (Exod. 12.23), believing God would kill the Egyptians' firstborn but spare the Israelites' children. Finally, in faith
29   he stretched his hand out over **the Red Sea** for the waters to go back that the people might cross confidently over and leave the Egyptians to drown. The faith that can move mountains (Matt. 17.20) can move the sea. That it was Moses' faith in God which caused the destruction of the Egyptians is shown by the fact that according to Exod. 14.27 he raised his hand a second time and the waters engulfed them. If this was their

faith, the writer seems to ask us as he looks back on these heroes, what about ours?

Mark 13. 5–13

Part of what is known as 'the little apocalypse of Mark' which precedes the narrative of the passion in this Gospel. Mark depicted Jesus speaking privately to his disciples, so that what he said was a revelation of God's secrets to his chosen ones.

An 'apocalypse' or 'revelation' was a form of literature not uncommon among the Jews in Jesus' day. Such works were composed by visionaries who were inspired to see in the events around them signs of that coming supernatural drama which would end the present world order and usher in the judgement of God on all the nations. They recognized in wars and
8 disasters **the birth-pangs of the new age,** testing the hearts of the faithful. This form passed into Christian literature and found its supreme expression in the Book of Revelation. By contrast, the apocalyptic discourse which Mark included in his Gospel is a comparatively restrained prophecy by Jesus of future events which would have happened by the time Mark wrote. The year A.D. 70 witnessed the Jewish revolt, when Titus' army occupied Jerusalem and destroyed the Temple: this seems to be in the background of the passage.

Jesus warned his disciples not to be deceived by those who would come
6 pretending to be the Messiah and using the divine title, **I am he.** There must have been pretenders, unknown to us, who in apostolic times claimed to be Jesus returned from heaven, such as those who fooled the Christians in Thessalonica into thinking that the end had arrived. Already the disciples may have heard rumours of troubles on the eastern
7 and northern frontiers of the empire which constituted **the noise of battle near at hand and the news of battles far away.** There were famines and earthquakes in the time of the emperors Claudius and Nero. Verse 8 is an adaptation of Isa. 19.2.

The unpopularity of Christians is attested in other sources. Tacitus (*Annals* 15.44) spoke of them as 'a class hated for their abominations' and of their religion as 'a mischievous superstition', and the Acts of the Apostles gives instances of Peter and Paul and other disciples appearing
9 **before governors and kings on my (Jesus') account to testify in their presence.** In one of the few references to the Holy Spirit in this Gospel, Mark recorded Christ's promise to his followers that when they were summoned before the courts they could rely on the power of the Holy

Spirit in guiding them what to say. Divisions would be created even within families—a terrible thing to contemplate from the viewpoint of
10 Jewish family solidarity. But before the end the Gospel must be proclaimed to all nations—a widespread vision of the Church's future growth.

FIFTH SUNDAY BEFORE CHRISTMAS
Sunday next before Advent

* 1 Kings 19. 9–18

Alone and unsupported, and in need of encouragement for his faith, Elijah set out to escape the vengeance of Jezebel, and reached Horeb, the holy mountain of the covenant and the law-giving, Sinai. It was the place where the true God revealed himself (Exod. 3.1ff, 33.18—34.9) and where the covenant had been concluded. Elijah entered that cave where Moses had crouched when the glory of God appeared (Exod. 33.22).

The storm, earthquake, and lightning, which in Exod. 19 had manifested the presence of God, did not contain the message that Elijah needed; they were only the heralds of the Lord's coming. The whisper of a light breeze signified that God is a spirit and that he converses intimately with his prophets; it does not mean that God's dealings with men are necessarily gentle and unnoticed—as indeed the career of Elijah was to demonstrate!

13   Elijah muffled his face in his cloak because the theophany had roused his fear at the presence of the Lord—though the theophany had been gentler than that on mount Sinai, an indication perhaps that God was now seen as communicating with men inwardly rather than through spectacular phenomena. Asked what he was doing on the mountain, Elijah explained that through the disobedience of the people he was the only faithful one left. The way was prepared for the later concept that God would work, not through the whole people, but through a faithful remnant, through one faithful man.

The task of anointing Jehu king was in fact performed by Elisha
16 (2 Kings 9. 1–13). The charge to anoint Elisha to be prophet in your place is a novel departure from OT practice. Anointing was usually

reserved for kings and priests. Since Hazael was not anointed but simply
told he would be king by Elisha (2 Kings 8.13), and since there is no
record of Elijah actually anointing Elisha, it is thought that the word
really means 'to set apart', which is what anointing signified.

17   The terrible slaughter prophesied in the words, **Anyone who escapes
the sword of Hazael Jehu will slay, and anyone who escapes
the sword of Jehu Elisha will slay,** is a foretaste of the idea to be
developed by later prophets that God uses war as an instrument of divine
18 discipline. The number **seven thousand** is a conventional one; kissing
an image of a god was a common expression of devotion in primitive
religions.

The story brings together the figures of Moses and Elijah; both
experienced a theophany of God on the holy mountain, and by it Elijah
understood that he was to continue the work of Moses in maintaining the
covenant and restoring the ancient faith of Israel.

Romans 11. 13–24

Paul's special commission was to go and preach the gospel to the Gentiles
(Gal. 2.7,9), but writing to Gentile Christians in Rome, he admitted
that he hoped it would come about that through the success of his mission
Jews would be brought to consider the gospel more carefully. The
14 conversion of **some of them** would be wonderful, for it would herald the
full return of all Israel to God—and when that happened it would mean
15 **nothing less than life from the dead!** By this, Paul did not mean that
the Jews would be rejuvenated. It was part of the common Christian
expectation that, when Israel was converted, the consummation of all
things would be at hand. Paul meant by 'life from the dead' that the general
resurrection would take place as the first act of the eschatological drama
at the end of time.

16   **If the first portion of dough is consecrated, so is the whole
lump.** The reference was to the sacrificial offering of the first-fruits loaf.
'Whenever you eat the bread of the country, you shall set aside a contri-
bution for the Lord' (Num. 15.19–21). The offering released the rest of
the bread for general consumption. The rest of the passage is an elaborate
working out of a metaphor of an olive tree (a symbol of Israel in the OT).
The root of the tree is like the first-fruits loaf: being consecrated, it
16 makes the rest of the tree holy. In the metaphor **the root** was intended by
Paul to represent the first Jewish Christians or, more probably, Jesus
Christ himself. The Gentiles' place in the saving work of God through
Christ is comparable to that of wild branches grafted on to the olive

tree; the Jews who rejected Christ, on the other hand, are like branches that have been lopped off. Those to whom the apostle was writing, then,

17 **have come to share the same root and sap as the olive.** All the grace and hope that has been given mankind has come through Jesus Christ as the one for whom Israel looked.

But the Gentiles had no reason to think themselves in any way
22 superior to the rejected Jews. If they fell away, God's **kindness** would become his **severity.** (The wrath of God has been described as the love of God as seen by the sinner.) Gentile Christians could be lopped off from the vine as well. Jews who repented, on the other hand, would be
24 grafted in again. **For if you were cut from your native wild olive and against all nature grafted into the cultivated olive, how much more readily will they, the natural olive-branches, be grafted into their native stock!**

Matthew 24. 37–44

In a series of sayings about the coming of the Son of Man (only Matthew among the evangelists used the word *parousia*) Jesus emphasized the need for watchfulness by drawing on the story of Noah and his family. The contemporaries of Noah were so corrupt that God had 'determined to make an end of all flesh' (Gen. 6.11–13 RSV). Here Christ merely men-
38 tioned their heedlessness: **In the days before the flood they ate and drank and married.** When the flood arrived, it took them completely
39 by surprise: **They knew nothing until the flood came and swept them all away.** Christians must be very different if they are to be ready when the Son of Man comes. Quite suddenly in the midst of their ordinary daily occupations one will be taken to join the elect in the Kingdom of heaven and the other left to face the last judgement.

The warning is further reinforced by the parable of the householder
44 and the burglar. **Hold yourselves ready, therefore, because the Son of Man will come at the time you least expect him.**

FIFTH SUNDAY BEFORE CHRISTMAS
Sunday next before Advent

* Isaiah 10. 20-23

The historical setting of these verses is uncertain, but the prophet seems to speak against the background of an Israelite surrender to Assyria, whereby Israel became once more its vassal. Isaiah looked forward to the
20 time when the people would **cease to lean on him that proved their destroyer, but shall loyally lean on the Lord, the Holy One of**
21 **Israel.** Those who did this would only be a remnant. This concept was central to Isaiah. He called his son Shear-jashub, 'a remnant shall return' (7.3), and he prophesied that in the end only a few would survive the final
22 judgement even though the people became **as many as the sands of the sea.** The destruction of the rest would be complete.

Romans 9. 19-28

Paul had been arguing that it was necessary to accept the predestinating sovereignty of God if God's dealings with men were to be seen as resting entirely upon his love and mercy. In developing this argument, the apostle had said that God's sovereignty even extended to making 'men stubborn as he chooses' (verse 18). At this point—which is where our passage begins—he forestalled the objection: if God treats men like this,
19 **then why does God blame a man? For who can resist his will** if it is God's purpose that a person should disobey him?

The apostle did not attempt to answer the objection, which comes in that mysterious region where the free will of man ends and where the overriding will of God is discerned even in acts which are contrary to his purpose and command. Instead, Paul said that, since man can never do anything other than as God's creature, he has no right to query the way God treats him. He is like a vessel of clay in the hands of the potter.
21 **Surely the potter can do what he likes with the clay.** (The analogy was drawn from Isa. 29.16, 45.9, etc.) A man's wisest course is to accept his position as a creature with humility.

God's predestined will is absolute, but Paul did not go quite as far as
22 to say that God pre-determines which vessels were to be **objects of**
23 **retribution due for destruction** and which would enjoy **the full wealth of his splendour.** He did not entirely rule out universal salvation in verses 22 and 23, though he certainly did not regard it as inevitable. If a man is damned, it is not because God has predestined him to this

fate but because that individual has, through his own free choice, rejected God's love and mercy.

The passage ends with quotations from the OT which Paul used to prove that it was God's purpose to call the Gentiles but that he called only a remnant of Israel. The first two quotations come from Hos. 2.23
25 and 1.10. In Hosea **not my people** and **the unloved nation** were the disobedient Israelites, but the apostle applied the words to the Gentiles (who were not regarded as God's people by Israel). The second quotation
27 comes from Isa. 10.22. **The remnant** is reduced to one—Jesus Christ. Henceforth those who were to be saved would be saved in him.

Mark 13. 14-23

Part of the 'little apocalypse' of Mark 13 (see pp. 59-60) in which Christ is depicted as disclosing his nature as Son of Man and Son of God and foretelling the signs of his second coming. This piece of Christian prophecy is thought by some scholars to be linked with the riots which took place in Jerusalem in A.D. 40 when the emperor Caligula attempted to have a statue of himself set up in the temple. To the Jews this was a repetition of the disaster of 167 B.C. when Antiochus IV Epiphanes profaned the temple by making it a sanctuary of Olympian Zeus (1 Macc.
14 1.54-64). Dan. 9.27 called it **the abomination of desolation**, playing on the Hebrew words for the title of the pagan god. Other scholars have linked Mark 13 with the destruction of Jerusalem in A.D. 70. The phrase, **let the reader understand**, indicates that the evangelist hesitated to be more specific about the reference.

The coming of the Son of Man would be preceded by disasters such
14 as those which happened in wartime. **Those who are in Judaea must take to the hills** because it was among the caves and crevices that the
15 people took refuge to escape the attention of an invading army. **A man who is on the roof** would have to escape down the ladder that went down to the ground outside the house without going indoors. Nursing mothers would be trapped. Winter was the worst time for such catastrophe.
18, **Those days will bring distress such as never has been until now**
19 **since the beginning of the world which God created—and will never be again.** The first part of this sentence is a quotation from Dan. 12.1, describing the moments before the final deliverance of the people
20 'to everlasting life'. Since the great tribulation would mean that **no living thing could survive**, God had for the sake of his own decided to **cut short the time.** The idea of shortening the days of tribulation has its origins in the OT.

Another of the signs of the coming of the Son of Man would be the
21 false prophets who would deceive people by saying, **Look, here is the
Messiah, or, Look, there he is.** There would also be impostors of
various kinds. Christ warned his followers to be on their guard against
them. The faithful disciples must be on the watch for the true advent
of God's Son.

ADVENT SUNDAY
Fourth Sunday before Christmas
See pages 28–29

* Isaiah 52. 7–10

The prophecies of the Second Isaiah originated in the period immediately
before and after the fall of Babylon to the armies of Cyrus, king of Persia
(539 B.C.) The prophet exulted in joyful anticipation of the exiles' return
to Jerusalem which God had made possible by anointing Cyrus as his
agent (44.28). The prophet's mission was to warn the people that
Yahweh's advent was imminent and that the Lord would reveal himself
not only to Israel but also to the whole world.

In verses 7 to 10 the prophet's work reaches its climax with the procla-
7 mation of his 'gospel'. It is the **good news** that, in spite of the past, God
is still king. Different voices are built into a crescendo of joy. There is the
single voice of the messenger, whose feet are lovely because of the news
he brings across the mountains which surround the holy city. There are
the voices of the watchmen on the ruined walls shouting when they see
8 the Lord **returning to Zion** (NEB footnote). And there are the voices of
9 those inhabitants within the ruins who learn that **the Lord . . . has
ransomed Jerusalem.** Verse 10 affirms that the Lord has shown his
strength and brought deliverance to Israel in the sight of all other nations
The belief that other nations, especially those who had oppressed her,
would see Israel's final vindication was an important element in the
prophetic tradition.

1 Thessalonians 5. 1–11
Jewish apocalyptic ideas about the Day of the Lord, when God would
bring to an end the present order with its sinfulness and corruption and

establish his rule, vindicating his people and eliminating his (and their) enemies, passed into Christian expectation concerning the Second Coming; and it is about this particular topic that Paul was writing in his letter to the Church in Thessalonica. The matter was of importance, for there were teachers among the congregation saying that the Second Coming had happened already and some were anxious about the fate of those who had died. Paul himself was in the full throes of his life's work and, convinced of the imminence of the parousia, wanted to bring the gospel to the Gentiles while there was time.

2   The arrival of the Day, he said, in words which echo Christ's own teaching (Matt. 24.43), will be as unexpected as **a thief in the night**. But he had no idea when that Day would be and could only repeat what Jesus himself had said (Matt. 24.36). He knew that it would come as suddenly as the labour pains of a pregnant woman—a simile used in Jewish apocalyptic for the messianic woes which, it was thought, would precede the coming of the Day.

Reference to the Day led the apostle's mind, by an association of ideas, to the contrast between daylight and darkness as a symbol of the light in which Christians walk and the sin from which they have been delivered.

5   We are **children of light, children of day**. We must be wakeful and sober, as those who watch. Since we are children of light, we have nothing to fear from the judgement of God which will occur on that Day. Employing one of his favourite metaphors (borrowed, perhaps, from contemporary Christian catechesis) the apostle urged the Christians to arm themselves with faith, hope, and love, the three virtues which are the subject of the hymn in 1 Corinthians 13. God has destined us all, living Christians as well as the faithful departed, to live in company with him through the sacrifice of Jesus Christ. The Thessalonians can strengthen one another with this belief.

At the time this letter was written, Paul was expecting the parousia within his own lifetime (1 Thess. 4.17). Later his views changed and he decided he would probably die before the Lord came.

Luke 21. 25-33

In answer to a question about the last times, Jesus had answered—according to the arrangement of his sayings in Luke—that there would be wars and natural disasters, persecutions for Christians, and Jerusalem itself would be destroyed (a prophecy which had been fulfilled in A.D. 70, when the Roman army under Titus seized the city and razed the temple to the ground. Luke may well have known about this when he wrote.) But

these would not necessarily be signs that the end was at hand. Luke's theological insight convinced him that Christ's coming must be delayed in order that all men might hear the gospel. The signs to look for would
25 be cosmic—universal in their implications. **Portents will appear in sun, moon, and stars**: the continuity and orderliness of the whole world would be interrupted. **The roar and surge of the sea** was a symbol for a momentary return to that state of chaos which ruled the universe before the Creator called it to order. **On earth nations will stand helpless**:
26 the event would reveal to all men their utter weakness. **The celestial powers will be shaken**: these were believed to control the destinies of men as unfolded in the movement of sun, moon, and stars. Before the last day, however—and here the Lucan eschatological scheme differs from those in other NT writings—there would be the return of the Son of Man. As at the transfiguration and the ascension, the glory of God would be manifested in this mysterious person from Daniel 7, identified in the NT with Jesus at his parousia. The cloud was a symbol of the divine presence, the *shekinah*, in biblical imagery.
28 What are Christians to do when these things happen? **Stand upright and hold your heads high, because your liberation is near.** They can be confident that the consequences of Christ's redemption are universal. In their Redeemer they will be saved from whatever overtakes this world and the men in it at the end of time. Christ told them to be watchful, to look for the signs as they might look for the first buds on the
29 fig-tree (**or any other tree** Luke adds, for the benefit of readers in whose territory the fig-tree might not flourish). The fig-tree is one of Palestine's few deciduous trees; it stands starkly bare in the winter, and only puts on fresh green leaves in the spring—rapidly, for the interval between winter and summer is short, March to mid-May. Like these rapid signs, so also will the portents of the Day of the Son of Man be, telling his
31 followers that **the kingdom of God is near.**

After the parable comes a declaration that these things will happen within a generation. Mark understood this prediction to include the Second Coming (Mark 13.30) but Luke, writing years later, seems to have interpreted it as a reference to the disaster of A.D. 70.

ADVENT SUNDAY
Fourth Sunday before Christmas
See pages 28–29

* Isaiah 51. 4–11
The OT lesson is in two sections (though the exegetical problems associated with these verses, not detailed here, go much deeper than that): the first is an address by God to the people (5–8); the second is an appeal or lament to God by the people (9–11).

First, the Lord directs the nation's gaze towards the coming world-judgement in which heaven and earth and those who dwell in it are to be destroyed. When the end of the world comes, there will be only one
6, 8 security—God's salvation which continues for ever (the phrase, **my saving power shall never wane/shall last for ever**, appears twice in the passage). The law of God, his divine instructions, will be vindicated and he will rule all nations. When the signs of the end appear, his people
8 are to look to him and to the **deliverance** from the judgement which he brings **to all generations**.

Secondly, the people cry to God for help. Their situation is that of the Babylonian exile or something very much like it, when they are surrounded by oppressors. God appears to be silent or inactive, so they appeal to him to awake and to do for them what he did in the past. Verses 9 and 10 link God's work of creation with his work of redemption at the
9 exodus. **Rahab** and **the dragon** are the figures from ancient eastern mythologies which depict the act of creation as the victory of God over primeval chaos, and the waters of that myth are associated with the waters of the Red Sea which also obeyed God's word. The anthropo-
9 morphism implied in the words, **Put on your strength, O arm of the Lord** speaks of an arming with weapons, an important feature in the ancient myths which tell of the struggle with chaos. When God acts for his people, as he did in the past, they will return to Zion with joy and their sorrows will be over. The lament asks God to let the new exodus begin.

Romans 13. 8–end
The whole of Paul's letter to the Church in Rome was directed towards showing what the love of God has achieved for us in Jesus Christ. Here he stresses that the love of our neighbour is the dynamo that energizes our Christian conduct. The charge to pay all outstanding debts, with which this passage begins, led him to say that there is one debt which we
8 can never repay—the debt of love to our neighbour. Yet **he who loves**

his neighbour has satisfied every claim of the law. We are no longer 'in debt' to the law. For example, the apostle said, take any of the commandments which govern our relationships with other people (and he cited four of them), and you will find that they are all summed up in the 9 one rule, **Love your neighbour as yourself**. With love as the motive, 10 nothing can affect our neighbours in an evil way: therefore **the whole law is fulfilled by love** (NEB footnote).

To emphasize his injunction, the apostle reminded his readers that they were living in critical times. The Greek word for 'time', *kairos*, is translated in biblical terms as 'the latter days' and refers to the eschatological era which has been ushered in by the death and resurrection of Jesus Christ. This critical 'time' is the age of salvation and is coextensive with the age of the Church on earth. Christians are emancipated from the age of this world and the kingdom of darkness and are already living in the age to come and in the Kingdom of God and his Son. Although Paul said less in this letter about the coming of Christ than he did in earlier writings, yet his idea was that the lapse of time between the conversion of Paul and his readers and the moment of writing was a significant proportion of the total interval between the resurrection and the parousia. The consummation of God's final act of redemption was near.

In the OT lesson the prophet and the people called on God to awake out of sleep; here it is the apostle who told the people to awake. The 'day' which is coming is not just the day of judgement: it is 'the age to come' (as night is 'this age'). The practical consequence of Paul's reveille is the moral life of the Christian, a putting on of the armour for the conflict with temptations and evil. It is possible that behind the exhortations there is a common form of catechetical instruction used by the apostolic Church to help the converts distinguish between walking in the light and walking in the darkness, as they put behind them the customs and standards of a pagan society. The armour is none other than Jesus himself.

Matthew 25. 31–end

One of a series of prophecies and warnings which in Matthew precede the narrative of the passion. They are set against the background of contemporary Jewish apocalyptic writings, but with some unique and striking features. One of these is that it is the Son of Man himself who will be 31 judge at the end of time. **When the Son of Man comes in his glory** is an image from Dan. 7.13–15 describing the solemn moment of divine judgement, but in the OT it is God himself who judges. Furthermore, Jesus described the Son of Man as sitting in state on his throne—another function in Jewish apocalypse attributed only to God. Into this picture Jesus brought the scene of the Palestinian shepherd pasturing his mixed flock of light-coloured sheep and dark-coated goats until he has to separate them; the animals represent the righteous and the wicked who remain together in this life until they are separated by the Judge (the basic meaning of the Greek word *krinein* 'to judge', is 'to separate'). The former inherit the Father's blessing, the latter are cursed and sent into the eternal fire—again Jesus used images from Jewish apocalypse.

Another unique and striking feature of the passage is the way in which Jesus identified himself with the needy and underprivileged. When he answered the question, On what grounds will a man be judged on the last day? he answered this entirely in terms of that man's conduct towards his neighbours. He would not be judged on his membership of the Jewish race or his success in keeping the Law of Moses, but on what he did for those around him. The list of needy and underprivileged is taken from Jewish lists commending acts of charity (except that of visiting prisoners). But who are these people? The whole of mankind? This is how the
40 passage is usually interpreted. But Jesus specifically said, **Anything you did for one of my brothers here, however humble, you did for me**: 'brothers' is the normal NT term for fellow-Christians. Jesus called 'brothers' those who, like him, could address God as 'Father'.

ADVENT 2
Third Sunday before Christmas

* Isaiah 55. 1-11
God's word has power to achieve all that he has promised, and in this passage he summoned Israel through the prophet to a new condition of salvation. The vendors in the market-place try to sell the essentials of life, water and bread; but God offers freely not just water and bread but
1 the fat of the land, **wine and milk** (NEB footnote). All the people have to do is to listen to God's word and to obey it. The prophecy seems to be addressed to those in exile in Babylon. God intended to make a lasting covenant with them, the content of which was compared to the favour he once showed David. What was promised for that king personally by God

 4 was extended for the whole nation. David was **a witness to all races, a
    prince and instructor of peoples**; now Israel was going to be blessed in
    such a way that other nations would see the glory of God revealed in her.
 6 **Inquire of the Lord while he is present, call upon him when he
    is close at hand** is basically a summons to worship, to offer oblations
    to God, and to pray to him in the temple. But as used by the prophets,
    it became a summons to worship God by obedience to him in daily life.
    This involved the abandonment of the ways and thoughts of the wicked,
    an act of repentance. The ways and thoughts of God are on a different
 9 plane: **For as the heavens are higher than the earth, so are my ways
    higher than your ways, and my thoughts than your thoughts.**
    The Creator of the world and the Lord of history has plans and designs
    for procuring Israel's salvation, and his word is as prolific as the fertile
11 cycles of rain and growth in the earth: **the word which comes from my
    mouth (shall) prevail; it shall not return to me fruitless without
    accomplishing my purpose.**

2 Timothy 3. 14—4. 5

Timothy was the son of a heathen father and a converted Jewish mother.
He first joined Paul's entourage at Lystra in Lycaonia at the beginning of
the latter's second missionary journey. He was already a Christian of some
standing, having probably been converted when Paul preached in the
neighbourhood a year or two previously. The apostle persuaded Timothy
to accompany him, but first circumcised him as a concession to Jewish
susceptibilities among Christians (Acts 16.1–3). He remained Paul's
constant companion and intimate friend, collaborating with him in several
letters (1 and 2 Thess., 2 Cor., Phil., Col., and Philem.) and being entrusted with important missions—to Thessalonica (1 Thess. 3.2) and
Corinth (1 Cor. 4.17). The apostle regarded him as his 'colleague' (Rom.
16.21) and 'a dear son and a most trustworthy Christian' (1 Cor. 4.17).
When Paul was setting out on his last journey to Jerusalem, Timothy was
in the party (Acts 20.4) and he was at his side during his Roman imprison-
ment. Indeed Paul drew special comfort from his presence and planned
to send him on a mission to the Philippian church (Phil. 2.19–24). At
the time of the Letters to Timothy, he was an apostolic delegate in temporary charge of the church in Ephesus. He was still relatively young and
needed the apostle's guidance and encouragement.

In this passage, Paul is urging him to stand by the truths which he has
learned and believed. He learned them from his Christian mother, Eunice,
and his Christian grandmother, Lois; he also learned them from the

'sacred writings' (the usual Greek expression for the Old Testament scriptures) from childhood—Eunice may have followed the normal Jewish custom of making her son memorize passages of the Law by heart. These make the Christian wise with the wisdom of God which leads him to salvation through faith in Christ Jesus.

A note of urgency is sounded at the beginning of Chapter 4. Paul was expecting martyrdom before the second advent of Christ. When Christ

4.1 came he would judge men living and dead—a phrase that is found elsewhere in the NT and that already sounds like a credal expression, as

2 in the Nicene Creed. Appearance is the English translation of the Greek *epiphaneia*, from which 'epiphany' is derived. He urges Timothy to preach the gospel at every opportunity, especially as he foresaw a time when Christians might refuse to listen to it and succumb to a morbid fascination for other cults. As an evangelist, Timothy must be a sound and resourceful teacher of the Christian truth.

The Old Testament was the only canonical scriptures for the early Church in apostolic times and for several generations afterwards. Irenaeus (*c.* 180) was the first to speak of a 'New Testament', though as early as 2 Pet. 3.15f Paul's letters were being ranked as 'inspired wisdom', while for Ignatius (*c.* 110) 'the gospel' was an equivalent authority to 'the prophets'. 'It was not through any human whim that men prophesied of old; men they were, but, impelled by the Holy Spirit, they spoke the words of God' (2 Pet. 1.21).

John 5. 36–end

Jesus has a testimony that is higher than that of John the Baptist. This testimony was given by the Father to John the Baptist at Jesus' baptism ('When you see the Spirit coming down upon someone and resting upon him you will know that this is he who is to baptize in Holy Spirit' 1.33). It was also given through the works which Jesus performed, as Nicodemus acknowledged ('We know that you are a teacher sent by God, no one could perform these signs of yours unless God were with him' 3.2). But the Jews were unable to see these testimonies because the word, the whole revelation of God, had found no home in them through their unbelief. In spite of their intense study of the scriptures—and intensive study of the scriptures was a mark of the devout Jews, for there was a rabbinic saying that 'He who has gained for himself the words of the law has gained for himself the life of the world to come'—they were unable to accept Jesus Christ as Messiah. Properly understood, the OT scriptures converge on Jesus who is their focus; but both the works of Jesus and the scriptures only testify to Jesus as one whom the Father has sent when we believe in him. Unbelieving Jews were failing to hear the Father's voice, and their failure corresponded to their unbelief.

From verse 41 Jesus asserted that, although he did not seek honour for himself, their failure to see that he was accredited by the Father was the same as rejecting God himself. They could not be blamed for not seeing God, for no one has done this (1.18), but they could be blamed for neglecting their opportunity of knowing him through his Son, to see whom is to see the Father (14.9). A further evidence of their failure was when a voice was heard from heaven and they misinterpreted it (12.28ff).

They were willing to welcome some self-accredited messiah (as in the case of Simon bar Kochba, leader of the Jewish revolt in A.D. 132–5), and they put their trust in Moses, the one who gave them the Law, but they did not believe in the one to whom the writings of Moses pointed. When the trial and judgement came, and their failure was exposed, it would be Moses himself, not Jesus who would accuse them. They had set their hope on the Law of Moses, only to find, as Paul did, that it simply ex-

46 poses men as sinners. **If you believed Moses you would believe what I tell you, for it was about me that he wrote.** Properly understood, Moses was a prophet of the gospel, the good news of God's mercy to the sinner.

ADVENT 2
Third Sunday before Christmas

* **Isaiah 64. 1–5**
The earthquakes on the mountains and the manifestations of fire described in the opening verses of the OT lesson are familiar features of God's epiphany: 'The earth trembled and quaked: the very foundations of the hills shook and were moved, because he was wroth. There went a smoke from his nostrils, and a consuming fire from his mouth: coals of fire issued from his presence.' (Ps. 18.7–8)

The trembling of the nations in the face of God's awful advent is also a regular feature of the theophanies: 'Mount Sinai was all smoking because the Lord had come down upon it in fire; the smoke went up like the smoke of a kiln; all the people were terrified.' (Exod. 19.18–19)

The present passage looks back to the great epiphanies associated with Israel's past. Can we hope, the prophet seems to ask, that they will ever come again?

Yet it is also a prayer that God will come again. There is no such God 4 as the God of Israel who takes **the part of those who wait for him** (a piquant phrase as we approach the feast of the Incarnation). To wait in hope is an attitude of faith towards God which he honours with his support and protection. He accepts completely those whose happy objective in life is to fulfil his will.

The prophet then confessed that, in spite of God's former anger against evil, the people continue to sin against him.

Romans 15. 4–13

Commences in the middle of a digression in Paul's discussion in this letter to the Church in Rome. A few verses earlier he had been dealing with the matter of the polarization of the Christian community (everywhere, not just in Rome) between those who were completely committed and well-instructed and those who were weaker in faith: 'Those of us who have a robust conscience must accept as our own burden the tender scruples of weaker men, and not consider ourselves' (15.1). Characteristically, he cited the example of Christ with a quotation from Ps. 69.9, 'The reproaches of those who reproached thee fell upon me' (15.3), to show from prophecy that Jesus put the interests of others first. In justifying this appeal to scripture—and this is where our passage (and the digression) begins—he reminded his readers that scripture is for the instruction and strengthening of Christians that they might be built up in hope. And he prayed that they will be enabled to live together in unity, understanding one another and praising God together.

Returning to his main theme in verse 7, he urged the stronger and 7 the weaker members of the Church **to accept one another as Christ accepted us, to the glory of God.** Pointing again to the example of Jesus, the apostle said that Christ became the servant of those who were, as far as religion was concerned, the most awkward and scrupulous of people; yet, because he was prepared to accept them as they were, the promises which God had given his people under the old covenant had been fulfilled. Furthermore, Jesus' acceptance of his servant role among 9 the Jews meant that all other nations, the Gentiles, were coming to **glorify God for his mercy** (an echo of today's OT reading). Paul assembled a number of scriptural texts to demonstrate that the blessing to the Gentiles was not an afterthought on God's part, but prophesied under the old covenant—an important argument in his debate with those Judaising Christians who wanted to make Gentile converts Jews by circumcision as well as Christians by baptism. The texts quoted by the apostle are: Ps. 18.49 (=2 Sam. 22.50), Deut. 32.43 (LXX), Ps. 117.1, and Isa. 11.10. The last text is a messianic prophecy envisaging the Messiah as one raised up by God not just for Jews, but for all peoples.

The passage ends with Paul's brief prayer that God, as the source and goal of Christians' hope, will so fill the apostle's readers with joy and peace through their faith in Jesus Christ that their hope will spill over to others as they are released in the power of the Holy Spirit. The
12 prayer comes out of the last text, **There shall be the Scion of Jesse, the one raised up to govern the Gentiles: on him the Gentiles shall set their hope.**

Luke 4. 14–21

The ministry of Jesus in Luke begins with his sermon in the synagogue at Nazareth, following the temptations in the wilderness. The passage describes the reading of the scripture and summarizes what Christ said. The service in the synagogue probably consisted of prayer (the Eighteen Benedictions came into use this way), two scripture readings (one from the five books of the Law, the Pentateuch, and the other from the Prophets), a homily and a blessing (Num. 6.22–27)—a framework not unlike the beginning of a Christian eucharist. It was usual for a member of the congregation to be invited to stand and read a lesson from the Prophets and then to sit and expound it. Jesus had already gained a reputation **as a**
15 teacher—he **taught in their synagogues and all men sang his**
16 praises—and when he visited a town, and especially **Nazareth where he had been brought up,** it was natural that he should be asked to speak. He may have welcomed opportunities to teach in the synagogues in this way, like the apostles after him, and many of his memorable sayings may have been heard for the first time in synagogues where Jewish communities assembled for instruction and worship.
14   Luke pictures Jesus as a great prophet, **armed with the power of the Spirit,** and also as one in whom the scriptures find their fulfilment.
21 The **today** of God's grace had arrived. The OT passage read by Jesus (Isa. 61.1–2, with an additional phrase from 58.6) is a familiar one in the NT: it is used to answer the messengers sent from John the Baptist
19 and it is echoed in the Beatitudes. Its theme is **the year of the Lord's favour.** It originated as an oracle which declared that after the Babylonian exile the people of Israel would once again be free to return to

Jerusalem and celebrate 'the jubilee year' (Lev. 25.10). According to the
Law, this was a year for the release from all outstanding debts and certain
social obligations, but by our Lord's time it was interpreted as a prophecy
of the messianic age—as yet unfulfilled, so the Jews believed. The
21 summary of Christ's sermon, **Today in your very hearing this text
has come true,** makes the stupendous claim that the messianic age has
dawned. Christ announces the OT witness to himself for himself.

ADVENT 3
Second Sunday before Christmas

* **Isaiah 40.1–11**
1 **Comfort, comfort my people** begins the book of Second Isaiah's
prophecy—from which it gets its title, 'the Book of the Consolation of
2 Israel'. Exiled Israel is soon to know salvation. (**Jerusalem** is the name
given to the people who are committed wholeheartedly to God); her
bondage is over, reparation has been made for her sin. (The passage
is linked with 52.11.) God's voice—or perhaps the voice of one of his
messengers—announces the beginning of a new exodus, a magnificent
pilgrimage back to the Holy City. The return of Israel from exile will also
in some sense be a return of the Lord himself in a theophany which the
watchmen in Zion will see (52.7ff). The highway must be prepared for the
5 coming of the King. The **glory of the Lord** is to be revealed and all
men will see it.
6   In verse 6 the Lord addresses the prophet. **A voice says, "Cry," and
another asks, "What shall I cry?"** It is his call, his commissioning.
He is to prophesy that, although mankind is weak and transient like grass,
yet the impossible will happen, for the word of God is strong and in-
transient. Verse 9 continues the prophecy. The revelation of God is
announced by a herald who speaks from the mountains, as God did in
9 former times. The **good news** (gospel) is that **your God is here.**
The arm of the Lord is a symbol of his power. He will lead his people
back like a shepherd and king.
10   **Recompense** is the payment due to a man who labours: the words
'recompense' and 'reward' are closely connected: they picture the Lord

as completing his work in restoring his people. The image of the shepherd is, of course, a continuing one through both Old and New Testaments. (See pages 234–238.)

1 Corinthians 4. 1–5

Earlier in this letter Paul had had to warn the Corinthian Christians against those who divide the congregation into factions, using the names of other apostles—Apollos, Cephas, or even his own—as party titles. Here he expounds the vocation of an apostle, and, beyond the apostolic office, of all who are called to exercise pastoral care in the Church, in
1 terms of **Christ's subordinates** (at the Lord's beck and call) **and stewards of the secrets** (RSV, JB 'mysteries') **of God**. *Mysteria* is the Greek word for the sacred rites of pagan religions and divine secrets revealed to a few initiates. In this sentence it is used to describe the plan of God for the salvation of the world, hidden from men in the divine foreknowledge until the time comes when it can be revealed to those whom he has chosen and, through them, to the whole of mankind. Christian theology employed the word for the sacraments of Baptism and the Eucharist—the celebration by the Church of God's saving work. The image of a steward is used elsewhere in the NT of Christians in general, but the apostle uses it in this passage for apostles and ministers. Their office is exercised within the Church, God's household (1 Tim. 3.15), and it is essential that such officials should be reliable.

But these are only preliminaries. Paul's main concern in his letter at this point is to answer criticisms about himself and his work. It does not matter, he says, how he is judged by his fellow men (he may have had at the back of his mind the distinction made by the Jewish rabbis between 'judgements of men' and 'judgements of heaven'). He does not judge himself. He has a clear conscience; but he adds that a clear conscience does not prove that he is innocent, **I have nothing on my conscience . . . that does not mean I stand acquitted**. The only competent
3 judge in these matters is **the Lord** (= Christ). So, he tells them, wait until the Lord comes again. The parousia will throw light on things that
5 men keep hidden in their hearts and minds. **Then will be the time for each to receive from God such praise as he deserves**.

John 1. 19–28

The fourth Gospel omits the details of John the Baptist's ministry and focuses on his witness to Jesus Christ. In an earlier verse John has been introduced as 'a man . . . sent from God . . . as a witness to testify to the light, that all might become believers through him'. He preached of Jesus, 'This is the man I meant when I said, "He comes after me, but takes rank before me"; for before I was born, he already was' (1.6, 15). The Jews, usually represented as hostile to Christ by this evangelist, question John on his ministry. He affirms that he is not the Messiah, nor is he Elijah, who was expected to return at the beginning of the messianic age (Mal. 4.5–6, a later addition identifying the 'messenger of the covenant' with the returning Elijah, whose task it would be to restore peace in the community and so avert God's wrath on the day of judgement). Nor, says John, is he the eschatological prophet promised by Moses (Deut. 18.15).

23 He is the herald of Isaiah, **crying aloud in the wilderness, 'Make the Lord's highway straight'** (Isa. 40.3).

The Jews go on to ask him about his baptism. The ceremony of immersion in water to symbolize purification or renewal was a familiar one in ancient religious practices. Washings of various kinds were a feature of cleansings for ceremonial purposes in Judaism (Num. 19.1ff, Exod. 30.17ff, etc.) and, together with circumcision and the offering of a sacrifice, were included in the rites for the initiation of a proselyte. The Qumran community used lustrations in their rituals. But John's baptism, although it had affinities with these ceremonies, was distinctive for three reasons. 1. It was a sign of moral conversion and purification, not merely of ritual washing. Men must live changed lives; tax-gatherers must not make extortionate claims; soldiers must not bully or blackmail (Luke 3.10–14). 2. It seems to have been offered once only and therefore had the character of an initiation. 3. It had an eschatological value in that it enrolled the baptized into the congregation of those who were preparing themselves for the coming Messiah and who could expect to be members of the messianic community. Because it had this preparatory nature, the Baptist

27 saw himself in the humble role of a servant: **I am not good enough to unfasten his shoes.** The **I am not** of John contrasts with the 'I am' saying of Jesus which this Gospel records (see p. 51). The figure of John shrinks before the person of the Word made flesh who comes to enlighten the world. John baptizes in water, but the one who comes after him is to baptize in Holy Spirit (1.33; see Epiphany 1 Year 2). Yet, in Jesus' own words, John was 'more than a prophet', for he lived in an age when prophecy had all but died in Israel.

ADVENT 3
Second Sunday before Christmas

* Malachi 3. 1–5
Malachi is the Hebrew for 'my messenger' (NEB footnote). The introduction to his book informs us that he was 'Ezra the scribe'. In 4.5 'the messenger' is identified with Elijah, though in this passage he is almost synonymous with the Lord himself. The situation envisaged is a restored temple, so the prophecy is dated after the exile. The people have said that the Lord does not concern himself with what is right, 'Where is the God of justice?' (2.17), but the prophet tells them that they will learn the truth when he comes. There is some doubt as to whether the advent described in verses 2–4, Who can endure the day of his coming? . . .,

2 refers to the coming of the Lord or to the coming of the messenger. But the effects are the same. God's judgements will be made from the temple, which is his dwelling-place and throne-room on earth, and the first to be purified will be the officials associated with it, the Levites. The work of purification will be analogous to the process whereby gold and silver is purified in the fire. Then the offerings of the people will be acceptable as in former times. This act of the community's purification is linked with the day of judgement, described in terms of a court. No individual dare be complacent on that day, for each one will be judged according to his conduct. The Lord will witness against all wrong-doers and those who have no fear of him.

Philippians 4. 4–9
Coming towards the end of Paul's letter to the congregation in Philippi, these verses strike a buoyant note of confidence and hope. 'I want you to be happy, always happy in the Lord: I repeat, what I want is your happiness' (verse 4 JB). He urges them to show that quality of toleration and

5 kindness—magnanimity—which can be recognized and valued by all men, especially as the advent of the Lord is imminent. The eschatological hope of the apostolic Church was high; they lived like men who expected the immediate and sudden return of their master (Luke 12.36). One of the earliest Christian prayers was *Maranatha*, 'Come, O Lord!' (1 Cor. 16.22, Rev. 22.20). Christians need have no fear, says the apostle, for they can commit themselves in complete trust to the Lord, who is the Lord of their future as well as the Lord of their past and their present.

Thanksgiving is an essential part of Christian prayer. It is in praising God that we demonstrate our assurance in his promises and purpose for

79

us, no matter how black our personal situation may seem to be. 'Give
thanks whatever happens; for this is what God in Christ wills for you'
(1 Thess. 5.17–18). By offering thanks to God in all circumstances,
we appropriate for ourselves by faith Christ's victory over all evil. Then
7 we know **the peace of God, which is of far more worth than human
reasoning** (NEB footnote). The peace which God gives is the gift of
himself to men. In scripture 'peace' is more positive than the absence of
strife. It is the restoration of God's order in creation—wholeness, wellbeing, safety—and it is the dominant characteristic of his kingdom. The
peace which Christ has made with men and which he alone can give
remains in the world by the operation of the Spirit of Christ (Acts 10.36,
John 14.27, Gal. 5.22). This peace guards the affections and ideas of those
who are in Christ.

It is notable that Paul's list of virtues is not a specifically Christian
catalogue: 'Everything that is true, everything that is noble, everything
that is good and pure, everything that we love and honour, and everything
that can be thought virtuous and worthy of praise' (verse 8 JB). He
may have come to recognize that there was a genuine capacity for moral
discernment in the pagan society around him and that things which
were counted honourable by good men were in fact worthy of a Christian's
9 honour too. **The lessons** and **the traditions** were evidently the moral
rules which concerned the life of congregations and individuals, together
with the summary of the gospel, which was expressed in the credal
statements then in the process of formation. To these were added the
facts of Christ's life, death, and resurrection, and the theological interpretation of them which we find taking shape in the earliest Christian
letters (1 Cor. 11.23, 15.3ff). When Paul speaks of 'the tradition he
received from the Lord' he means the teaching which he had been given
through the mediation of the Church.

The passage is typical of a Pauline ending to a letter. The reason for the
apostle's joy is his recognition of the way in which the work of God has
progressed. The proximity of the Lord's advent is cause for Christian
joy—proximity which is not to be thought of now just in terms of time
but also in terms of the imminence of the Lord's activity. Christian
eschatological thought has shifted, through the influence of Christ's own
teaching, from an expectation of the Day of the Lord in Jewish theology
to the return of the Lord himself.

Matthew 11. 2–15
According to Josephus, John the Baptist was imprisoned at Machaerus,

east of the Dead Sea, at the southern border of the tetrarchy of Herod
Antipas, who had arrested him. Some of his disciples continued to be
loyal to him and to assist him in prison, and it was through them that he
heard what Jesus was doing. There is a problem in the story. If John had
recognized Jesus at his baptism in the Jordan, why should he require
further assurance? Some commentators have suggested that John's faith
was shaken as a result of his experiences; others that the message from
John is merely an occasion for Jesus to assert his messianic role in fulfilment of scripture. At any rate, what Jesus is doing is, for the evangelist,
sufficient evidence to show that he is the true Messiah. Christ refers to
the messianic signs in Isa. 29.18, the healing of the deaf and blind,
Isa. 35.5, the lame, Isa. 61.1f, the good news to the poor. Those who do
6 not find Christ a **stumbling-block**—Jesus means here those, like the
disciples of John, who recognize the messianic claims—are blessed. They
see that the messianic age has been inaugurated.

Christ now continues to address the people on the subject of John. Did
they expect him to be as common as the cane grass which grows on the
banks of the Jordan? Did they expect someone in luxurious clothing—
a hint of sarcasm directed at Herod? Instead, Jesus declares that John
was the mysterious messenger of the prophet Malachi.

Yet, great as John is, his greatness is only comparable with the greatness
11 of the old covenant. **The least in the kingdom of heaven is greater
than he**, not through any personal achievement, but because of the
privilege which God's gift brings. Jesus' disciples are 'greater' in this
sense because they are already in the Kingdom, within its empowering
borders. (We can perhaps understand that John the Baptist's personal
12 entry into the Kingdom was after his death.) **Ever since the coming
of John the Baptist the kingdom of heaven has been subjected
to violence and violent men are seizing it** is a difficult verse to interpret. The NEB footnote gives an alternative: . . . **has been forcing its
way forward, and men of force**. . . . Either the Kingdom of heaven is
subject to violence in that Jesus and his disciples and all that he teaches
is being opposed by men, or the Kingdom of heaven has been progressing
and keen and daring men are taking hold of it. In whatever way it is
interpreted, the next verse goes on to state that John the Baptist's ministry
is the last of a long line of ministries stretching back to Moses and the
prophets, who foretold the coming of the Kingdom in the person of Jesus
15 Christ. Jesus emphasizes his saying by crying, **If you have ears, then
hear.**

ADVENT 4
The Sunday next before Christmas

* Isaiah 11. 1–9
The oracle of the prophet celebrates the advent of a descendant of David,
1 a new king **from the stock of Jesse**, who will restore the nation to its
former glory. With the spirit of the Lord resting upon him, he will rule
as the representative of God; anointed for his office, he will be equipped
with the spiritual gifts required to govern wisely and well. The charisms
are linked in pairs: wisdom, the divinely-inspired insight into the ways
of God; resolution and the ability to carry out his decisions; and a piety
which gives a deep reverence for the Lord and his will. What was original
about Isaiah's prophecy was that it saw the authority of the king conferred
not by a single, temporary gift, but by a series of apparently permanent
gifts. With these gifts the new David will exercise the regal duty of arbitra-
ting between disputants and administering justice impartially in accordance with the justice of God. He will not rely on appearances or rumours to
decide between right and wrong; he will uphold the rights of the weak
and destroy those who attempt to oppress them. His power will be such
that he can send wicked men to their deaths at a word of command.

The prophet then sees a vision of a return to a paradisal state of affairs,
reminiscent of Eden, when the peace of God mediated through the Davidic
king will remove all inclinations to violence in nature. Even the most
fierce of the wild animals will become so tame that a small child will be
able to lead them about in safety. In the midst of this vision is the holy
mountain of God, and at the end of our passage the prophet sees the whole
land filled—could we say 'baptized'?—with the knowledge of the Lord.
The revelation of God to man will be complete.

1 Corinthians 1. 26–end
In the midst of his assertion that what God has done in Jesus Christ is a
contradiction of man's ideas about wisdom and power, Paul illustrates
God's paradoxical way of working by telling the Corinthian Christians
to consider themselves. Look at the kind of persons the Lord has called
together in Corinth and the nature of the community that has been formed
as a result of the divine call. It ought to be obvious that God has other
standards in these matters than man has. If we wanted to make friends
and influence people, we would gather round us the worldly wise, the

men who can get things done, and the socially respectable. But the Corinthian church was very different from this. While there were a few well-to-do (a synagogue official, Acts 18.8), there were also slaves (7.21). They may have included the poorer sort of Corinthian inhabitants, for Christianity was noted later for appealing to the lower classes in society. God has, therefore, not only rejected the world's standards but over-
26 thrown them. **He has chosen things low and contemptible, mere nothings, to overthrow the existing order** may have been rhetorical, but the apostle's meaning is clear: God has humiliated the world's pride and negatived man's wisdom even within the Church. Paul had a special purpose in refuting notions of worldly wisdom, for trouble had been caused at Corinth by some who had made 'mere men a cause for pride' (3.21). He forcibly reminds them that they are in Christ, not through any strata-gem or foresight of their own, but because of what God has done for
30 them. **Jesus is our wisdom** through God's gift.

In Jewish thought wisdom came to be personified as the mediator between God and man in creation and in communicating to man the knowledge of salvation (Prov. 8.22–31; Wisd. 7.22). 'The Lord created me (Wisdom) the beginning of his works, before all else that he made, long ago'; 'She (Wisdom) is but one, yet can do everything; herself un-changing, she makes all things new; age after age she enters into holy souls, and makes them God's friends and prophets, for nothing is accept-able to God but the man who makes his home with Wisdom' (Wisd. 7.27). Sometimes Paul appropriated the concept of wisdom to Christ's functions, but here he directly appropriates it to Christ himself. True wisdom, he says, is not to be found in eloquence or theological speculations; it is to be found in God's plan for the redemption of the world which, for all its own wisdom, had fallen away from him.
30   **Christ is our righteousness**—another word which Paul uses to express the mediatorship of Christ. Man cannot be judged as righteous, so righteousness is given to him by God, and in these circumstances his faith is accounted to him for righteousness (Rom. 4.3, Gal. 3.6, both quoting Gen. 15.6). Christ becomes righteousness for man (2 Cor. 5.21) and God as judge views man, not as he is in himself, but as man is in Christ. Man can only draw near to God if he is holy, and he can only be made holy in Christ. Similarly it is only in Christ that he can be redeemed, liberated.

Finally, Paul concludes this passage with a quotation from Jer. 9.23f, 'If any man would boast, let him boast of this, that he understands and knows me'. A man has no standing whatever before God except that which he has been given in Christ.

Luke 1. 26-38a

The ancestry of Jesus' earthly family is significant, for Joseph belonged to the house of David and Mary was a relative of Elizabeth, who was of Aaronic descent. The family tree foreshadowed the royal and priestly character of Jesus as Messiah.

In early Jewish texts 'the angel of the Lord' meant the Lord himself (Gen. 16.7, etc.), but with the development of the doctrine of angels their distinction from God becomes sharper and they emerge as heavenly messengers, conveying the word of God to men from the transcendent

26 God. **Gabriel** (the word means 'man of God' or 'God has shown himself mighty') was one of the seven archangels in the Hebrew celestial hierarchy.

28 **Most favoured one** is the modern equivalent of the more familiar 'full of grace': grace is divine favour. The supernatural naming of the child recalls the naming of Ishmael (Gen. 16.11), Immanuel (Isa. 7.14), and John the Baptist (Luke 1.13). Verses 32–33 tell the reader that the prophecies of Isa. 9.6ff are being fulfilled, with messianic titles and

32 offices: **Son of the Most High, the throne of David,** and **king of Israel**. The OT associated the messianic descendant of David with son-ship of God, since the word of the Lord for David had come to Nathan: 'I will set up one of your family . . . to succeed you . . . I will be his father, and he shall be my son' (2 Sam. 7.12ff); 'He shall call unto me "Thou art my Father: my God, and the Rock of my salvation". And I will make him my first-born: highest among the kings of the earth' (Ps. 89.26–27). The promise of an everlasting reign for the Messiah recalls Mic. 4.7, 'The Lord shall be their king on Mount Zion now and for ever'.

34 Mary's question, **How can this be when I have no husband?** implies that her conception is to be virginal. The birth of Jesus is to be brought about by the power of God the Holy Spirit (just as the Church was born out of that same power at Pentecost). The 'overshadowing' of the Most High is another theophany such as that at the transfiguration, the divine *shekinah*. From the time of Irenaeus, Mary's obedience has been contrasted by Christian theologians with the disobedience of Eve. Like Abraham, Mary accepted the divine call with faith; she assented to

38 God with an Amen, **Here I am**. She recognized herself as the Lord's servant in the role to which her nation had been called. Every word of Mary's is full of messianic interest. God is already with her, 'gracing' her for her task. She is Mary, Miriam. It would be unrealistic to ask if she

understood who the holy child to be called 'Son of God' might be. She only faintly saw what her vocation was to be, but she trusted in God. And, like Hannah, whom Mary resembles (1 Sam. 1.11), her faith was rewarded.

ADVENT 4
The Sunday next before Christmas

* **Zechariah 2. 10–end**
The prophecies of Zechariah seem to date from a period when the temple in Jerusalem was being built after the Exile, and the concern of the prophet is to assure the people that God is going to return to the Holy City. Although the signs of the times are not auspicious, Zechariah assures them that God will come. The passage is the climax of a series of visions on the advent of God—the third being the man with a measuring-line making plans for the rebuilding of the city. The Lord is coming and is going
10 to make **his dwelling** (the word is significant—see p. 86) among his
11 people. Furthermore, many other nations will become the people of God on **that day**, for the scope of the divine advent is universal. The passage ends with a call to silence in adoration and awe, for God has al-
12 ready begun his progress towards **the city of his choice.**

Revelation 21. 1–7
Like the OT reading, the epistle is also from the climax of a prophecy. John's visions culminate in a picture of the eternal city, the new Jerusalem, coming down from above after the first heaven and the first earth (the present order) had passed away. Part of God's plan was that all evil would be destroyed. The sea was a horror and a wonder to people like the Hebrews, who were never a seafaring people; in Babylonian mythology it represented the chaos which God had to overcome before he created the
1 world. So the saying **and there was no longer any sea** meant that the element of disorder in the universe had been conquered. Notwithstanding God's conquest over the waters at the creation of the world, the sea had remained on earth and in heaven as a symbol of a victory still to be claimed, a barrier between God and man through which the martyrs had to pass in the new exodus.
The bridal image is a common one for the people of God, both the old

Israel and the new, but here the new Jerusalem represents the fulness of
the Kingdom of God, the Church triumphant in its ultimate sense. The
3 use of the word **dwelling** ('tabernacle') takes us back to the OT and the
sojourn of Israel in the wilderness. There the sacred tent in which God
was believed to dwell was called the tabernacle. In later times the Hebrew
word for the tabernacling of God, the *shekinah*, was used as a reverential
way of referring to God, rather in the same way that we speak of 'the
Presence' today. In the prologue to the fourth Gospel the author used it to
describe the incarnation of the Word of God: 'The Word became flesh;
he came to dwell (to tabernacle) among us, and we saw his glory, such
glory as befits the Father's only Son, full of grace and truth' (John 1.14,
see Christmas Day, page 96). The author probably chose the Greek
word *eskēnōsen* because it recalled the sound of the Hebrew word
shekinah. He wished to assert that the presence of God had come down
among men. John uses the same word here for **his dwelling** and **he
will dwell**.

From one aspect the vision is a picture of the future and of what will
happen. Yet from another aspect it is absurd to speak of 'the future' when
we are concerned with eternity. Eternity is not 'a long time'; it is a condition which is altogether outside time. When we interpret this prophecy,
then, we must remember that we are not just seeing into the future, but
also that the truth of what has begun to happen in the past and what is
happening in our own day is being revealed to us. The eternal can be
dimly discerned in the temporal—its past, its present, and its future.

3   **They shall be his people.** The ancient promise to the Jews is given
to those who, refusing to be at home in the old order, have lived as citizens
of an abiding city whose designer and builder is God. Along with the sea,
other elements in the old order will vanish—tears, mourning, death.
5 **Behold! I am making all things new!** Re-creation, the process by
which the old order is being transformed, is continuing all the time. Paul
wrote of a new creation in the lives of men and women (2 Cor. 3.18,
4.16–18; Col. 3.1–4, see Easter 3 Year 2). John sees the same transforma-
tion taking place on a cosmic scale. **I am the Alpha and the Omega.** The
6 first and the last letters of the Greek alphabet signify the fact that when
men and women find themselves in the presence of the living God, they
confront the beginning and the ground of their being and the goal of their
living. All that man has and all that man is—his salvation and his hope—
are gifts of God. What God requires is that man should desire **the
6 water-springs of life.** The reward for the one who is victorious is the
privilege of divine sonship.

86

Matthew 1. 18–23
The Matthean narrative of the nativity begins boldly with the assertion
that it tells the story of the birth of the Messiah. There is no delicate
unfolding of the truth as in Luke. The virginal conception of the child is
explained from the beginning. Jewish betrothal customs meant that a
fiancée could already be regarded as belonging to her future husband,
but he could release himself from the engagement by an act of repudia-
tion of the marriage contract. Mary's pregnancy, if discovered, would cause
19 a scandal. **Being a man of principle**, Joseph could not condone it.
But in order not to make the matter public, he had decided to repudiate
the contract and leave Mary's family free to deal with the shame she had
brought on them as best they could. But the angelic visitor informs him
that the conception is a miraculous act by the Holy Spirit and that he is
not to fear the consequences of completing the marriage. The name
21 **Jesus** is a form of the Hebrew *Yehoshua*, 'God saves'. The quotation from
Isa. 7.14 has 'a young woman' in the Hebrew but 'a virgin' in the LXX.

In this Gospel interest in the nativity story is centred on Joseph, whose
genealogy is traced earlier in the chapter back to David. It is Joseph who,
as head of the family, receives the annunciation, not Mary. Behind the
narrative are the traditions of the miraculous births of the OT—Sarah
(Gen. 18.11–14), Rebekah (Gen. 25.21), and Hannah (1 Sam. 1.4–20),
when future great men were brought into the world through divine
intervention. Angels appear in the NT in moments of such divine intervention. The word means 'messenger' in Hebrew and Greek, but in
English denotes a supernatural being.

CHRISTMAS DAY
See pages 23–28

Isaiah 9. 2–7
The theological basis of the monarchy in Judah was the covenant that
God made with David (2 Sam. 7.16, 'Your family shall be established and
your kingdom shall stand for all time in my sight, and your throne shall be
established for ever.') These promises were reaffirmed at the accession
of a new king, and the people hoped that each new monarch would make

the dynastic ideal an actual fact. It was from this theology of the monarchy that the messianic hope developed.

The passage, then, can best be seen against the background of a royal enthronement. When the successor came to the throne, he was given the religious and ceremonial titles of his ancestors. On the coronation day he was hailed as an adopted son of God (Ps. 2.7, and other 'royal psalms') and to him were ascribed the virtues of Moses and the patriarchs, the courage of David, the wisdom of Solomon. More importantly, he was seen as a new fulfilment of God's promise to David. Even though he was still a child, the titles were bestowed upon him.

It is in this setting that the prophet sees the possibility of an ideal king, a new David emerging. The theophany of God at his accession would be as a light in the darkness. (Although the verbs of this passage are in the past tense, they really speak of a 'prophetic perfect', affirming the certainty of something hoped for.) The joyful people would be like victorious warriors dividing the spoil, since oppression would be lifted from them, as in Gideon's day (Judg. 6–8). The grisly debris of the battlefield would be cleared. The ideal king would be born as a child to grow up and to put into effect the royal titles of his proclamation.

It was not a prediction of the Messiah in the strictly Christian sense, but the Church is entirely justified in seeing as fulfilled in Jesus this prophecy of a great and good king who would rule in justice and righteousness.

Isaiah 62. 10–12

The Third Isaiah took over words and phrases from the Second Isaiah to address a different situation. The prophet was not speaking to exiles
10 but to Israelites living in Jerusalem. He instructed them to **Go out of the gates, go out, prepare a road for my people,** to get ready for the return of exiles. The building up of the highway could be meant metaphorically—the removal of obstacles which prevented Israelites living abroad from returning to Jerusalem. **To raise a signal to the peoples** means setting up a flag or ensign to tell pilgrims that the city was now open to them.
11 Verses 11 and 12 contain the Lord's message: **Behold, your deliverance** (LXX 'your saviour') **has come. His recompense comes with him**—the redemption which he brings his chosen people, who through
12 this gift are known by a list of titles, **Holy, Ransomed, Long-sought, Not Forsaken.**

Micah 5. 2-4

In one of the OT's most direct prophecies about the Messiah's place of
origin, Micah says that the Lord is going to resume his work in Bethlehem, which is where he began it in earlier times when he raised up David.
The promised son of David, born of the same Ephrathah clan, would rule
over the united kingdom of Israel and Judah, and he would be a true
shepherd of the people of God. (The role of the monarch in Israel was
traditionally interpreted in terms of shepherding.) And when would this
3 be? **Only so long as a woman is in labour shall he give up Israel.**
Perhaps Micah is echoing Isa. 7.14–16, when he says that God will do this
in a period of time equivalent to a woman's pregnancy. The Hebrews
lacked a word for our modern concept of 'time'. The word most frequently
used has a sense of 'a period of time' or 'a point of time'. The rule of the
4 new king would be upheld by God and would extend **to the ends of the
earth.**

Ephrathah originally denoted a clan related to Caleb (1 Chron. 2.19)
that settled in the neighbourhood of Bethlehem. Jesse, David's father, was
an Ephrathite (1 Sam. 17.12).

Titus 2. 11-14; 3. 3-7

Much of this charge to the apostolic delegate in Crete, Titus, is concerned
with the importance of teaching Christian conduct, but at the point in the
letter where today's epistle begins Paul, or his editor, moves away from
the practicalities of godly behaviour to the fount and inspiration of that
conduct, namely, what God has done for his people. It is possible that
some of the phrases in this passage had their origin in an early Christian
hymn.

God's great gift and blessing has now come and been made known
11 to us, he says. The divine favour has **dawned upon the world.** The
Greek word for 'dawned' ('appeared' RSV, JB) comes from the noun
'manifestation' (*epiphaneia*). This was a technical term in the language of
contemporary Hellenistic religion for the self-disclosure of a god or
semi-divine being (e.g. a king, or, in the imperial cult, the emperor). It
could refer to the god's birthday, or to some other occasion when he
miraculously displayed himself or his divine power, or to the anniversary
of a king's coronation, or to his homecoming from a journey abroad. In
2 Tim. 1.10 it is used to describe Christ's first coming, his incarnation;
here and in 2 Thess. 2.8 it is used to refer to the second coming instead
of the more usual word, parousia. In his early days Paul had anticipated
that he himself would live to witness Christ's glorious return (1 Thess.

2.19, 3.13, 5.23, etc.). If the present passage is genuinely Pauline, then it shows that he later came to realize that as far as he himself was concerned, its date lay in the more distant future.

12   By God's grace we are **disciplined to renounce godless ways and worldly desires.** To be disciplined is to be made into a disciple, a follower. Renunciation of the world, the flesh, and the devil is a preliminary to baptism, when the pagan life—so often recalled in this letter—was firmly
12 set aside. **In the present age** echoes the Jewish belief that the present order is under the dominion of the devil and will be overthrown when God establishes his kingdom. Used in this context it demonstrates how, for the Christian, the kingdom of God is at hand, even though he must still look
13 forward to its fulfilment in the second coming. **Our great God and Saviour Christ Jesus** is a striking but rare example of the way in which the NT confers divinity on Jesus (and is probably to be preferred to the NEB footnote, which distinguishes between **God and our Saviour Jesus Christ**). 'God and Saviour' is a phrase from contemporary pagan theology.

The reference to Jesus leads into a summary of Christ's work. Jesus
14 **sacrificed himself** in order to redeem us (to ransom us), **to make us a pure people marked out for his own, eager to do good.** The concept of a pure people is basic to both OT and NT. The Israelites were cleansed by the blood of the covenant (Exod. 24.8); the new Israelites are cleansed by the blood of the new covenant ('We are being cleansed from every sin by the blood of Jesus', 1 John 1.7). The phraseology goes back to the LXX version of the OT and denotes that God has redeemed his people from slavery and that they are therefore his own in a very special way. Titus has every authority to teach these things.

As a gesture of humility Paul associated himself with Titus's Cretan Christians (many of them probably former Jews) in his reminder of what
3 he and they were before their baptism: **We were slaves to passions and pleasures of every kind. Our days were passed in malice and envy; we were odious ourselves and we hated one another.** It sounds as if the apostle might have been indulging in rhetorical exaggeration. Surely there were some good pagans, even in Crete! ('Cretans were always liars, vicious brutes, lazy gluttons'—1.12!) But Paul was looking back on his former life and theirs from the viewpoint of one on whom has
4 shone **the kindness and generosity of God our Saviour,** and from that enlightened perspective the sin of the unbeliever was for the apostle very dark indeed.

At this point he characteristically reminded Titus that God had saved

mankind, not as a reward for anything that men and women might be
5 capable of, but **because he was merciful**. Then he went on to teach
that this salvation is made effective through baptism, **the water of
rebirth and the renewing power of the Holy Spirit**. Although Paul
did not use the term 'rebirth' (or 'regeneration') elsewhere in relation to
baptism, Christian initiation is described as a new birth by other NT
writers (e.g. John 3.3–8, 1 Pet. 1.3, 33) and the idea of baptism as the
beginning of a new life is implicit in the images of dying and rising with
Christ and becoming sons of God that Paul used in Rom. 6.4 and 8.14.
The word 'renewing' or 'renewal' (NEB footnote) enriches the concept of
baptism as the beginning of that process whereby God through the power
of the Holy Spirit is restoring the world in the age of the Messiah. These
eschatological notions were current in NT times (e.g. in the saying about
'the new world' in Matt. 19.28 RSV) and reached their climax in the vision
of the new heaven and the new earth in the Book of Revelation. If the
question is asked, why is there no reference in this passage to the necessity
for an individual's repentance and faith? the answer is that the apostle
was here concerned with the effects of baptism, not on the preconditions
necessary for Christian initiation.

6 **He sent down the Spirit upon us plentifully through Jesus Christ
our Saviour**. 'Sent' is, of course, a perfectly acceptable word to use in
this context, but the RSV and JB translations—'poured out upon us richly'
—is surely better. The verb 'pour' associates the sending of the Holy
Spirit more closely with baptism itself and in the Greek, Paul used the
same verb as that used by Luke in Acts 2.17 and 33, where Joel 2.28 is
quoted, '**I will pour out on everyone a portion of my spirit**.'

7 God's purpose is summed up in the sentence, **So that, justified by
his grace, we might in hope become heirs of eternal life**. Baptism
is the outward and visible sign by which a man or a woman, repenting of
their sins and turning to Jesus Christ as their Saviour, are accepted by
God through the power of the Holy Spirit into a renewed relationship
with him as his son or his daughter—a relationship which has been made
possible for them because they have been justified, set right, through the
sacrifice of the Son of God. The passage brings together neatly the great
Pauline themes of justification by faith and of union with Christ by
baptism.

1 John 4. 7–14

The epistle's discussion on faith and love reaches its climax in this
passage which affirms that love is what our redemption is all about. In-

deed, this is what God is all about. But love is not, in John's mind, something neutral; it is an activity which demonstrates its nature by what 9 it does. **God sent his only Son into the world** because of his love for us. This love, then, means giving up what is most dear, or thinking about others more than about ourselves. All this is lifted to a divine plane above 10 personal reactions and feelings. **The love I speak of is not our love for God, but the love he showed to us in sending his Son as the remedy for the defilement of our sins.** We believe what it is, and we describe it by recounting the message of our salvation; but we cannot define it. God acts for love, and is himself love; and it is in the act of loving one another that the divine presence is manifested in us. The gift of the Holy Spirit is the assurance of his indwelling, and he bears witness to the sending of the Son as the Saviour of the world.

Alongside the belief that 'God is light' (1.5) we must then set the belief that 'God is love'. John does not mean that light is God or that love is God: rather, he means that loving is the most characteristic activity of the Godhead, such love as was demonstrated on the cross. His desire is that Christians should treat one another as God has treated them.

Hebrews 1. 1–5 (6–12)

The opening verses of the letter to the Hebrews set out a summary of the redemptive acts of God which the Bible described. They form one of those great NT passages which embrace the work of God in Jesus Christ, and they can be compared with John 1.1–14 and Phil. 2.5–11. Behind these verses is the belief that what we know about God, man, and the universe, is what God has chosen to disclose to us—and no more. Our knowledge of God is not primarily the result of our quest for truth: it is the result of God's intention that the truth should be known. While that knowledge comes partly from the world around us, God has chosen a special way to communicate to us the truth about his nature and his purpose, and this way involved a particular community at a particular moment in their history in order that, through them, he might reveal his truth to the rest of mankind.

The passage begins, then, by stating that, having made himself and his intention partially known to and through the old Israel, the community chosen for that purpose, God has now finally disclosed all that men need to know to be at one with him, and he has also done what needed to be done in order to establish that relationship with himself through Jesus Christ. God himself, his mind, his purpose and his nature, have been expressed in terms of human personality. The entrance of Jesus Christ onto the stage of history is mankind's most decisive hour; it is the culmination of God's revelation of himself and the key to all knowledge of him. It is, therefore, the most significant moment since creation.

1   The **forefathers** to whom God spoke are the Israelites of the old covenant, seen from the Christian viewpoint as those who preceded the new People of God, the Church. The **prophets** through whom he spoke included men like Abraham, Moses, Aaron, and Elijah. They had different glimpses of the truth—Hosea the extent of God's love, Isaiah the splendour of his glory. No prophet was shown all of the truth, but each in his own way and according to his experience of God was shown part of it. The author of Hebrews demonstrates this in the later verses of chapter 1 where he quoted a series of four testimony-texts from the OT. Yet the revelation was incomplete because they told of a promise not yet fulfilled. The full revelation could come only through someone who was himself one with God.

That revelation was given by Jesus—not just in what Jesus taught, but also through the whole act of God in Christ from the incarnation to the ascension. The writer distinguishes between the revelation that had gone before and that which had been given in Jesus Christ, and he also points to Christ's unique place in the universe. What the writer means by 2 **Son**—'the one who is a son', to give a literal translation of the Greek— he now goes on to say:

He is **heir to the whole universe**. Jesus is identified with the Messiah, who is made heir in Ps. 2.1–9,

'I shall give thee the nations for thine inheritance:
and the uttermost parts of the earth for thy possession'. Cf. Isa.
11.1–10.

Jesus spoke of himself as the heir in the parable of the vineyard (Mark 12.1–10), implying his unique relationship to God and his authority over the vineyard, Israel. Thus Jesus inherits, on behalf of the new Israel, the assurance of God's presence and power which were promised to the 2 old. **Through him he created all orders of existence.** Jesus is identified with the creative power of God. In the OT the creative act of the Word of God (Gen. 1.3) or the Wisdom of God (Prov. 8) came to be regarded in the intertestamental period as personal emanations of God which could be paralleled with the *Logos* of Greek philosophy, the immanent Reason which created and directed the universe. The pre-existence of Jesus is indicated by his own self-consciousness and identification of himself with the Father. If Jesus was what he claimed to be, and if he had the power that only God can have to heal, to forgive, and to change men's lives, it follows that he must have been eternally present with God. The Wisdom-Logos idea made possible the communication between God and man. The interest of Christian teachers was not theological or philosophical but missionary. In using terms like 'Logos' or 'Word' (John 1.1–4,14), or in other ways identifying Jesus with the creative and sustaining power of God in the universe (Heb. 1, Col. 1.14–17), the NT writers were endeavouring to adapt the concept of the Messiah and all that he meant in Jewish tradition to the language and ideas that were familiar in the Greco-Roman world into which the gospel spread.

3   He was **the effulgence of God's splendour**. The radiance and reflection of God's glory is his divine nature as it is manifested to man. The light and the power and the holiness of God are visible and comprehensible to man only to a degree; beyond that they are past his understanding.

3   He was **the stamp of God's very being**. The image is that of a stamp on a wax seal or a die from which a coin is cast. Christ's character is such that we see in him the image of God perfectly demonstrated in human terms.

3   He **brought about the purgation of sins**. The rest of the epistle gives an elaborate explanation of Christ's death and resurrection and ascension in terms of the most important of all the ritual sacrifices described in the OT, the offering of the Day of Atonement. Here the first words are written to introduce the great theme. It is not individual sins that have been done away, but the effect of sin: the author is to explain what Paul calls justification in cultic terms.

3   He **took his seat at the right hand of the majesty on high**. The symbolic phrase (Ps. 110.1 and Mark 16.19) suggests the royal authority of the one who sits while his subjects stand or kneel. It is the attitude of one whose task is accomplished and whose relationship with God the Father is unique. The Son is both priest and victim, and in virtue of his completed sacrifice he has been exalted to take the highest place in heaven which is his by right. His session is at the throne of God.

4   He was **raised . . . far above the angels**. His superiority is over all spiritual beings as well as over mankind, as the writer goes on to prove with a series of quotations from the OT (thought by some scholars to be drawn from a collection of such texts used regularly in the apostolic Church for teaching purposes: some of them are found elsewhere in the NT). Taken from the LXX version, they are as follows:

Ps. 2.7 demonstrates the eternal generation of the Son from the Father, and 2 Sam. 7.14 shows that the Son enjoys a relationship with the Father that is superior to that of the angels. Deut. 32.43 argues that for this reason the angels worship the Son. Ps. 104.4 teaches that the angels are created beings, like winds and flame, made to carry out God's commands, but in contrast—with the quotation from Ps. 44.6—the Son has been raised above them, anointed by the Father to share in his divine rule. Ps. 101.25–27 is addressed to Jesus as Lord and as the agent of creation.

10 In the Psalmist's universe **the earth's foundations** and **the heavens** were the most enduring things imaginable, but in comparison with God's unchangeableness they appear in this song to be only transitory.

* **Luke 2. 1–14 (15–20)**

Luke skilfully focuses Israel's history on the birth of Christ. Great men of the past looked forward to the redemption of Israel; Bethlehem is associated with the most famous of Israel's kings. For Luke, the infancy narrative is the fulfilment of God's promise that 'the morning sun from heaven will rise upon us, to shine on those who live in darkness, under the cloud of death, and to guide our feet into the way of peace' (1.78–79)—a promise which has a universal implication, not just a Jewish one.

1   There are difficulties in identifying the **registration . . . made throughout the Roman world.** Such a census did take place in A.D. 6–7 under Quirinius (Luke mentions it in Acts 5.37) but Herod (mentioned in 1.5) died in 6 B.C. It is possible that this particular census was a local one towards the end of Herod's reign; this would have been while Saturninus was governor of Syria and Quirinius was holding a less important post in Syria. Scholars on the whole favour the latter explanation, so that Jesus' birth is dated about 6 B.C. (the error in the difference between that date and our own calendar is because in the sixth century Denis the Small made a faulty computation in taking Luke's thirty years too literally).

At Bethlehem under the church of the Nativity there is a cave which according to Origen has been venerated as the traditional grotto of the nativity since the third century. Before that, the place had been a pagan sanctuary. One explanation of the physical circumstances of the birth is that the house was either the front part of the cave walled in and the manger for the animals was at the back, or that there was a separate house where the occupants used a cave on their premises for animals.

Although the image of a shepherd played such an important part in the OT and NT, at the time of Christ these men were often regarded as the poorer members of the community, contrasted with the more sophisticated members of the city and towns. Bethlehem is about four miles south of Jerusalem. Luke describes how the divine *shekinah*, which had once shone over the temple in Jerusalem, now lightened the Bethlehem fields and the infant in the manger. The message of the angel assures the shepherds that the time of fear is over and the time of rejoicing has been inaugurated.

7   There is a profound significance in being a **first-born**. The most ancient strata of the OT demanded the sacrifice of the first-born (Exod. 22.29), illustrated in the story of Abraham and Isaac (Gen. 22.1–9). In the NT Christ is also *the* first-born (Rom. 8.29, etc.), and offered to the Lord in
11   accordance with the Lord's instructions (Luke 2.21ff). **Deliverer** (Saviour) is a more familiar word. In the OT God is the saviour of his people from their enemies and natural disasters. The name 'Jesus' connects the child with God acting as Saviour. During his ministry there were hopes that Jesus would save Israel from political oppression. But in Acts Luke calls Jesus Saviour in a deeper religious sense (5.31, 13.23) and in Eph. 5.23 Christ is 'the Saviour of the body', the Church. The angel announces him as the **Messiah, the Lord,** or **the Lord's Messiah** (footnote), titles with divine authority.

The song of the heavenly host (cf. the vision of Dan. 7.10) is of special interest because it is thought that it may have originated, like other hymns in Luke 1 and 2, in an early Jewish-Christian hymn.

The haste with which the shepherds resorted to Bethlehem depicts the speed with which the poor and the outcast react to Christ's preaching during his public life; being without hope; they recognize someone in whom they may have hope. When they had seen the child, the shepherds
20   returned **glorifying and praising God for what they had seen and heard**—a typical reaction to divine interventions in OT times.

19   Mary **treasured up all these things and pondered over them** in the same way that Jacob meditated about Joseph's dream (Gen. 37.11) and Daniel about the vision of the son of man at the throne of God (Dan. 7.28). The reaction of the disciple who is faced with a mystery that he does not fully understand is to reverence it because he knows it is of God.

* **John 1. 1–14**

1   **When all things began, the Word already was,** or, **the Word was at the creation** (NEB footnote). John saw the work of Christ as the beginning of a new Genesis and introduced his Gospel in the same terms ('In the beginning God created heaven and earth', Gen. 1.1, NEB footnote).

The use of Word, *logos*, was particularly inspired. To the Jew the *logos* of God meant the manifestation of divine wisdom, power, and love. God manifested himself through his Word at creation ('God said, "Let there be light", and there was light', Gen. 1.3) and revealed himself through his Word to his prophets ('Hear the word of the Lord', Isa. 1.10).

96

Among those whose Greek vocabulary took a particular meaning through the influence of the Stoic philosophers, on the other hand, the *logos* was the rational principle that permeated and governed the universe. In the years immediately before the formation of the NT, Hebrew Wisdom literature under this influence interpreted 'the Word of the Lord' in personal terms, almost identifying it (or him) with divine Wisdom: 'All things were lying in peace and silence, and night in her swift course was half spent, when thy almighty Word leapt from thy royal throne in heaven into the midst of that doomed land like a relentless warrior' (Wisd. 18.14–15). John must have chosen the term *logos* deliberately because of its far-reaching implications to both his Jewish and his Gentile readers.

1   **The Word dwelt with God, and what God was, the Word was.** John affirmed the pre-existence, the personality, and the divinity of the
3   Word. **No single thing was created without him.** In the Genesis story of creation the Word brought light and order and goodness out of chaos; in the Johannine theology of redemption the Word brought light and union with God to a world darkened by sin and death. That is why
5   Christ **is the light that shines on in the dark, and the darkness has never mastered it** (or, 'understood it': the Greek word has this other meaning as well).

There is a reference to the ministry of John the Baptist as 'the lamp, burning brightly' (5.35), but he was only the forerunner of the **light absolute, enlightening every man born into the world** (NEB foot-
9   note). The created world did not recognize the Word of God, although it
11 owed its existence to him; his own people (the Jews, the most likely meaning of **his own realm**) did not receive him. **But to all who did**
12 **receive him, to those who have yielded him their allegiance** ('confessed Jesus to be the Son of God' JB), **he gave the right to become children of God.** The implications of this rebirth were discussed more fully with Nicodemus and related to baptism by water and the Spirit (3.1–8, see Trinity 23 Year 1).
14 So the Logos took human nature and **came to dwell** among mankind. The OT expectation found its fulfilment. In ancient days God tabernacled, 'pitched his tent' (Gk) with his people; now the Word pitched his tent among men by becoming a man. 'They shall live under the shelter of my dwelling; I will become their God and they shall become my people' (Ezek. 37.27). John saw this prophecy fulfilled, not in the establishment of a new sanctuary in Jerusalem, but in the incarnate Lord, who is the true temple (2.21).

SUNDAY AFTER CHRISTMAS DAY

Isaiah 7. 10–14

An anti-Assyrian alliance that included Syria (Aram) and Israel threatened Jerusalem, where king Ahaz was being urged by his court to pay tribute to the Assyrians and seek their aid. Ahaz may have decided to do this before Isaiah approached him (2 Kings 16.1–9). The prophet urged the king, 'Have firm faith, or you will not stand firm' (verse 9). Judah was not to ally herself with a Gentile nation; she was to trust in the power of God. Through Isaiah the Lord offered the king any kind of sign he cared

11 to choose, **from the lowest Sheol or from highest Heaven.** Ahaz said he trusted the Lord without asking for a sign (pious cant, if he had already made up his mind to appeal to the Assyrians!). But his lack of faith provoked the prophet. A sign was to be given whether he wanted it or not. Within the time that it takes for a woman to bear a son, and for that son to grow sufficiently to know right from wrong, Syria and Israel would be desolated and Judah herself made subject to Assyria.

14 The child's name was prophetic: **Immanuel, God is with us.** If the young woman was one of the king's wives, the name assured him that God would remain with the dynasty of David, as he had promised. The hopes of the people had rested on the permanency of that dynasty since Nathan's prophecy (2 Sam. 7.1ff). But the naming of the child was later interpreted as pointing beyond the dynasty of David and, together with other passages in Isaiah, 9.1–6 (see Christmas Day) and 11.1–9 (see Advent 4 Year 1), to God's intervention and the establishment of his messianic kingdom. Although biblical scholars have found many difficulties in this text, Christian tradition has accepted it as a hidden prophecy of the birth of Jesus Christ (Matt. 1.23). The Hebrew, *almah*, meaning either a young girl or a recently married woman, was rendered in the Greek LXX as *parthenos*, 'virgin'.

Galatians 4. 1–7   See Pentecost 4 Year 1

* **John 1. 14–18**   For verse 14, see Christmas Day

The Baptist apparently testified to the pre-existence of the Word of

15 God when he said, **Before I was born, he already was.** We can understand this in the sense that John recognized Jesus as the crown of Israel's history, foretold in that tradition of OT prophecy of which the Baptist was himself the supreme example.

16   The result of the incarnation is that **out of his full store we have all received grace upon grace.** The **full store** is the totality of God's graciousness towards men (*pleroma*, 'fulness' RSV). *Pleroma* was the word used by Paul in the sense of the fulness of God in Christ—'In him the complete being of God . . . came to dwell' (Col. 1.19). That grace was mediated in some measure by **the Law . . . given through Moses,** but
17 fully (the divine attributes of **grace and truth) through Jesus Christ.**
18   **No one has ever seen God**: it was John's belief, as it was the belief of later Judaism, that no one could see God and live. The OT encounters with God (e.g. by Jacob, Moses, etc.) had been manifestations of God's glory, not of God himself. But John's point is, Christ **has made him known.** God has fully manifested himself in the man Jesus Christ (the original theme of the feast of the Epiphany) and thus Christ's earthly life as recounted in the fourth Gospel is a revelation of God's glory from the baptism to the cross.

1 Samuel 1. 20–end

Hannah had prayed in the temple at Shiloh (twelve miles south of Nablus) for a son and promised God that, if her request was granted, she would give her son back to the Lord and dedicate him to the Lord's service. And God intervened, as in the case of Isaac, Samson, and John the Baptist. Hannah despite her age bore a child, and he was called
20 Samuel. Although the text suggests that the name means **I asked the Lord for him,** in fact it means 'the Name of God' (*Shem-El* = Samuel). The verb used in the sentence puns with Saul, and this has led some scholars to suppose that what is recounted here is the birth of Saul.

Elkanah prayed that his wife would fulfil her vow. Eventually the time came for the child to be dedicated to the Lord's service, and this was
25 done with the offering of sacrifices. **They slaughtered** presumably refers
28 to the attendants in the sanctuary at Shiloh. Behind the phrases **I lend him to the Lord** is the idea that the child belongs to his family but that during his life he is given back to God for divine purposes. It is a curious reversal of our normal concept of vocation.

Interest in the passage also centres on the picture it gives, long before the period of the monarchy, of an annual festival attended by individuals like Elkanah as well as the twelve tribes. Pilgrimages such as this each year would nourish the people's common faith and their unity, especially when the areas settled by them were not contiguous. At the celebrations the emphasis would probably fall on recalling those traditions which all the tribes claimed as a heritage from the past: the promise to the patriarchs,

the deliverance from Egypt, the covenant and the law-giving on Sinai.
It may have been an early celebration of the feast of Tabernacles.

Romans 12. 1–8

The passage is taken from that part of the letter to the Romans where
Paul moves from his dogmatic exposition of justification by faith to his
explanation of its consequences in the life of a Christian. Man's response
is in loving obedience to God's revealed will, as a sign of that gratitude
which a redeemed and justified man must feel for what God has done for
1 him in his mighty acts (celebrated by the Church in her festivals). **My
brothers, I implore you by God's mercy to offer your very selves
to him: a living sacrifice, dedicated and fit for his acceptance, the
worship offered by mind and heart**—behind these phrases is the vocabulary of the cult (technical words are used in the Greek, 'offer', 'sacrifice',
'dedicated', 'fit for his acceptance', 'worship'). The kind of worship we
should offer is that which springs from our whole being as one created by
God with a mind and a will (as the NEB footnote brings out). The concept
of a life in obedience to God as one that is 'a living sacrifice', and 'worship
offered by mind and heart' has its roots in the OT. The psalmist realized
that what was acceptable to God was 'a troubled spirit, a broken and con-
trite heart' (Ps. 51.17). After the destruction of the temple in Jerusalem
in A.D. 70, it was said by the rabbis that although other sacrifices ceased,
the oblations of praise and thanksgiving remained.

2   Paul is able to speak about men's minds being **remade** and their
natures **transformed** because this renewal has begun in conversion and
baptism, and it is advanced in every act of obedience in a Christian's life
according to the will of God. Further, as the Christian continues in obe-
2 dience, so he is able to **discern the will of God, and to know what is
good, acceptable, and perfect.** This is an inward understanding which
has little to do with obedience to a written code or law.

The apostle then goes on to plead for humility, because all that a
Christian possesses is given by God; *charismata*, 'grace-gifts', within the
Body of Christ. The strong link he forges between the charisms and the
unity of the Church is similar to his theme in 1 Cor. 12–14. There may
have been some who possessed special or showy charisms and despised
others in Rome, as some did in Corinth. So he briefly outlines the right
6 use of these gifts. **Inspired utterance** ('prophecy' RSV JB) . . . **in proportion to a man's faith**: like OT prophecy, this was primarily a direct
communication of God's word to his people; the **proportion** of faith
means much the same as the measure of faith in verse 3, the power given

by God to men to do certain things (not 'faith' in the more usual sense
7 in this letter). **The gift of administration** (*diakonia* = 'ministry' or
'service') aligns practical tasks in the Christian community with charisms.
Teaching, exhortation, generosity, leadership, and charitable works of
mercy all follow in the list. Charisms in this passage refers to those
practical expressions of the grace (*charis*) of God under which the
Church of God stands. In this sense the whole life of the Church, and not
just its ministry, is 'charismatic'.

* **Luke 2. 22–40**
   Lev. 12.3 lays down that a child should be circumcised; Exod. 13.2,12,
   that the first-born should be presented to the Lord. These laws may go
   back to a primitive age when the first-born were offered to the Lord in
   sacrifice—at least in theory: it is doubtful whether the first-born sons of
   Israel were ever killed for this reason. One of the lessons behind the story
   of Abraham's offering of Isaac (Gen. 22.1–12) seems to have been that
   human sacrifice is contrary to the will of God. See Tuesday before Easter
   Year 2. Anyway, as obedient members of the people of God, Joseph and
   Mary obeyed the law and brought Jesus up to Jerusalem for the presentation.
      Two representatives of the old Israel came forward to witness the work
   of God in Christ. They were not officials of the temple but devout and
25 faithful Jews. Simeon was one **who watched and waited for the
   restoration of Israel, and the Holy Spirit was upon him.** The
   'comforting of Israel' (JB—Gk *paraklesis*) was expressed in Isa. 40.1ff,
   'Comfort, comfort my people, says your God', and looked forward to the
   fulfilment of God's promises in the messianic age. Simeon was given a
   prophecy concerning the Messiah and, recognizing him in the infant
   being presented at the temple, he utters an oracle which has passed into
   Christian liturgy, the *Nunc dimittis*. The hymn gathers together words and
   thoughts from Isaiah. The universal scope of the Messiah's deliverance is
   proclaimed and the special place of Israel in God's revelation is acknowledged. It is a chant of praise for the fulfilment of God's promises
   and for the light which he has brought into the world. As an act of devotion, it stems from the borderland of Jewish and Christian faiths and may
   have originated as an early Christian canticle. The old man also warns
35 the parents: the prophecy about being **pierced to the heart** has a double
   meaning—the pain that Mary would feel at the crucifixion, or the pain
   that Judah (personified in Mary) would feel when the sword passed
   through the land (Ezek. 14.17).

The second representative of the old Israel was Anna, a prophetess. The revival of prophecy in these two figures is offered by Luke as one of the signs of Christ's birth. It was believed that the Spirit would raise up prophets again in Israel as the messianic age drew near, especially among

38 those **who looked for the liberation of Jerusalem** (a technical name for that age). The first chapters of this Gospel are full of references to the Spirit's activity: Zechariah was told that his son John would be filled with the Holy Spirit (1.15), Mary that she would conceive a son by the Holy Spirit (1.35), Elizabeth was filled with the Holy Spirit at the news of Mary's conception (1.41), Zechariah was filled with the Spirit when John was born (1.67). These references, including those of Simeon and Anna in this passage, culminate in the descent of the Spirit on Jesus at his baptism (3.22).

YEAR I

THE SECOND SUNDAY AFTER CHRISTMAS

Ecclesiasticus 3. 2–7

Ben Sira (Jesus son of Sirach in the Greek title of the book) seems to have been a professional teacher of the OT. 'Come to me, you who need instruction, and lodge in my house of learning' (51.23) suggests that he may have presided over an academy in Jerusalem where he lectured young men on religious and ethical subjects. About 180 B.C. this Jewish scribe committed to writing the wisdom he had accumulated over years of teaching, and in this passage he is giving advice about filial duty and its reward.

In accordance with Jewish doctrine he believed that the observance

3 of the Mosaic law was meritorious: **Respect for a father atones for sins, and to honour your mother is to lay up a fortune.** The injunction echoes the fifth commandment: 'Honour your father and your mother, that you may live long in the land which the Lord your God is giving you' (Exod. 20.12). It is a view that contrasts sharply with the teaching of Jesus Christ, 'When you have carried out all your orders, you should say, "We are servants and deserve no credit; we have only done our duty" ' (Luke 17.10). Nevertheless, the wisdom of Ben Sira explains why the family has had such a powerful influence in the lives of individual Jews through the centuries.

Ecclesiasticus is the last great example of the type of wisdom literature represented in the OT Book of Proverbs, and the first specimen of that form of Judaism which subsequently developed into the rabbinic schools of the Pharisees and the Sadducees.

Exodus 12. 21–27

The feast of the Passover was originally celebrated in family or kin-groups. The account of its institution in this chapter indicates this domestic setting: 'Let each man take a kid for his family, one for each household' (verse 3), and the ritual of daubing the lintel and doorposts with blood. Only after the reform of Josiah about the year 622 B.C. (2 Kings 22ff), when Jerusalem was made a focus of worship, was it connected with a sanctuary. Then Passover became one of the pilgrimage feasts which brought devout Jews to the holy city each year. But even then it was not celebrated in the temple. The Passover lambs were slaughtered within the sacred precincts but the meal was eaten in the homes, lodgings, and tents in and around Jerusalem where the pilgrims were staying.

Some have seen behind the ritual details a more ancient, pre-Mosaic ceremony in which the entrances to houses were smeared with blood on a certain night to protect those who dwelt in them from a destructive 23 demon. This might explain why **the destroyer** is mentioned (the demon in this narrative becomes the angel of death, charged with the execution of God's **judgements**). It might also explain why one interpretation of the phrase, **he will pass over that door and will not let the destroyer enter your houses to strike you**, is that the Lord will pass over *into* the house to protect those within. The title of the feast is probably from the Hebrew *pāsah*, 'to skip' or 'to pass over'—either the angel of death's passing over the houses, or the Lord's passing over the threshold into the houses.

What is particularly interesting for the theme of this Sunday is that the account of the institution of the feast contains within itself the means by 27 which it is to be handed on through successive generations. **When your children ask you, 'What is the meaning of this rite?' you shall say, 'It is the Lord's Passover, for he passed over the houses of the Israelites in Egypt when he struck the Egyptians but spared our houses.'** The annual recital of the story of the Passover is a catechism through which the children of the household are instructed about its meaning. Traditionally it is the youngest in the family who asks the questions.

22 **Marjoram** is an aromatic plant used for various rites of purification.

On the threshold (footnote): it is possible that at some time there was a hollow in the floor of the house for this purpose.

Romans 8. 11–17

In this part of his letter Paul has been making it clear that an individual's conversion and baptism into the Church are not an end but a beginning, and that the Christian must expect to be faced constantly with a series of choices which can only be made with the guidance of the indwelling Spirit, who gives new life to our mortal bodies.

12   **It follows, my friends, that our lower nature has no claim upon us; we are not obliged to live on that level.** By 'lower nature' (JB 'our unspiritual selves') Paul meant that natural side of our personality which is incapable of good in itself: 'I know that nothing good lodges in me—in my unspiritual nature, I mean—for though the will to do good is there, the deed is not. The good which I want to do, I fail to do; but what I do is the wrong which is against my will: and if what I do is against my will, clearly it is no longer I who am the agent, but sin that has its lodging in me' (7.18–20). The unspiritual man may think of the natural way as the way to life, but in reality it is the way to death. Augustine, looking back on his life before his baptism, remarked wistfully, 'Such was my life—but was *that* living?' Our lower nature is occupied by sin if it is not submitted to the Holy Spirit.

14   The Spirit claims us for God. **For all who are moved by the Spirit of God are sons of God.** Sonship, like marriage, is used to convey the intimate relationship which exists between God and his faithful people; and it is as the Christian is filled with the Spirit that he enters into that intimate relationship. But the mastery of the Spirit is not the kind of lordship that a slave experiences (and slavery was a common feature of the world in which Paul lived). Rather, the Spirit liberates us into the status of sonship with God and guarantees our future salvation. To put it another way, the Spirit establishes our salvation in the present by anticipating what we inherit in the future. Our adoption as sons can be compared in Pauline theology with our justification. Justification, which is a verdict of the last judgement, is brought forward into the present through our faith in God's manifestation of his righteousness in Christ and in us by his Spirit.

The practice of adoption was not known in Jewish circles, where other provision was made for parentless children, but it was common in Greco-Roman society. A wealthy man might adopt a young slave, if he was childless, to inherit his possessions. Just as children of a household might look forward to receiving a portion of their father's possessions, so Christians as sons of God will one day enter into their heavenly inheritance as Christ, their Elder Brother, has already done. The Spirit of God, by bringing this inheritance forward into the present, enables us to address 15 God as Abba! Father! The Aramaic word—an intimate, family term of address—is followed in the text by the Greek translation. Though not liturgical in origin, Paul's use of it recalls contemporary practice in Christian prayer, as witnessed in the Lord's Prayer and the prayer of Christ in the garden of Gethsemane (Luke 11.2, Mark 14.35). But there is a condition attached. For Christ the path of glory involved suffering. For his fellow-heirs it is the same.

* Luke 2. 41–end

It was the custom of Joseph and Mary, as devout Jews, to pilgrimage to Jerusalem to observe the Passover. The rabbis expected children to keep the Law fully from the age of thirteen. The presence of Christ at the pilgrimage at the age of twelve suggests that his parents were introducing him to the practices of their religion early in life. We are told that he was 'full of wisdom' (2.40), that he had learned the ways of God from the study of the scriptures, and so we can assume that the questions he put to the teachers in the colonnaded forecourts of the temple turned on the interpretation of certain passages in the OT. Could it be that all who 47 heard him were amazed at his intelligence and the answers he gave were listening to the uniquely fresh exposition of the scriptures which were to be a well-remembered feature of his future ministry?

The story contrasts the relationship of Jesus to his heavenly Father with his relationship to his earthly parents. Jesus recognized God as his Father long before the voice from heaven spoke at his baptism by John in the river Jordan. He was not 'adopted' at his baptism, as some have claimed all through the Christian era. Yet his obedience to Joseph and Mary is set in this context as a model of Christian family relationships.

The story has close affinities with that of Samuel, whose parents, like the parents of Jesus, used to observe the feasts year by year and who also, as he grew up, 'commended himself to the Lord and to men' (1 Sam. 1.7, 2.26).

THE SECOND SUNDAY AFTER CHRISTMAS

Isaiah 60. 1–6

1, 4 The passage hinges on two imperatives, **Arise** and **Lift**. In the first the mourning people were summoned to raise themselves from their prostrations to see the glory of God shining over them; in the second they were shown that the light that shines on them is a centre upon which the peoples of all nations are converging.

Verses 1–3 contain a magnificent picture of the fulfilment of the biblical promise to Israel. The motif of the Lord's epiphany to his people is an old one, but the elements of warfare and of natural phenomena which accompanied the manifestation of God in other OT passages are missing. All that remains of the latter is the light of God shining in the darkness, the sign of God's presence at the Exodus, but now employed in a way that resembles the NT use of darkness and light—particularly John's—rather than the OT. God's advent is not identified with the people's return to Jerusalem, as it is elsewhere in this collection of prophecies. Instead, other nations come to Jerusalem as a result of God's saving act.

Verses 4–6 demonstrate the universal scope of God's work in the vision of the kings and their peoples making pilgrimage to the holy city in mighty caravans across the deserts of Syria and Sinai (Midian and Ephah from north Arabia; the descendants of Sheba, like their famous queen, from southern Arabia) and from across the sea (the maritime
4 powers of Phoenicia and Greece). With them come **your sons** and **your daughters**, Hebrews of the dispersion, bringing the riches of the nations with them. The foreigners themselves will be heralds of the Lord's praise.

Revelation 21. 22—22. 5

22 There was **no temple** in John's vision of the New Jerusalem because the whole city radiated the presence of God. There was no need for a
23 special sanctuary. Similarly, **the glory of God** was no longer limited to momentary theophanies. God's glory, mediated through the Lamb, gave all the light that was imaginable.
24 **The nations** were the heathen who, having trampled the holy city underfoot and having been seduced by the great whore earlier in the vision, were finally subject to the armies of Christ; **the kings of the earth** were those over whom Christ had asserted his authority at the cost of suffering to his people. These now came in pilgrimage to the new Jerusalem bringing valuables with them. Although the picture is univer-

27 salist in its implications, the only ones allowed to enter the city were those who are inscribed in the Lamb's roll of the living.

John's main OT sources for his vision, Ezekiel's new Jerusalem and
22.1– the garden of Eden, came together when he saw the river of the water of
2 life . . . flowing from the throne of God and of the Lamb down the middle of the city's street. God's curse over the old creation has been lifted and the tree of life now brought the healing of the nations. With
3 the worship of God's servants, bearing his name on their foreheads and gathered round the throne, the picture of the beatific vision is complete.

* Matthew 2. 1–12, 19–23

Although the Gospel of Matthew has a strongly Jewish bias, it begins and ends with reference to the worldwide mission of the Church. At the end of the Gospel Christ's disciples are commissioned to go into all the world; at the beginning the birth of Christ is reverenced both by Jews (Joseph and Mary) and by Gentiles (the magi).

Bethlehem, 'the house of bread', is situated about four miles south of Jerusalem. Herod the Great was a puppet king of Palestine who was maintained by Roman authority from 40 to 4 B.C. According to Matthew's dating (and as implied by Luke's) the birth of Jesus took place before 4 B.C. Astrologers (Gk. *magoi*, Latin *magi*) originated from a tribe of the Medes who became a priestly caste among the Persians. In this sense the magi were wise men, observers of the stars. The word later acquired a more sinister meaning of 'magicians' or 'sorcerers' (Acts 8.9, 13.6,8),
2 though this is obviously not meant here. The rising of his star was associated with the birth of great men—e.g. Alexander the Great. The
4 chief priests were the families from which the high priests were chosen; the lawyers were the experts in the Law, frequently Pharisees, though not always. With the high priests and the elders they constituted the Grand Sanhedrin in Jerusalem.

The gifts of the magi represented the wealth of Arabia, but the early Christian fathers saw in them symbols of royalty (gold), divinity (incense) and the passion (myrrh). The adoration of the magi fulfilled the prophecies that homage would be paid to the God of the Jews by the nations (Isa. 49.7, 60.6; Ps. 72.10–15).

Matthew saw in the murder of the children and the flight of Jesus' parents into Egypt a repetition of the events which led to the exodus. Once more a king killed Jewish children; once more one child was saved from the slaughter (Moses, Jesus); once more God's purpose was ful-
19 filled when he called his son out of Egypt. The Lord appeared in a

dream: a familiar way in which God communicated with his servants in
20 the OT. The men who threatened the child's life are dead: Herod
and those he commanded to carry out the massacre. Archelaus succeeded
his father in 4 B.C. and ruled until A.D. 6, when he was replaced by a
23 Roman procurator. He shall be called a Nazarene: the source of this
prophecy is not known, but it has been suggested that it comes from
Isa. 11.1, 'A shoot shall grow from the stock of Jesse, and a branch
(Hebrew *nēitzer*) shall spring from his roots.'

The desire for a saviour was not confined to Jewish circles. There is a
good deal of evidence to show that in a world distracted by social up-
heavals and civil wars, the men and women of the centuries either side
of the birth of Christ longed for a release from the uncertainties they
experienced in daily life. There was a move away from the formal and
conventional worship of the Olympian gods to the cults from the East
which professed to offer divine guidance and protection in return for
moral and ritual purification within a close brotherhood of initiates. Thus
the Son of God came as a saviour to men awakening to their need on a
universal scale, not a narrowly Jewish one.

YEARS 1 AND 2

THE EPIPHANY OF OUR LORD
(January 6)
See page 27

Isaiah 49. 1–6
The second of the four songs of the servant of the Lord in Second Isaiah.
The servant of God proclaimed the true faith and suffered to atone for the
sins of his people, but God exalted him in the end. Who was the Servant?
Some commentators have suggested he was an individual closely related
to one of the sources of Second Isaiah; others have seen him as the
personification of the people of Israel themselves, or a group of them; **you**
3 **are my servant, Israel, through whom I shall win glory.** The
problem may never be solved; both suggestions are to be held together,
since they point forward to the identification of the servant with Christ,
and of Christ with his Church—an identification which is so intimate
that Paul could speak of 'helping to complete, in my poor human flesh,
the full tale of Christ's afflictions still to be endured, for the sake of his
body which is the church' (Col. 1.24).

God called the servant from his birth—indeed before it, as in the cases of
1 John the Baptist and Jesus Christ, for he **named me from my mother's
   womb**—and equipped him with the ability to speak words that pene-
2 trated like **a sharp sword** and ranged far and wide like **a polished arrow.**
   Concealed me under the cover of his hand may indicate that the
   first part of his life was hidden until he came out into the open to prophesy;
   it could also mean that he enjoyed the protection of the Lord.

His task was to glorify God. He set aside the disappointment of his
previous failure. Though men had thought that his work had miscarried,
4 God was going to accept it and vindicate it: **my cause is with the Lord
   and my reward is in God's hands.** His new task was to restore Israel
   as in the days of promise after the return from exile in Babylon, but with
6 a greater responsibility: **I will make you a light to the nations.** The
   Gentile world was to be included in God's saving work.

Ephesians 3. 1–12

The writer, perhaps a later editor of the apostle's works, introduces the
apostle as one who prays in captivity for the Gentile Christians. He is
1 **the prisoner of Christ Jesus** in the spiritual sense that he was captured
   by the risen Lord on the Damascus road; he was also a prisoner in the
   physical sense when his arrest in Jerusalem (Acts 21.17–40) led eventually
   to a martyr's death in Rome. He is the one whom God has chosen to
   bring the gospel to the Gentiles.
3   This was the **secret**, 'mystery' in the contemporary sense of that word
   (see p. 77), that was **made known to me** when Paul was called by God.
4 **The secret of Christ** was that the Church, Christ's Body, should be the
   means of bringing all mankind into unity. The Jews had been the ex-
   clusive heirs of the promises of God under the covenant, of which circumcision was a sign. The Gentiles, 'separate from Christ, strangers to
   the community of Israel, outside God's covenants and the promise that
   goes with them' (2.12), had now been given access to God in Christ
   through his reconciling death. This divine plan was unknown in previous
   ages, but God has willed to disclose his eternal purpose, and by special
   revelation entrusted Paul with the task of proclaiming it to the Gentiles.
4   **A brief account** may refer to 1.9–10 or perhaps to part of another letter,
5 Colossians. **Prophets** are probably members of the Church with charismatic gifts who shared the work of proclaiming the gospel with the
   apostles, or they may be OT prophets who only had an obscure and
   imperfect vision of the work of the Messiah.

The change in outlook involved in accepting all men as potentially

members of the people of God was one which many early Christians from a Jewish family found difficult to accept, and behind the NT writings are echoes of the controversy. It was only slowly that Jewish Christians came to see that Gentiles who had repented and sought baptism need not be circumcised—i.e. become Jewish proselytes—before they were admitted into the fellowship of the Church. Paul, as the apostle to the Gentiles, insisted on this again and again in his letters, and the lesson was repeated in the early chapters of the Acts of the Apostles until the council in Jerusalem laid down conditions under which Gentiles would be admitted to communion with former Jews in the Church (Acts 15). Paul's anxiety to stress this equality of Gentile and Jew under the new covenant emerges
6 in his use of phrases like **joint heirs with the Jews, part of the same body, sharers together in the promise made in Christ Jesus.**

The Greek original of verse 9 is difficult. A literal translation would be something like this: 'To me . . . was this grace, to preach to the nations the unsearchable riches of Christ, and to bring to light what (is) the stewardship (*oikonomia*—a household term) of the mystery hidden in the ages from God'. JB translates it: 'I . . . have been entrusted with this special grace, not only of proclaiming to the pagans the infinite treasure of Christ, but also of explaining (showing clearly to all, *Vulg.*) how the mystery is to be dispensed'. Earlier the letter had spoken of the unity of Jews and Gentiles in the Body of Christ; here the writer is asserting that the God, who brings about that unity through the redeeming work of Christ, is also the God who creates and rules all things. So the unity achieved in the Church is a permanent revelation of the very essence of God's nature. He is the one whose nature is love, and love unites men to him and to one another.

The mystery now revealed is 'that through the Gospel the Gentiles are joint heirs with the Jews, part of the same body, sharers together in
10 the promises made in Christ Jesus' (verse 6). The reference to **rulers and authorities in the realms of heaven** can mean that the Church declares the purpose of God to all the universe, but it is more likely to imply that the existence of the Church is a sign to the cosmic powers of evil that they have been defeated in the victorious purpose of God. The priestly office of Christ, taught in other NT writings (e.g. Rom. 5.2, 1 Pet.
12 3.18, Rev. 1.5f), is presented in a Pauline manner: **In him we have access to God with freedom, in the confidence born of trust in him.**

* **Matthew 2. 1–12** See Christmas 2 Year 2

EPIPHANY 1

1 Samuel 16. 1–13a

Another tradition attributed the anointing of David to the men of Judah and then to the elders of Israel at Hebron (2 Sam. 2.4, 5.3). This story of his anointing serves to demonstrate the charismatic succession of leadership between Samuel and David, once God had rejected Saul.

David's family tree, that of Jesse at Bethlehem, was deeply rooted in Israel and therefore powerful support for the claim to kingship. He was a man of Judah through and through. Saul, on the other hand, came from Benjamin, and as the divisions in Israel intensified, with Judah opposed to the other tribes, Saul with Benjamin came to be regarded as apostate.

Samuel's status was somewhat ambiguous. He was fearful of Saul's power and had to adopt a subterfuge in order to travel to Bethlehem, yet he was vested with such authority that the elders of Bethlehem hurried out to find out what he wanted. The fact that Samuel said he had come to make an oblation and invited them to cleanse themselves with a ceremonial washing indicates that Bethlehem occupied a special place in the religious life of the people. It was a place of sacrifice.

The selection of the new king proceeded on romantic lines. The three brothers were inspected, but rejected by God, although Eliab was tall and handsome (as Saul was, 'a head taller than any of his fellows', 1 Sam.

7 9.2). These are not qualities that impress the Lord; **he does not see as man sees; men judge by appearances but the Lord judges by the heart.** It was the youngest, the eighth, son (eight being the number of perfection) who was chosen and anointed. Samuel was guided not to proceed with the sacrificial meal until this son had been brought forward.

13 After the anointing, **the spirit of the Lord came upon David,** as the spirit of the Lord had come on Saul at his anointing (10.6,10). Verse 14 says that the spirit had left Saul, implying that it was only upon the leaders of the people that the spirit was expected to work.

Acts 10. 34–48a

The Gentile Pentecost in the house of Cornelius, the centurion in the Italian Cohort, who lived in Caesarea and who sent for Peter from Joppa, marked the Church's decisive step out of Judaism into a world mission in the Acts of the Apostles. Luke drew up the story as a model of the kind of response to the Gospel that evangelists should expect from the

36 Gentile world; the word of God is preached: **the good news of peace through Jesus Christ, who is Lord of all** (words from Isa. 52.7; the

last phrase is an interesting fragment of an early Christian credal statement); the Holy Spirit comes upon all who are listening, and they are
baptized. The usual order—preaching, repentance, baptism, gift of the
Holy Spirit—was perhaps reversed on this occasion because of the need
to show Peter and the Jewish believers with him that God was moving
out into the Gentile world and that they must follow.

    Peter's speech is a short gospel of its own. Like the earliest Gospel,
Mark, the apostle began with the baptism of Jesus by John. Jesus was
God's Messiah, Peter taught, quoting Isa. 61.1, for it was at his baptism
38 that the Father **anointed him with the Holy Spirit** (Messiah = 'the
anointed one'). The ministry of Jesus is summarized as beginning in
Galilee and culminating at Jerusalem on Calvary. Peter referred to the
crucifixion only briefly, for he wanted to pass on to the good news of the
41 resurrection. The risen Christ appeared, **not to the whole people, but
to witnesses whom God had chosen in advance—to us, who ate
and drank with him after he rose from the dead.** The reference to
eating and drinking (the meal at Emmaus, the supper by the lakeside) was
a proof of the reality of the apostles' fellowship with Jesus after his
resurrection. The special office of an apostle was to be a witness of the
42 resurrection and **to proclaim him to the people, and affirm that he is
the one who has been designated by God as judge of the living
43 and the dead.** Finally, with a reference to scripture, **it is to him that
all the prophets testify,** Peter declared that everyone who believed in
Jesus Christ **receives forgiveness of sins through his name.** The OT
has its indispensable place in the divine plan of salvation for Gentiles as
well as Jews.

44   Perhaps Peter had intended to say more—he was **still speaking**—
when the Holy Spirit descended on his listeners and, like the apostles
on the day of Pentecost, they spoke in tongues. Glossolalia was the sign
of receiving the Spirit in Acts 10.42 as in 2.4. It is a form of praise and
46 thanksgiving for **acclaiming the greatness of God,** and it convinced
Peter and his companions that those Gentiles should be baptized in the
name of Jesus Christ.

    * **Matthew 3. 13–end**
In describing the baptism of Jesus, Matthew seems to try to answer the
question, Why should the sinless one submit to the baptism of John?
Jesus would more fittingly baptize John. Indeed, John had already said
of him: 'I baptize you with water, for repentance; but the one who comes
after me is mightier than I. I am not fit to take off his shoes. He will

baptize you with the Holy Spirit and with fire' (3.11). But Jesus pressed
15 to be baptized: **We do well to conform in this way with all that God
requires.** Jesus is one with the people and must join with them in those
acts which express their response to God's spokesman. Divine judgement
is coming, and Israel must repent and be baptized and prepare by obedience for the kingdom of God. By being baptized Christ also validated the
rite for all future generations of Christians.

The descent of the Spirit of God, pictured by the evangelists as a dove
—a symbol used in Jewish literature to depict both Israel herself and
divine wisdom—does not mean, of course, that Jesus had not been possessed by the Spirit before. Rather, it means that the Spirit comes
dynamically to those whom God chooses for his work to give them power
and guidance to fulfil their vocation. The descent of the dove represents
the anointing of Christ (= 'the anointed one') for the next step in his
ministry, the withdrawal into the desert to do battle with the devil (see
Lent 1 Years 1 and 2), and the choice of the disciples (see Epiphany 2,
17 Years 1 and 2). **Beloved** means 'chosen of God'.

Patristic commentators long recognized the baptism as a theophany of
the Holy Trinity—the Father's voice from heaven, the Son's baptism, and
the Spirit's descent. Jesus' stepping down into the waters of the Jordan
was seen as a symbol of his crushing underfoot the power of evil (associated in Jewish mythology by water). The event looked forward to Christ's
death and resurrection and the sending of the Spirit on the Church, his
Passover, which he called 'a baptism to undergo' (Luke 12.50).

EPIPHANY 1

Isaiah 42. 1–7
Part of the first of the songs of the servant of God, which form a special
strand within the prophecies of the Second Isaiah. The prophet saw God
1 selecting someone and nominating him: **Here is my servant, whom I
uphold, my chosen one in whom I delight.** The servant's vocation
3 was to **make justice shine on the nations.** Justice in this context means
almost the same as what Paul meant by 'righteousness' when speaking of
the salvation which God accomplishes for man. As far as the Gentiles
are concerned, their gods are as nothing. Israel's Lord alone is God. This

does not mean, however, that the servant was to go and preach to other nations. His was the way of suffering among his own people, and others would see through his acceptance of that *via dolorosa* the salvation of God.
1   For this vocation God equipped him: **I have bestowed my spirit upon him.** This is the spirit of God which stirred the prophets, the out-pouring of which was a sign of the messianic age. When he promulgated judgement, the servant would not follow the usual custom and announce it in public. Instead, he would make God's justice prevail in such a way that he avoided the harsh law of the world, which allows those who are
3   weak and defenceless—**a bruised reed, a smouldering wick**—to perish.

Verses 5–7 are another section of the song. An eulogy for God's power and wisdom in creation and for bestowing life on the human race intro-duces the Lord's further call to the servant. The reason why he has been chosen is that through him the nations will receive light and salvation (and be drawn into the covenant, NEB footnote); the effect will be as if the blind are given their sight and the prisoners are brought out into daylight. These two classes of unfortunates typify the dimensions of human suffer-ing: the first class suffer as a result of natural affliction, the second as a result of man's cruelty. These verses were quoted by the NT writers with reference to Jesus' work.

But who was the servant? Sometimes he is an individual bearing the burden of Israel's sins; sometimes he is the collective representative of Israel as a nation, called by God to suffer as a witness to all the nations of the earth.

Ephesians 2. 1–10
A summary of Paul's gospel, probably written by one who was collating his teaching in a new letter: God has brought man into the sphere of his forgiveness and love, replacing the dark life of sinful hostility to God with a new life within the divine will. It is all the difference between life and death. The man who receives God's grace in Christ and the man who is still in bondage to sin are as different as a living being and a corpse.
2   **The commander of the spiritual powers of the air** is Satan. According to the NT outlook, the existing world has fallen at least par-tially under his control; and just as goodness is produced by the Holy Spirit at work in men's hearts, so evil is produced by Satan **at work**
2, 3   **among God's rebel subjects. We too were once of their number:** perhaps the writer was aligning Paul with his fellow-Jews to distinguish them from the Gentiles to whom he is addressing the letter. Like them, Paul and those to whom he refers also lived in such a way that their lives

3 tended to be oriented away from God and towards their own concerns: **in our natural condition we, like the rest, lay under the dreadful judgement of God.**

The rest of the passage teaches what God has done. In his love and mercy he completed his great work through Jesus Christ to bring new
5, 8 life to dead sinners. The phrase, **it is by his grace you are saved,** is repeated twice. What God has done is in no sense deserved by us, the writer emphasized. Then he followed the Pauline teaching of dying and rising again with Christ, though without saying that the Christian must
6 die with his Lord (in baptism), and adding that we shall **be enthroned . . . with him in the heavenly realms** (an idea not found in Paul). Like John, he was concentrating entirely on the wonderful way in which the deadness of a soul is transformed into vigorous spiritual life as a result of fellowship with Christ. This led him, in his enthusiasm, to speak as if the believer was already in heaven with his exalted and enthroned Lord. There is, of course, a real sense in which this is true, in that eternal life is something in which we begin to share here and now. Salvation is for
7 eternity—**in the ages to come.**

The last two verses of the passage compress into few words Paul's doctrine of justification by faith in dependence on the unmerited grace of God. It is a doctrine which expresses itself in the life of the individual Christian through the good deeds for which God designed us. This is what we were created for; this is what, in Jesus Christ, God makes it possible for us to do.

* John 1. 29–34

The fourth Gospel handles the story of Jesus' baptism in its own distinctive way. The role of the Baptist is reduced so that he is little more than a commentator introducing the advent of Jesus and a witness to the descent of the Holy Spirit upon him. The actual baptism of Christ is not described.

29 **There is the Lamb of God; it is he who takes away the sin of the world.** The Baptist's announcement is rich in OT association. The lamb was the sacrificial offering of the Passover. In early Christian theology Jesus was recognized as the new paschal lamb: 'Our Passover has begun; the sacrifice is offered—Christ himself' (1 Cor. 5.7), 'Praise and honour, glory and might, to him who sits on the throne and to the Lamb for ever and ever!' (Rev. 5.14, etc.). If the Aramaic word for 'servant' has been mistranslated as 'lamb' (though this is doubtful), then the announcement would look back to the Servant of God of Isaiah who was 'led like a sheep to the slaughter', and who 'bore the sin of many'

(Isa. 53.7,12). Lambs were offered daily in the temple, not however to seek the remission of sins: that oblation was made with a goat on the Day of Atonement (Lev. 16.21f). The figure of Christ as the Lamb of God has been associated with the Christian Eucharist from earliest times, and it is not impossible that it already had this association when the fourth Gospel was being written. Above all, **Lamb of God** is a synonym for Messiah. The Baptist saw in Jesus, who was of Davidic descent, the destined

31 leader of God's people: **I myself did not know who he was; but the very reason why I came, baptizing in water, was that he might be revealed to Israel.**

33   **This is he who is to baptize in Holy Spirit.** According to Mark, only Jesus saw the Spirit in the form of a dove. In Matthew and Luke the dove was seen by the people, but in the fourth Gospel it was John who saw the sign and interpreted it. His had been a preparatory ritual of baptism in water; Jesus was the one sent from God to baptize in Holy Spirit. This Gospel distinguishes between 'the spirit' as a gift to men from 'the Spirit' as the one who gives it (the Spirit is always spoken of as 'he', indicating that he is as personal as the Word). It is the Spirit who continues the work of the Word among the faithful: 'When he comes who is the Spirit of truth, he will guide you into all truth' (16.13). To be baptized in Holy Spirit is to be immersed in his life and power by Jesus. Baptism, then, is not just a forgiveness of sins; it is a full participation in the life of God.

34   **This is God's Chosen One, the Son of God** (NEB footnote). Israel of old thought of herself as the chosen people or son of God: 'When Israel was a boy, I loved him; I called my son out of Egypt'. The Baptist testifies that the only true Chosen One or Son of God is the man Jesus of Nazareth.

EPIPHANY 2

Jeremiah 1. 4–10

The ministries of prophets such as Amos, Hosea, Isaiah, and Ezekiel resulted from an encounter with God; the details were different in each case, but the form was the same—a command from God that was irresistible, despite excuses the one called might offer. This passage describes the call of Jeremiah. Even before he was conceived in his mother's womb, his ministry as a prophet was determined in the eternal counsels of God. God 'knew' him for his own in a knowledge that is profound and un-limited—the meaning of the Hebrew word embraces what we understand by 'to love' and 'to elect'—and had set him apart (consecrated) him to a task that would give him the power to set up or overthrow not just Judah, but nations and kingdoms. The call of Jeremiah came about 627 or 626 B.C., when the weakening powers of Assyria and the rise of Babylon made the situation around Israel dangerously fluid. Jeremiah was subsequently much involved in the political situation that led up to the exile.

6   Jeremiah protested that he was too young: **I do not know how to speak; I am only a child.** He may at the time of his call have been about twenty years old. But God's purpose is paramount. The word of the Lord is placed in the prophet's mouth, a power which God injects into human history like a fire, or like a hammer that splinters rock (Jer. 5.14, 23.29). The authority which the prophet received from the Lord foreshadowed the authority which the apostles were to receive from Jesus Christ when they were commissioned (Matt. 16.19, 18.18, John 20.23, 1 Cor. 13.10).

Acts 26. 1, 9–20
Herod Agrippa II was brought up in the court of the emperor Claudius, was made a king of Chalcis in the Lebanon region about A.D. 50, and later took over the tetrarchies of Philip and Lysanias (cf. Luke 3.1) with certain cities in Galilee and Peraea. Paul's speech, therefore, was given to the highest representative of the Roman power in that part of the empire. In our passage the apostle's flattering form of address (verses 2–3) and his assertion that his Christian faith in the resurrection of the body is shared by the Pharisees (verses 4–8) are omitted.

The stretching out of the hand is the gesture of an orator. Some versions says that Paul spoke with boldness and with the 'advocacy' or 'encouragement' of the Holy Spirit.

This is the third account of the conversion of Paul in Acts, and his description of the way he persecuted the Church is fuller than in the previous accounts. For Paul, a devout Pharisee, hunting down Christians was his duty as a devout Jew, and his zeal for the task led him to track down Christians among the Jews of the dispersion (though only Damascus is mentioned in earlier accounts, he refers here—perhaps rhetorically—

11 to **foreign cities**). The extent of the persecution following the martyrdom of Stephen was, perhaps, greater than indicated by Luke. The theophany

affected the men travelling with Paul—the light denoted the presence of God to them as it had done to the shepherds at Bethlehem. The saying 14 about **kicking against the goad** is a Greek proverb for useless resistance: the ox kicking against the goad only succeeds in hurting itself.

Paul was called directly by the risen Christ in a vision to which he could not be disobedient; he was to go to the Gentiles as God's servant and convert them to the God of Israel. The commissioning is in the terms of an 15 OT prophet. **Rise to your feet and stand upright** recalls Ezek. 2.3. The charge to be a 'servant and witness' puts Paul on a level with the Twelve, although Luke does not give him the title of 'apostle'. Verses 17 and 18 echo the mission of the servant of God who was 'to open the eyes that are blind' because God would 'turn darkness into light before them' (Isa. 42.7, 16). The conversion of the Gentiles **from the dominion** 18 **of Satan to God**, had been a prophetic expectation in OT times; under the new covenant they would enjoy, like Judaeo-Christians, the forgiveness of sins which is effected by the breaking in of the Kingdom of God. 18 They would have **a place with those whom God has made his own.**

* **Mark 1. 14–20**

The conclusion of John the Baptist's ministry is the signal for the beginning of Jesus' proclamation of the gospel. The manifesto, drawn from Isa. 40.9, 52.7, and 61.1, sums up the substance of Christ's preaching and the meaning of his public ministry. The time of waiting is over, the sovereign rule of God so long expected had begun, and the moment set by God for the coming of the Messiah had arrived. Jesus did not seek recognition as the messianic figure bringing in the Kingdom of God; on the contrary, he silenced such recognition as there was among his followers and took careful steps to hide his identity. He deflected his hearers' attention away from himself and challenged them about their attitude to God's rule. The call to repent shows how men must respond to the Kingdom: there must be a radical reorientation of their lives towards God, and they must believe the gospel. This was the appeal of early Christian preachers, a turning of the whole person to the message which God's prophet brings us.

John the Baptist had called on people to repent, but his baptism was a sign of a washing away of sin; the repentance of those who turn to Christ requires much more, an acceptance of the gospel. Turning to God meant unconditional obedience, even to the extent of leaving homes and occupations and closest ties of kinship.

This is what the first disciples did when they were called. Simon,

Andrew, James, and John were the closest of the Twelve—Simon, James, and John especially. They would hardly know what it meant to be
17 fishers of men, though early Christian art saw in the image a picture of the Church gathering men into the Kingdom (as, indeed, Christ himself did in Matt. 13.47). They would be drawing men out of the waters of this world into the net of the eschatological life of the age to come.

EPIPHANY 2

1 Samuel 3. 1–10

Samuel was called to be a prophet, to be a messenger of God's word to his people, by an experience of God's presence like Isaiah (Isa. 6) and Jeremiah (Jer. 1.4–10.) Like Isaiah, too, he received his call while he was in a temple. According to Jewish tradition, Samuel was twelve at the time (the age of Jesus when he talked with the teachers in the temple at
1 Jerusalem, Luke 2.40–52), but the word **child** can also mean 'young' and may mean 'inexperienced' rather than juvenile. **In those days the word of the Lord was seldom heard, and no vision was granted**: the comment can mean either that the religious life of the people was at a low ebb (contrasted with the later age of great prophetic activity) or that the disobedience of Eli's sons had resulted in a withdrawal of God's favour. With the call of Samuel a new era began, the era of a mighty prophet.

Eli the priest and Samuel his acolyte were asleep at their appointed 'stations' in the temple, and the sanctuary lamp, which normally burnt all night, had gone out (perhaps it was nearly dawn). Samuel himself was too young and inexperienced to have had any personal knowledge of God. What 'to know the Lord' means is unfolded in the parallelism
7 of verse 7: **to know the Lord** is to have **the word of the Lord . . .**
4,6,8 **disclosed to him. Here I am,** repeated three times, may be compared with Isaiah's 'Here I am; send me' (Isa. 6.8). Something within the servant of God compels him to respond to the divine call.
10   **The Lord came and stood there, and called, Samuel, Samuel.** The narrative conveys a vivid sense of God's presence by describing the Lord as coming and standing by the ark. Tradition associated the ark of God with a chest that had accompanied the Israelites in the wilderness.

In its early form it may have been a simple, transportable shrine in the form of a box; later it was thought to have been highly ornate (Exod. 25.10–22; 37.1–9). This story of Samuel's call originated in the later source of the Book of Samuel from the time when the veneration of the ark was at its peak in Israel.

Galatians 1. 11–end

One of Paul's objectives in writing this letter was to justify his claim to apostolic authority. To do this he recounted the circumstances of his conversion and the way in which the gospel was given to him by the Lord. It is problematical precisely what Paul intended to convey by **I did** 12 **not take it over from any man; no man taught it me; I received it through a revelation of Jesus Christ.** He wanted to stress that he received the gospel from the same source as the Twelve and that, like them, he had encountered the risen Christ. He could have meant that all, or most, of what he knew about the Christian faith came to him as a gift of knowledge on the Damascus road. In that case he was claiming that God, who had set him apart from before his birth, had revealed his Son to him in such a way that Paul needed no further instruction. But he could also have meant that, as a result of his conversion, he needed no further persuasion from any Christian evangelist but, knowing the basis of the gospel, spent years afterwards meditating on it and working out its 14 implications. This he was well fitted to do for, as one who **was outstripping many of my Jewish contemporaries in my boundless devotion to the tradition of my ancestors,** he had been trained as a rabbi. The period in Arabia may have provided the opportunity for adjusting his ideas when he worked out his distinctive doctrine of salvation through faith and not through the Law. He also came to see that Christ was the Lord of all men, not just of the Jews, pointing Paul to his mission to the Gentiles.

We have here, then, a piece of autobiography. The details of the conversion are not given as fully as in Acts. Presumably they were well known to the Galatian Church. The way Paul said that he spent the seventeen years after his conversion (1.18 and 2.1) do not exactly fit in with the account of his life in Acts, but the difference can be explained if we take into account the possibility that Luke may have been selective in the sources he used.

* John 1. 35–end

John the Baptist witnessed to Jesus as the paschal Lamb sent by God for

the redemption of the world and, hearing this, two of the Baptist's disciples left John to follow Christ. The process by which Jesus would draw all men to himself had begun. John was content to become less while Christ grew greater (3.30). The disciples asked where Jesus was staying; they assumed that, as a teacher, he must have a school somewhere. Jesus
39 replied by inviting them to **Come and see**. They accepted his invitation and spent the rest of the day with him, but that 'day' was to be the whole of their lives and the entrance to eternity. The place where Jesus 'stays' is the Christian community, where his disciples dwell in him and he in them (15.4ff).

One of the two was Andrew; the other may have been John the son of Zebedee. Andrew became the first home missionary, for his first action (next morning?—NEB footnote) was to find his brother Simon and tell
41 him that the greatest of all possible discoveries had been made, **We have found the Messiah**. Christ gave Simon the name of 'Rock Man', *Cephas*; *Petra* is the Greek equivalent of the Aramaic name. In the Gospels Peter is more of a waverer than a rock, but Jesus was prophesying through that new name what Peter would one day become, after he had witnessed the resurrection and received the Holy Spirit.

Bethsaida, 'Fishertown', was also the home of Philip and Nathanael, who is usually identified with Bartholomew: the name means 'gift of
45 God'. Philip told him, **We have met the man spoken of by Moses in the Law, and by the prophets: it is Jesus son of Joseph, from Nazareth**. He believed Jesus was the person to whom so many passages in the OT pointed, the Messiah, the Christ. Nathanael was dubious. The Messiah was supposed to be *incognito*. Besides, Nazareth was not even mentioned in the OT as the Christ's place of origin. Again the invitation was repeated, **Come and see**: the best way of presenting the gospel is to see it in action in men's lives. And when Nathanael came, Jesus recognized him as one who had nothing false in him (the RSV phrase, 'without guile', hints at Gen. 32.28: Jacob's new name was 'Israel', but he remained
47 a man of guile; Nathanael, without guile, is **an Israelite worthy of the name**). Christ, the good shepherd, had recognized one of his own sheep
48 (10.3). To a Jew the words **under the fig-tree** would suggest the domestic bliss of a place for studying the Law, for the rabbis recommended men to meditate on the law 'under their own vine and fig-tree'. Nathanael
49 pronounced Jesus as **Son of God . . ., king of Israel**. He had not yet understood that Jesus is the Saviour of all men and his Kingdom is not of this world.

The passage closes with the promise to Nathanael and the others,

51 I tell you all, you shall see heaven wide open, and God's angels ascending and descending upon the Son of Man. The allusion to Gen. 28.12 is unmistakable: 'Jacob dreamt that he saw a ladder, which rested on the ground with its top reaching to heaven, and angels of God were going up and down upon it.' The vision reveals the office of the one who bears the mysterious title 'Son of Man': he was to be the link between heaven and earth, and his destiny was to be played out in both.

EPIPHANY 3

Exodus 33. 12–end

Moses was anxious because he had to take the people into strange territory. He asked God who would be sent to go with him. In doing so, Moses invoked the relationship which God had established with him when he had revealed to Moses the divine Name and told him that he had
13 found favour with God. **Teach me to know thy way, so that I can know thee and continue in favour with thee, for this nation is thy own people,** Moses said. The Lord promised that he himself would go with Moses and the people in person and that he would set their mind at rest (in Num. 10.33 the Ark of the Covenant of the Lord set out a day's journey ahead of the company to find a site in Canaan). The request and the reply are repeated in verses 15–17, with the added indication that it was the presence of God in Israel that made the nation distinct from all the other peoples on earth.

Then Moses, emboldened by the response to his first request, made another. He asked the Lord to grant him a full manifestation of the divine glory. This was daring indeed, for it was believed that God is so holy that he cannot be seen by the eyes of sinful men. Man must perish if he looks on God (Exod. 20.19). Moses (Exod. 3.6) and Elijah (1 Kings 19.13) and even the seraphim covered their faces in his presence (Isa. 6.2). The Lord did not grant all that Moses requested, but he pronounced his name in the hearing of Moses, an act indicative of an intimacy with God of a very profound kind, and he permitted Moses to see his back, not his face. In Exod. 24.9–11 the vision of God is presumably at some distance; here God passed by a cleft in the rock on which Moses stood.

Elijah was granted a similar favour (1 Kings 19. 11f). Moses and Elijah, then, were the only two in the OT who looked on God in an intimate way, and it is they who shared the glory of God in the transfiguration of Christ on the mountain (Matt. 17.3, etc.).

1 John 1. 1–7

The theme of 1 John is communion with God: eternal life, which depends on the incarnation of Jesus Christ, and on the brotherly love within the apostolic community of those who believe in him. This passage is the prologue to that epistle, introducing this theme.

1   As in the Gospel, Jesus Christ is the divine Logos, **the word of life**. The pre-existence of the divine Logos is acknowledged in the first few words of the passage, and then the author, speaking on behalf of the apostolic witnesses, declared that the Logos made eternal life known in the historical Jesus. A succession of verbs, used to emphasize the encounter with the historical Jesus—**heard it, seen it, looked upon it**—sum up all that is contained in the word 'epiphany'. It was the act of God in Christ Jesus to manifest himself in human terms.

The manifestation of God in Christ was not made to the apostles for their own benefit, however; it was made so that they, as witnesses to what God has done and is doing, might declare it to others and with them share in the common life which joins them to God the Father and his
4 Son Jesus Christ. **And we write this in order that the joy of us all may be complete.** It is only as others share in that life that Christians themselves find fulfilment.

5   **God is light, and in him there is no darkness at all.** It was widely believed in Hellenistic religion that there were two realities—light and darkness—and that the way of escape from the uncertainties and miseries of this world was to enter into the divine light. Traces of this belief can be found in Jewish sources such as the Community Rule of Qumran: 'Those born of truth spring from a fountain of light, but those born of falsehood spring from a source of darkness. All the children of righteousness are ruled by the Prince of Light and walk in the ways of light; but all the children of falsehood are ruled by the Angel of Darkness and walk in the ways of darkness' (1QS iii). But the author is not content with an
7 outlook of mere dualism. If Christians **walk in the light as he himself is in the light**, then that reality will be manifest in their everyday conduct. We cannot claim—like certain heretical teachers during the first century (and since)—to be without sin. But, knowing that **we are being cleansed from every sin by the blood of Jesus**, we can seek his forgiveness so that our lives will reflect more gloriously the light of God.

* John 2. 1–11

The fourth evangelist's word for 'miracle' is 'sign', an act of Jesus Christ which is not simply a wonderful demonstration of power but one which shows forth or manifests the meaning of his life, his ministry, his death,
11 and resurrection. It was through these signs that **Jesus revealed his glory and led his disciples to believe in him.**

The first sign, the changing of water into wine at the wedding at Cana-in-Galilee, has long been associated with the feast of the Ephipany because of its significance as a manifestation. The circumstances were straightforward; Mary's remark was hardly a request for a miraculous
5 intervention by Jesus, yet he seemed to take it so: **My hour has not yet come.** It was not the time to show forth his glory, which in the fourth Gospel reaches its culmination in the *hour*, the death on the cross. We note in passing that Mary was present when Jesus manifested his glory the first time in this sign; she was also present when he manifested his glory on the cross (19.25–27). This was the hour when he showed his glory: it was when he was crucified and returned to the Father's right hand. Elsewhere in the Gospel Christ said the hour was determined by the Father and cannot be anticipated. But the miracle worked through Mary's comment is a prophetic sign of the hour. The reluctance of Christ to respond to the invitation from his mother is understandable if we remember that he had set aside the temptation to use his authority for his own purposes (Matt. 4.3f, Luke 4.2–4). He performed the miracle for the simple reason that he wished to save his host embarrassment.

It was an appropriate occasion for the first manifestation of the glory of God in Christ, for a wedding feast was a parable of the messianic kingdom. Jesus sanctified marriage by his presence at Cana, and made marriage a symbol of his own relationship with his Church. The substance of the miracle has been variously interpreted: the purifying waters of the old covenant now give place to the superabundant wine of the new covenant; the new life that is Christ's gift replaces the old. Large quantities of liquid were involved, between 120 and 180 gallons! Christ's wine is the best. The secret of its quality was known, not to the guests or even to the steward, but to the ordinary servants who had drawn the water.

EPIPHANY 3

Deuteronomy 8. 1–6

The preacher began with a call to obey God, and continued by telling the people to remember the forty years in the wilderness. It was then that they had experienced God's fatherly guidance. The Lord had used it as a time to humble them and to test them, building them up in discipline, sometimes through scarcity, sometimes through blessings, to reach a mature understanding of his ways and of his law.

The reference to the manna is interesting because it illustrates a fresh interpretation of the miracle from the standpoint of a later writer. In Exod. 16 it was regarded as simply a miracle wrought by God to supply his people's need; here the miracle is declared to be a lesson from God 3 to teach his people that **man cannot live on bread alone but lives by every word that comes from the mouth of the Lord.** The Lord's word is life to Israel. The miracle of the clothes and the shoes which did not wear out is not mentioned elsewhere in the OT. It is an example of the way in which the preacher had access to traditions about Israel's past which have since been lost.

Philippians 4. 10–20

The occasion of Paul's letter to the congregation (*ecclesia*, used in the sense of 'local church') at Philippi, the Roman colony in Macedonia, was to thank them for financial assistance they had given him. Normally the apostle avoided doing anything that might give the impression that he was making money out of preaching the gospel (Acts 18.3f). But he seems to have been on terms of intimate trust with his converts in Philippi, for they had supported him at Thessalonica, at Corinth, and later commissioned Epaphroditus to take further contributions to him. The letter was written to tell them that he had received the gifts and to express his gratitude.

Yet, even so, he endeavoured to make it clear to them that it was their consideration for him and their fellowship with him that gave him joy; they shared the burden of his troubles through what they gave—that was what really mattered to him. Their gifts were inspired by their love for God and were therefore as valid as any sacrificial oblation made in 18 the temple ritual: **a fragrant offering, an acceptable sacrifice, pleasing to God.**

Within this expression of thanks Paul conveyed the sense of his opti-

mism and faith in the goodness of God. He knew what it was to be poor
or to be comparatively comfortable, but he gave thanks to God whatever
13 his circumstances, because through Christ he had **strength for anything
through him who gives me power.** That is where true riches are; what
he wanted was that the Philippians might lay up for themselves treasures
18 in heaven. And through his 'thank you' letter—the phrase **I give you my
receipt** is the common one for acknowledging a financial transaction—
Paul was subtly urging the Philippians to imitate him in dependence upon
God who would supply all they required whatever their social or financial
status.

* **John 6. 1–14**
The feeding of the five thousand is set in the fourth Gospel against the
background of the Passover—the second of the three references to this
feast in John (the first is at the cleansing of the temple, 2.13, the third
at Christ's passion). It gives the incident the atmosphere of a Passover
celebration, or, rather, a looking forward to the paschal eucharistic
celebrations of the people of God after the resurrection. This impression is
strengthened when we remember that it precedes the great Bread of Life
discourse in this chapter. Some commentators have doubted the miraculous element in the story, saying that it represented an act of mutual sharing by the people inspired by the presence of Jesus. Others have pointed
out that the miracle is credible if Jesus is believed to be the incarnate
Word, through whose agency creation came into existence. Whatever the
explanation, the evangelist seems to be using material from an oral tradition which was independent of the synoptic Gospels.

   Jesus did not sit down to teach, as in the synoptics; the teaching came
next morning (6.22ff). The Galilean lake was sometimes called Tiberias
after the Gentile city Herod Antipas had built on the lake shore in honour
of the emperor Tiberius. In John it was Jesus, not the disciples (as in the
7 synoptics) who noticed that the people lacked food. A **denarius** (NEB
footnote) was a day's pay for a hired labourer—bread, even the barley
bread of the poor, was relatively more expensive in relation to other food
in the ancient world than it is today. Pickled fish was added as a relish.
As it was April, the grass was green; it dries up under the hot sun in May
and June.
11   **Jesus took the loaves, gave thanks, and distributed them to the
people** is reminiscent of the Last Supper. The usual Jewish prayer of
thanksgiving was offered over the bread by Jesus, acting as the head of the
table for the meal. When the meal was over, the order to collect what

remained was inspired not by economic considerations but by feelings of reverence, and may well reflect later Christian concern for the disposal of the eucharistic elements. The bread which God had provided was the new manna pointing to Jesus the true Bread from heaven, and it must not be wasted. Each disciple found his basket full. The feeding therefore becomes in John a kind of Galilean Last Supper, an acting out of the parable of the great supper told in Luke 14.15–24. The messianic significance of the
14 occasion was recognized by the people, for they called Jesus **the prophet that was to come into the world** (Deut. 18.15, a messianic reference).

EPIPHANY 4

1 Kings 8. 22–30
Solomon offered his prayer for the dedication of the new temple in Jeru-
22 salem **standing in front of the altar . . . spread out his hands;** that was the normal attitude for prayer in the ancient Near East. To stand is the attitude of an inferior before a deity, who is normally represented sitting. That it was Solomon who offered the prayer and not a priest reflects the sacerdotal status of the king in pre-exilic times. The monarch was not only the divinely appointed sovereign over the people; he was also the mediator between God and the community.

The prayer, which shows signs of later editing, opens with an ascription to the Lord reminding him of the covenant he had made with the people at Sinai, conditional upon their faithfulness, and recalls also the new covenant which the Lord made with David and his house. A new element in the religion of Israel, this is elaborated: **Thou hast kept thy promise**
24– **to thy servant David my father; by thy deeds this day thou hast**
25 **fulfilled what thou didst say to him in words. Now therefore, O Lord God of Israel, keep this promise of thine to thy servant David my father: 'You shall never want for a man appointed by me to sit on the throne of Israel, if only your sons look to their ways and walk before me as you have walked before me.'** The introduction of the promises to David into the covenant prepared the way for the conception of the Messiah as a descendant of this monarch, as one of the house of Jesse.

Solomon's prayer goes on to acknowledge that the Lord cannot be limited to a building. The temple is only a place where, or towards which, men can address their petitions to God. He is present only in the sense that his Name is there. God's true presence, where he ultimately receives ('hears') all intercession, is his transcendent dwelling in heaven.

1 Corinthians 3. 10–17

The reading comes from that part of the Corinthian correspondence where the apostle introduced the concept of the Church as a building—a concept common in other NT writings. Where the reading opens, he developed the metaphor, seeing himself as a skilled ('wise' with God's
10 wisdom) master-builder, one who supervises the work of others. As the first evangelist at Corinth, he had laid the foundations of the local church there, leaving it to others to continue the superstructure. Perhaps he had in mind Apollos and Peter, who seem to have visited Corinth as well. By the foundation, however, Paul means, not the first converts in themselves, but their faith in Jesus Christ who is himself the only true foundation of the Church. There can be no other foundation, such as a party loyalty to a particular apostle (there were groups in the Corinthian congregation who claimed a special allegiance to Apollos or to Peter, 1.12–13).

If it is an error to attempt to build on the wrong foundations, it is another error to use the wrong materials. Paul listed the various kinds of materials, some worthy, some unworthy, and pointed out that when they are tested the unworthy materials will be burnt away. The day of judgement will reveal the true value of what each has contributed to the building up
13 of the Church. For that day dawns in fire, and the fire will test the worth of each man's work.

God's approval of work done is expressed in terms of a reward; God's disapproval, however, the apostle sees in terms of destruction by fire. The day of judgement will be a day of conflagration, and the workman who is caught in his own badly-constructed house will run the risk of being engulfed by flames unless he escapes by a quick dash through them.

Paul then develops the metaphor a stage further by describing the
16 Church as God's temple. The building erected on the foundation of Jesus Christ is the meeting place for God and man, where man offers God the worship and obedience due to him. The presence of God in this living temple of the baptized is effective through the Holy Spirit. The apostle warns that those who destroy the Church will themselves be destroyed. How this destruction of the Church might be brought about the apostle

does not specify. He was, of course, thinking of the Church as a local congregation; and perhaps he had in mind those who tried to import elements into it—excessive legalism, for example, from Judaism—to destroy its nature as a family living under the grace of God. Congregations have been destroyed in Christian history through heresies as well as through persecutions.

* **John 2. 13–22**
In the synoptic gospels the cleansing of the temple occurs before the passover when Jesus was crucified. In John it is the opening act of Jesus' public ministry. It therefore assumes the character of a prophetic demonstration of the Messiah's advent: 'Suddenly the Lord whom you seek will come to his temple. . . . Who can endure the day of his coming? Who can stand firm when he appears?' (Mal. 3.1–2); 'When that time comes, no trader shall again be seen in the house of the Lord of Hosts' (Zech. 14.21).

The cattle, sheep, and pigeons were sold in the temple precincts for the purposes of the sacrificial cult—their suitability as oblations was guaranteed by the temple authorities—and the money-changers exchanged coins bearing effigies forbidden in the temple for the shekel and half-shekels required for paying religious dues and offerings. Even though the traders made a profit out of their business—Jesus said they were making the temple 'a robbers' cave' (Mark 11.17)—their stalls must have been convenient for pilgrims and worshippers. According to this evangelist, however, it was not the dishonesty of the traders that Jesus attacked but
16 the pursuit of commerce within the holy place. **Take them out; you must not turn my Father's house into a market.** The personal pronoun stresses the unique sonship of Jesus. It is *his* Father's house that they are desecrating. Judgement begins at the house of God, and Jesus the Messiah began his ministry by acting judgementally in the temple
17 to expose the Jews' impiety. **Zeal for thy house will destroy me** (Ps. 69.9) asks God to vindicate the righteous man who has been oppressed because of his eagerness for the things of God. Here the verse becomes a prophecy that the zeal which Jesus showed would lead to his own destruction.

Jesus' answer to the Jews' request for a sign appears evasive. In the fourth Gospel signs are used to confirm faith, not to convince sceptics. So Jesus refused to give them a sign and uttered a warning instead. The unbelief of the Jews will lead to the destruction of the temple, but Jesus will raise a new temple in three days—a saying which was quoted in a garbled version against him at his trial (Mark 14.58). Typically the Jews missed the point. Herod began his rebuilding of the temple about 20 B.C. so it must have been completed—or the major part of it completed (Josephus records that it was not entirely finished until A.D. 63) by about 20 A.D. 26, a year or two before this incident. **Are you going to raise it again in three days?** they asked him.

21   But Jesus **was speaking of his body.** His resurrected physical body is the new temple, but, although John does not say so here, we may understand that the new temple is also his Body in the Pauline sense, the Christian Church. Thus the cleansing of the temple at Jerusalem takes on a more profound meaning. It was not only a demonstration against an improper use of the Lord's house; it was also a sign that the sacrificial worship associated with that house was coming to an end, because of the one perfect and sufficient sacrifice which the paschal Lamb of God was to offer in Jerusalem in two years' time (the cleansing of the temple took place during the first of three Passovers mentioned by John, 6.4 and 13.1, the last one being the occasion of the crucifixion). As the gospel replaced the Law, so Jesus replaced the temple where God dwelt and where men worship him. The new temple, the community of which Christ is the living Head, fulfils the prophecy of Isaiah, quoted in Mark 11.17, that God's house 'shall be called a house of prayer for all nations'.

EPIPHANY 4

Jeremiah 7.1–7   See Pentecost 17 Year 1

Hebrews 12. 18–end
The passage contrasts Judaism and Christianity in their ability to bring men face to face with God. Moses, who was the mediator of the old covenant, stood trembling at the foot of mount Sinai where God manifested himself in a terrifying theophany. The author deliberately stressed the awe-fulness of that occasion by recalling the details of the event—the fire, the darkness, the wind, the trumpet, the voice of God. Coupled with this was the knowledge that the holiness of the mountain meant death to anyone who trod upon it. But Jesus, who is mediator of the new covenant, brings the Christian to the foot of another mountain, Zion, the heavenly reality of which the earthly mountain is but a shadow.

Mount Zion was traditionally the hill of Moriah on which Abraham sacrificed Isaac and where the Jebusites later built a fortress which was captured by David. Solomon's temple was built there, also the second temple, and the temple of Herod. It was there that God was to be worshipped with joy and gladness (Ps. 65.1) and it was there that the Messiah would be manifested (Ps. 2.6). In the New Testament Zion was seen as the foreshadowing of the heavenly Jerusalem (Gal. 4.26, Rev. 3.12, 21.2), an idea also current in contemporary Judaism. The earthly sanctuary was but a copy of the heavenly.

Myriads of angels, the messengers and ministers of God according to the religious ideas of the time, are described as gathered in festal
23 array. With them were **the full concourse and assembly of the first-born citizens of heaven** (there is disagreement as to who these might have been: some scholars say they were the first-born of new Israel, the Church triumphant, others that they were the angels themselves who were 'first-born' because they were created before man). God was seen in heaven in his office as Judge—justice is closely connected with the
23 concept of God in this letter. With him were the saints, **the spirits of good men made perfect,** those who in virtue of their faithful lives have passed the scrutiny of the Judge and have been rewarded with eternal life. The order in which they appeared may mean that they were the saints of the Old Testament, though the author would not have seen them as having been saved apart from the sacrifice of Christ.

In the midst of the heavenly Jerusalem was Jesus, the name being used to emphasize that Christ's status is as a man as well as Son of God. He it was who sacrificed himself and who through the cross inaugurated
24 the new covenant. The phrase **sprinkled blood** recalls the inauguration of the old covenant, when Moses sprinkled the blood of the sacrifice over the altar and the people (Exod. 24.6–8, Heb. 9.19). The blood of Jesus is so much more effective than other blood that had been spilt. The blood of Abel, regarded by the Jews as the proto-martyr, only demanded vengeance (Gen. 4.10); the blood of Christ proclaims forgiveness.

But the fear which the inauguration of the old covenant inspired has its lessons for Christians. Those who refused to hear the voice of God spoken through Moses ('Moses received the living utterances of God, to pass on to us' Acts 7.38) did not see the Promised Land, but died in the desert; similarly, those who do not listen to the voice of God spoken by Jesus, who came from heaven, will never enter the promised land of eternal life with God. If the circumstances under which the old covenant was promulgated were frightening enough, that is nothing compared with

25 the results of apostasy from the new covenant. **Those who refused to hear the oracle speaking on earth found no escape; still less shall we escape if we refuse to hear the One who speaks from heaven.** The author quoted Hag. 2.6 in support of his contention. The shaking of mount Sinai would be followed by a second shaking at the end of time,—the earthquake was a signal of the end of all things, an apocalyptic sign of consummation. Heaven and earth would pass away (Mark 13.31) and only what was endurable would remain—the Kingdom of God which Christians are being given. The present tense denotes a continuous process, not a completed one. The Christian, then, stands before God to give thanks to him in reverence and awe, knowing that he worships a
29 God whose holiness is as **a devouring fire.**

* **John 4. 19–26**

The question as to whether mount Zion or mount Gerizim was the place of worship was an ancient contention between Jews and Samaritans. After the return from the exile, the Jews had debarred the Samaritans from access to the temple in Jerusalem, and the Samaritans had set up a rival shrine on mount Gerizim, which with mount Ebal encloses the valley, at the mouth of which Canaanite Shechem once lay. The two summits control the important approach from the north to Jerusalem and most of Palestine is visible from the top. From the slopes of mount Gerizim Joshua and other religious leaders pronounced the blessings which come to those who keep the law (Deut. 11.29, 27.12f; Josh. 8.33–35); hence its name, 'mount of blessings'. The temple was destroyed by John Hyrcanus about 128 B.C. and was never rebuilt, but for centuries afterwards it was regarded as a holy place by the Samaritans.

After recognizing that Jesus had unexpected insight into her immoral life, the woman at the well of Samaria put to Jesus a question about this ancient dispute on the two sanctuaries (Gerizim is visible from Jacob's well). Jesus' reply informed her that the relevance of the dispute was passing away; a new era was beginning in which local religious rivalries
21 would yield to a true and universal worship. The phrase **Believe me** introduces his prophecy.

Nevertheless, Jesus did not entirely ignore the Samaritan heresy. As a Jew, he confronted the woman with the truth about her religion as it had
22 been up to that point. **You Samaritans worship without knowing what you worship, while we worship what we know.** Samaritans denied any revelation of God through the prophets and the psalmists; their scriptures consisted only of the Pentateuch. They virtually worship-

ped an Unknown God. The Jews, on the other hand, worshipped the God who had been revealed to them, and this was why Jesus could say it is 22 from the Jews that salvation comes. 'The commonwealth of Israel was the school of the knowledge of God for all nations' (Athanasius).

But the ancient grievance must be forgotten. With the breaking in of the new order, symbolized by the living water which had featured earlier in the conversation (see verses 7–15), the worship of God the Father had been lifted to another dimension. The Spirit, who comes through Christ into the people of God, inspires a new principle of worship. God is 24 spirit—what is stressed is God's essential being—and because he is spirit it is in a spiritual dimension that worship must be offered. God's mode of operation is in the realm of life-giving power, and it is only those who receive this power through Jesus Christ who can offer to God real worship. To worship 'in truth' is to worship in such a way that one's worship is utterly real, the only kind of worship that meets the conditions revealed by God through Jesus Christ. The truth in which God is to be worshipped points away from both mount Gerizim and mount Zion to God's faithfulness in fulfilling in Christ that to which both Gerizim and Zion, in their varying ways, pointed. It is, perhaps, worth adding that 'spiritual worship' does not mean worship without rites and ceremonies; the Christian sacraments derive their validity through the union of the spirit and the flesh in the divine Logos to which all the baptized are united. Yet there is a lesson to be learned from Isaiah's condemnation of a cult unrelated to moral and spiritual values, nevertheless.

Like the Jews, the Samaritans also looked for the Messiah. They called him 'the Restorer'—*Ta'eb*. 'The Lord will raise up a prophet from among you like myself, and you will listen to him', Moses said in Deut. 18.15. And the woman acknowledged this. Her confession led to Jesus' remark- 26 able disclosure. The I am he echoes the act of divine revelation when God answered Moses with his name (Exod. 3.14); and the Deuteronomic prophecy, 'You will listen to him', seems to be reflected in the words of Christ: I who am speaking to you now.

EPIPHANY 5

Proverbs 2. 1–9
The Book of Proverbs is a collection of religious and moral instructions such as that given to Jewish youth by professional sages of the post-

exilic period. It contains much older material from various sources. Such training was considered necessary if one was to live a good life. Proverbs is the most typical example of a 'wisdom' book in the OT (compared with Job and Ecclesiastes) with its emphasis on morality based on religion, its teaching that reward and punishment follow in this life, and its appeal to the lessons of experience rather than to revelation. The book is founded on the belief that wisdom cannot begin without a right religious disposition ('The fear of the Lord is the beginning of wisdom', 1.7), and wisdom itself is seen as a charismatic gift dispensed by the teacher.

These verses advise the pupil on how he is to listen to his teacher. He 1 is to receive the words of the master in his **heart** and in his **mind**; he is not to waste his energies on criticizing or approving what he hears but 3 he is to **summon discernment** to his aid and **invoke understanding** so that he is able to embrace the instructions totally. Wisdom is like treasure buried in a field (Matt. 13.44f) and Yahweh bestows it on those who are morally qualified. Its effect is to guard the way of his servants 8 (**the course of justice** is the path to righteousness which Yahweh has prepared for them) and to enable them to fulfil their journey along that way.

Ecclesiasticus 42. 15–25

Ben Sira (see p. 102) saw in creation itself the omnipotence and om- 15 niscience of God. **By the words of the Lord** the universe was brought into existence (an early appearance of the doctrine of the creative word of God, Gen. 1 and John 1.1ff) and it reflects his glory like the rays of the sun. Even the angels lack sufficient power to declare all his mighty 18 works. **The signs of the times** are probably the stars which, according to an ancient belief, foretell the future for those who are able to read them. The Hebrew of verse 24 reads, 'All things are different from each other, and there is nothing superfluous.'

1 Corinthians 3. 18–end

The apostle continued his discussion about wisdom and folly, which arose out of his opposition to party conflicts in Corinth, by showing how false were the premises on which both the Corinthians' arguments and partisanship rested. Those who think themselves wise fall into the error of self-deception, for no one can advance in divine wisdom through human wisdom. On the contrary, if a man is to advance in divine wisdom, he

19 must be prepared to negate the wisdom of the world. **The wisdom of this world is folly in God's sight** because—and here the apostle quotes scripture, Job. 5.13 and Ps. 94.11, to give authority to his conclusions— even those who expound worldly wisdom are, in any case, no more than instruments in the hand of God. Since all men are only God's instruments, it is equally ridiculous to set one's ambitions and hopes in any man. You may think of yourselves as belonging to Paul, Apollos, and Cephas, he told them, but in fact you are not these men's, but Christ's.

22   **The addition of the world, life, and death, the present and the future** to the apostles' names seems puzzling at first sight. Obviously the world does not belong to the Church in the same way that Paul did. But Paul's thought had moved on as he wrote the names of his apostolic colleagues to the truth that, as Christ is sovereign Lord over the apostles, the Corinthians, and the Church, so he is also Lord of these other things— he has overcome the world, he has conquered life and death through his crucifixion and resurrection, and he is Lord of the future as well as the present because all things belong to him. These things, then, could be

23 said to **belong** to the Christian Corinthians because they belonged to him. And Paul rounded off this extension of his argument by reminding the Corinthians that Jesus is the willing agent of the Father, and that through him they owed obedience to God. In a later passage Paul was to amplify the meaning of this: 'When all things are thus subject to him, then the Son himself will also be made subordinate to God who made all things subject to him, and thus God will be all in all' (15.28). The Son, being of one substance with the Father, is differentiated from the Father precisely in this, that he renders the obedience of perfect love to the perfectly loving will of the Father.

* **Matthew 12. 38–42**

38 Master (*didaskale*, 'teacher') is a form of address which Matthew reserved for those who were outside the circle of Christ's followers (perhaps to imply that Jesus was more than a teacher, just as John the Baptist was more than a prophet). The request by the doctors of the law and the Pharisees for a sign (that is, a miracle) was refused without explanation in Mark 8.38 (see also, 1 Cor. 1.22–24, 'Jews call for miracles, Greeks look for wisdom; but we proclaim Christ—yes, Christ nailed to the cross; and though this is a stumbling-block to Jews and folly to Greeks, yet to those who have heard his call, Jews and Greeks alike, he is the power of God and the wisdom of God'); Matthew used it to introduce further

135

sayings about Jonah and the Queen of Sheba in which Jesus warned those who questioned him that they were in danger of making the same mistake as their forefathers.

39   A wicked, godless generation (RSV, 'an evil and adulterous generation') was one that, like the people in the OT, was faithless to God. God's relationship to his people was depicted as a marriage, and the latter committed spiritual adultery when they disobeyed God's commandments.

39   The sign of Jonah the prophet. Jonah had been one of the successful prophets. The people of Nineveh had listened to him and had repented (much to his disgust!). But Nineveh was a Gentile city! That was one interpretation of 'the sign of Jonah'—a warning to the Jews that Gentiles might repent before they did! But in this passage Jesus gives another interpretation (according to the evangelist). Jonah's experience in the sea-monster's belly is a prophetic sign of the death and resurrection of Christ. The contrast between this 'wicked, godless generation' and the Ninevites, then, is twofold: (1) the Ninevites repented, whereas Jesus' listeners did not, and (2) the Ninevites acted on the preaching of Jonah while Jesus' listeners had done nothing, even though Christ's preaching
41 and miracles told them that one greater than Jonah was among them.

42   At the Judgement the Queen of the South will be raised to life together with this generation and ensure its condemnation (NEB footnote). This time the contrast is threefold: (1) The Queen of Sheba came to Solomon (1 Kings 10.1ff) but this generation has not come to Jesus; (2) she came from the ends of the earth, but this generation will not believe Jesus, one of their own nation; and (3) she heard the wisdom of Solomon, but this generation would not receive the greater wisdom of Christ, the proclamation of the kingdom of God.

EPIPHANY 6

2 Samuel 12. 1–10

The Lord sent Nathan to the king with his famous parable designed to stir the king's conscience. The power of the parable is that it revealed the truth to one who was blinded by his sin. An irony in this story is that before David realized the implications of the parable, he said that the offender in it deserved to die—and unwittingly condemned himself. But

God's love for the man he had chosen and anointed king over Israel was such that he spared him this punishment. Others were to suffer instead— a strange comment on God's justice, yet one which lingers behind all forms of suffering. The son born to David and Bathsheba would die, and
10 David's other children would meet a violent end, **Your family shall never again have rest from the sword**—referring to the deaths of Amnon and Absalom.

Romans 1. 18–25

Greeting the Church in Rome, Paul declared that for a long time he had wanted to visit them to share their faith in the Gospel, 'the saving power of God for everyone who has faith' (verse 16). Then he began to explain why the Gospel is necessary—and it is at this point our passage opens.
18 Because they need salvation from **divine retribution**—God's opposition to everything that is evil. **In their wickedness (men) are stifling the truth.** For knowledge of God is available to anyone who will reflect on the wonders of the created universe around him. Paul is not laying the foundations of a natural theology but expressing a belief that is drawn from the Old Testament, namely, that the world bears the signs of the Creator.

> The heavens tell out the glory of God,
> the vault of heaven reveals his handiwork
>   (Ps. 19.1).

> Have you not perceived ever since the world began,
> that God sits enthroned on the vaulted roof of earth?
>   (Isa. 40.21–22).

21 **Knowing God, they have refused to honour him as God, or to render him thanks.** Whatever we may think, the apostle is convinced that there is a revelation of God in his creation which is clear enough for men to worship him; but they have not done this. Not only have they rejected what has been revealed to them, they have made idols of created
22– things: **They boast of their wisdom, but they have made fools of**
23 **themselves, exchanging the splendour of immortal God for an image shaped like mortal man, even for images like birds, beasts, and creeping things.**

Idolatry in any form—and it can be the worship of created things in a sophisticated age as well as the primitive idolatry depicted by the apostle —leads to wrong behaviour, and God's judgement of mankind begins in handing them over to the effects of their sinful desires: their bodies, created in God's image for his worship, are degraded by their wickedness (sexual immorality was associated with certain forms of idolatry in the ancient world). It is as if God, having held his protecting hand over the men and women he had created, had withdrawn it and let them take what they deserved. If this seems a particularly harsh teaching, we have to remember, (1) that Paul was here only writing the introduction to his great exposition of God's salvation of mankind in Jesus Christ, and (2) that he recognized there were some good pagans, those 'who do not possess the law (yet who) carry out its precepts by the light of nature' (2.14) and were therefore better than those Jews who ignored God's commandments.

The passage ends with a brief doxology.

* **Matthew 13. 24–30**   See Harvest Thanksgiving, page 432

NINTH SUNDAY BEFORE EASTER
Third Sunday before Lent

Isaiah 30. 18–21
Isaiah's protest against Judah's policy between 705 and 701 B.C. had been rejected, and he had warned the people of impending disaster. But at verse 18 the prophet's message changed. The Lord now promised that he would act on behalf of his people, and this was followed by an acclama-
18 tion in the form of a beatitude: **Happy are all who wait for him!** This is expanded in verses 19–21. At the right moment the Lord will show his favour and mercy, so there need be no more weeping. In spite of suffering,
20 linked in the prophet's thought with the **bread of adversity and water of affliction** of the exodus, God would lead his people by teaching them his law. Furthermore, he would guide them in the right way by revealing himself: **with your own eyes you shall see him always.**

1 Corinthians 4. 8–13
The dominant thought at the beginning of this passage is that no man should boast of his gifts or his status, because all things come from God. The Corinthians were behaving as if they were so far in advance of their teachers that they considered the various gifts they manifested as entirely

due to their own efforts. Paul therefore resorted to irony to bring their spiritual pride out into the open. They were acting as if the age to come had already been consummated, as if they now had their heavenly reward and possessed the Kingdom of God. Paul went on with sad sarcasm to remark that he wished it was already true, for then they could share it with apostles like himself!

Then he turned to contrast their attitude and mode of living with that of the apostles. These leaders of the Church had no feeling of superiority and self-satisfaction, such as the Corinthians had, for theirs was a life of constant shame, suffering, and slander. Those who are greatest in God's plans certainly come low in human estimation. The apostles were like the wretches brought in at the close of a display in the arena, men condemned to death at the hands of gladiators or in the paws of wild animals. Their fate provides entertainment for the whole of the created universe (a prophecy of what the Church was to suffer in the next two and a half centuries). The contrast sharpens: **We are fools for Christ's sake, while**
10 **you are such sensible Christians. We are weak; you are so power-**
11 **ful. We are in disgrace; you are honoured.**

The journeyings and difficulties of the apostles are then pictured in terms designed to move the self-satisfied Corinthians. For a teacher to have to work with his hands was scandalous to the Greeks: the educated
13 ought never to engage in manual labour. **They curse us, and we bless; they persecute us, and we submit to it; they slander us, and we humbly make our appeal** echoes parts of the Sermon on the Mount— indeed, the picture we are given is a working out of the principles of the Beatitudes in apostolic life. In the final half of verse 13, the words for **scum** and **dregs of humanity** may have a special sense of victims chosen for pagan sacrifice in times of disease, disaster, or famine, to avert the anger of the gods.

* Matthew 5. 1–12

Matthew, particularly sensitive to the Old Testament setting of the new covenant, introduced events on mountains in his narrative at key points— the temptations (4.8), the sermon (5.1), the transfiguration (17.1) and the resurrection (28.16). The mountain was the meeting-place of God and man in the old covenant, and in the new dispensation inaugurated in Jesus Christ, mountains still figure in the background as symbols of divine presence. The old law was given on mount Sinai; now, on another mountain, the new law is promulgated by God through Jesus Christ. Earlier in the Gospel he had called on the people, 'Repent; for the

Kingdom of heaven is upon you' (4.17). Now Christ listed the characteristics of those who are being called into that Kingdom.

The new law is not a series of commandments restraining conduct, obedience to which earns divine favour. Rather, the new law is expressed in terms of the spirit which prompts human conduct, those signs in a man's attitudes which denote the indwelling and overflowing of the Holy Spirit, who is given to those who repent and believe the gospel. It is by an inner quality of life known to God that spiritual progress is assessed, not by external acts; though these, of course, may be expressions of that inner quality.

The rabbis sat to teach. Christ taught as a rabbi, sitting and speaking to his disciples, though we understand that there were crowds present.

The beatitudes are in three groups:

verses 3–5, three contrasts with the standards of the world;
verses 6–9, four characteristics of the Christian life; and
verses 10–12, the world's reaction to them.

To be 'blest' means to be happy in the sense of a deep quality of contentment and security, the joy that passes understanding for those whom God loves and who know that he loves them. The JB translates 'How happy are....'

3   **How blest are those who know their need of God, the kingdom of Heaven is theirs.** The NEB brings out the meaning of 'poor in spirit' (RSV, JB). In the OT 'poor' is sometimes synonymous with 'saintly' and 'God-fearing', though such are often neglected and downtrodden (Ps. 9.19, Isa. 66.2). Although the beatitude applies to those who are materially rich as well as materially poor, Jesus usually has in mind actual poverty, and set himself the example of the poor and the humble. Spiritual poverty among the rich is only maintained by strict stewardship. Matthew may have modified Luke's version of this beatitude.

4 **How blest are the sorrowful; they shall find consolation.** (RSV 'Those who mourn . . . be comforted.') Christ did not mean those who mourn for the loss of a loved one, or who are weighed down by life's sorrows, but those who have a capacity to enter into spiritual sorrow for the sins of the world. This is not found in a mournful morbidity, but in a recognition that it is difficult to 'sing the Lord's song in the land of our captivity' (Ps. 137.4). The consolation they shall receive was promised to all those who waited for deliverance, like Simeon (Luke 2.25).

5 **How blest are those of a gentle spirit; they shall have the earth for their possession.** The word is taken from the Greek version of

Ps. 37.11, 'The meek-spirited shall possess the land: and shall delight in abundance of peace'.

6 How blest are those who hunger and thirst to see right prevail; they shall be satisfied. (RSV 'righteousness') These are they to whom the fulfilment of God's purposes is the fundamental need in this life.

7   How blest are those who show mercy, mercy shall be shown to them. The beatitude is found in the Lord's Prayer. Luke 6.36 comments on this, 'Be compassionate as your Father is compassionate'.

8   How blest are those whose hearts are pure; they shall see God. Purity has the connotation of chastity, but it means (and includes) more than this: it is a single-minded application of the gospel to one's life, putting one's hand to the plough without looking back. Such will 'see God'—and 'to see God' meant to appear before God, both in worship and at the end of time.

9   How blest are the peacemakers, God shall call them his sons. The Christian is called to be one who reconciles and builds right relationships, not only of man with man but also of man with God (2 Cor. 5.18ff). This was the office of the Son of God; sharing in this work, the Christian shares in the divine sonship.

10   How blest are those who have suffered persecution for the cause of right; the kingdom of Heaven is theirs. Christ had in mind the prophets, who suffered for proclaiming God's word, and also those who would suffer for the gospel—as verses 11 and 12 indicate.

The beatitudes have affinities with Isa. 61, the first verses of which Christ chose to introduce his ministry to the congregation of the synagogue at Nazareth (Luke 4.16). Modelled on the way the Wisdom writers described the wise and favoured ones of God, they also give us a picture of Christ's own human personality.

NINTH SUNDAY BEFORE EASTER
Third Sunday before Lent

Proverbs 3. 1–8
The Book of Proverbs is the best representative of the Wisdom literature of Israel. Some of its sources can be traced back into the ancient history of Egypt and Assyria, where aphorisms or sayings of a moral and ethical

nature developed in folk or government circles for the guidance of the young. The sayings were usually divided into 'instructions', which command or exhort giving reasons for the action or the attitude taken, and 'proverbs', observations of a more impersonal nature which were not ordered or explained but allowed to stand by the authority of their own inherent wisdom. When adopted and developed by the wise men of Israel, these sayings were moulded into the religious piety which regarded the God of Israel as the one who punished evil and rewarded virtue. In its later development, the sayings of the sages came to be attributed to a personified Wisdom, (though the strong monotheism of the Jews prevented any idea of ascribing divine nature to her). Christian theologians developed this by seeing in the figure of Wisdom the Word of God.

Chapters 1 to 9 are an introduction to the Book and in their present form are ascribed to the post-exilic period, perhaps the fifth century B.C.

The earliest sections of the book, chapters 10—22 and 25—29, are attributed to Solomon who, according to 1 Kings 4.32 was the author of three thousand proverbs. They may well have been current at his time.

The master addressed his pupil as 'my son'. **Years in plenty** translates
2 the Hebrew *shalom*, 'peace', of which a long life is an adjunct. The teachings of the sage should be inscribed on a tablet worn round the neck as a sign that they are indelibly moulded into the young man's character.
5 Total reliance on God is the keynote: **Put all your trust in the Lord and do not rely on your own understanding.** The one who follows God's ways faithfully will be kept in good health.

1 Corinthians 2. 1–10

Paul was not, according to references in 2 Cor. 10. 1 and 10, an eloquent speaker, 'so feeble' and 'beneath contempt'. His writing is graceful, and, in spite of its semitisms and Jewish influence, represents notable examples of fine Greek prose (Rom. 8 and 1 Cor. 13). His lack of eloquence, however, strengthened rather than weakened the authority of what he said. The Corinthians, so concerned about their wisdom, had to be told that
1 mere cleverness was not the vehicle of **the attested truth of God.** The NEB marg. reflects some doubt as to whether the original Greek word was 'attested truth' in the sense of 'the gospel' or 'secret purpose' in the sense of 'divine mystery'.

The apostle was not, of course, rejecting human wisdom in its entirety. The skilful marshalling of facts and the sensitive engagement in dialogue have their proper place. But what Paul was suspicious of was the use of human wisdom for personal ambition, to sway people and to gain power, when it so easily became subject to those evil powers which Paul, like his contemporaries, believed ruled the destinies of men if they did not commit themselves to the greater power of God.

This power of God was demonstrated through the cross of Jesus Christ 'to those of us on the way to salvation' (1.18). It was this that Paul
3 preached **nervous and shaking with fear** (a biblical cliché for men acting under the authority of God). What brought the Corinthians to faith in God was not the persuasiveness of Paul's speeches but the influence of the Holy Spirit in their minds and hearts as they listened to the gospel: 'In my speeches and the sermons that I gave, there were none of the arguments that belong to philosophy; only a demonstration of the power of the Spirit' (JB verses 4–5).

Not all are ready or able to be moved by the Holy Spirit in this way, said the apostle; words of wisdom can be appreciated only by those who are mature in the Christian faith, 'people who have the Spirit' (3.1).
6 Those who belong to **this passing age**—and here Paul adopted the terminology of Jewish apocalyptic thought which saw the present order as giving way to the messianic age and the establishment of God's Kingdom—had only the wisdom of this age and would not appreciate
6 the word Paul spoke; the **governing powers**—the evil influences which were believed to influence the course of men's lives—could not recognize it. What Paul declared (the word 'speak' has an authoritative
7 connotation) was God's **hidden wisdom, his secret purpose** in redeeming mankind through his Word, who was active from the beginning of all things. The saving work of Jesus fulfils the concept of the Wisdom of God personified in the OT: 'Hear how Wisdom lifts her voice . . . "Men, it is to you I call . . . Understanding and power are mine . . . The Lord created me the beginning of his works, before all else that he made, long ago. . . . Happy is the man who keeps my ways. . . ."' (Prov. 8.1ff).

Paul himself summarized this secret purpose later in the letter: 'There is one God, the Father, from whom all being comes, towards whom we move; and there is one Lord Jesus Christ, through whom all things came to be, and we through him' (8.6). This was unknown to the authorities who crucified Jesus, acting as they were under the influence of evil spirits who were also ignorant of God's plan. But through them the
8 **Lord of glory**—Paul did not hesitate to attribute to Christ the glory of the Godhead—was crucified, and as a result it is in that glory that we are called to share.

Men come to know these things only because they are revealed by

God and because their minds are enlightened by the Holy Spirit to recognize and to rejoice in their relevance and importance. The Spirit is the agent of the messianic age into which Christians have been brought, and it is a sign of their maturity that they can grasp the divine purpose.

The quotation from Isa. 64 in verse 9 is not word for word; the apostle was apparently quoting from memory.

* **Luke 8. 4-15**
The parable of the sower might be called more aptly 'the parable of the soils'. The message it conveys applies the quality of different soils to the kinds of minds and hearts of those to whom the gospel is proclaimed. It was addressed to the people who had gathered in large numbers, but the exposition was given only to the disciples. Associated with it is a saying
10 from Isa. 6.9, **they may look but see nothing, hear but understand nothing.** To grasp the meaning of this puzzling remark we have to go back to the context of the quotation in the book of Isaiah. It comes within the call of the prophet and tells him not to be dismayed by the apparent failure of his message. The verse did not mean that the people's obstinacy had been directly willed by God, but that he had foreseen it and taken it into account in his plan. 'They did not open their minds to love of the truth, so as to find salvation' (2 Thess. 2.10). The parable set a truth before its hearers. Those without discernment would fail to perceive its teaching and importance, but those who were enlightened would recognize that it contained the word of life.
10   **The secrets of the kingdom of God** are those inner mysteries which reveal God's intentions for the establishment and nature of his Kingdom. In the gospels they are taught both directly and in parable form; they tell of God's plan in time, the word and destiny of the Messiah, and the way people will enter the Kingdom and belong to it.

The parable was particularly applicable to the Church's preaching
13 after Pentecost. Phrases like **receive the word with joy when they hear it,** and **bring a good and honest heart to the hearing of the**
15 **word, hold it fast, and by their perseverance yield a harvest,** indicate the manner in which converts embraced the faith. In early
12 Christianity **to believe and be saved** was almost synonymous with 'to
13 become a Christian' and to **desert** was to apostatize.

The failure of the seed which fell on stony ground was explained more fully in Mark 4.5, 'on rocky ground, where it had little soil'. The fate of the seed which fell into the first three kinds of soil might well typify the
14 effects of the world, the flesh, and the devil: **choked by cares and**

13 wealth and the pleasures of life (the world), have no root (the flesh),
12 and the devil comes and carries off the word from their hearts.

EIGHTH SUNDAY BEFORE EASTER
Second Sunday before Lent

Zephaniah 3. 14–end

Zephaniah was an aristocrat, a great-great-grandson of King Hezekiah; apart from this we know little about him, except that he lived in the reign of King Josiah or King Jehoiakim (if the reference in 1.1 is a later and mistaken addition). Like Jeremiah, he re-echoed the teaching of the eighth-century prophets, continuing Amos', Hosea's, and Isaiah's denunciations of foreign superstitions, social wrongs, and false prophets and priests. National misfortune is God's punishment for sin, and he warned of a Day of Wrath in a passage which later inspired the *Dies Irae* (1.14–16).

These last verses of his book, however, exult in messianic joy at the protection which the Lord will give to Israel, when God will stand among them as a king and warrior. The faith and hope that is so often found towards the end of the prophetic books expresses the inspired authors' (or their editors') confidence in a God of mercy and forgiveness, who will provide Israel with all her needs. The joyful shout of these verses is in the spirit of the Second Isaiah.

Verses 14–15 and 16–18 are psalms of joy, the former echoing Ps. 48.9–14, one of those set for today. The last section of the passage, verses 18b–20, may be of a later date, echoing the promises made to the Jews exiled in Babylon. The time of their vindication is near. The day will be one in which all their foes are overthrown, their scattered members will be gathered together, and they will be brought back to Jerusalem amidst the
20 wonder of all other nations. **When the time comes for me to gather you, I will bring you home. I will win you renown and praise among all the peoples of the earth, when I bring back your prosperity; and you shall see it.** The final words give the prophecy the stamp of authority: **It is the Lord who speaks.**

James 5. 13–16

We are given here a tiny picture of the early Christian congregation to which the epistle was addressed, in its care for the troubled, the sick, and the sinful.

Prayer is not just a remedy for those in trouble, says the writer. We should pray when things go well, too, but then our prayers will take the form of praises. In illness the elders of the congregation are to pray over 14 the sick man and anoint him with olive oil in the name of the Lord. Oil had a medicinal purpose (Isa. 1.6, Luke 10.34) for soothing bruises and wounds; it was used among Christians not only for its natural qualities but also because it was regarded, like touching and the laying on of hands, as a vehicle of miraculous healing power. The twelve healed the sick by anointing them during their first mission (Mark 6.13). That it was done 'in the name of the Lord' gave it a sacramental significance— it has continued in the use of unction in the Church down to the present day (though as 'extreme unction' it was, for centuries, regarded more as a preparation for death).

We are not able to deduce much about the organization of the New Testament Church from this passage, except that apparently in this local congregation the Christian elders had the same status as the elders of the synagogue in the Jewish community. This was the pattern in many local churches in this period.

Forgiveness was also offered to those who were sick. People in the ancient world often concluded that there was a correlation between sickness and sin. The disciples believed that a man blind from his birth was suffering the consequences of his own sin or that of his parents (John 9.2). 15 The Lord will raise him from his bed recalls the miraculous healing that Jesus effected; the Church's ministry of healing is a continuation of Christ's work.

Reference to confession of sin led the author to recommend the practice generally among all Christians. It was assumed that they would confess their sins to one who was close to God and whose prayers would be heard. There is no suggestion of confessions being made only to the elders. In fact, confession of sins to holy men (that is, laymen) was customary in the Church, especially among the Orthodox who confessed to holy monks, down to the middle ages.

* Mark 2. 1–12

The incident took place in one of the common dwelling-places of the time, with an outside staircase and a roof of wood and clay that could be easily opened up and repaired. Jesus was addressing a large crowd in the space in front of the door when four men brought the paralysed man to him on a stretcher. Unable to get close to Jesus, they took the patient round the back of the house and on to the roof, lowering him into the room beside Christ.

The real point of the story is that Jesus is the bringer of forgiveness, and to demonstrate this authority the remission of a man's sins is made outwardly visible by the healing of his paralysis. The ancient world was well aware of the link between sin and suffering (in ways that modern psychosomatic research has sometimes vindicated) and the particular disease from which the man was healed can also be taken as a sign of the paralysing effect of sin. The story has been used as an illustration of the Church's liturgy of penance from early times, the four men being seen as those who intercede in faith for the forgiveness of the penitent (an important feature of the early discipline, where the public acts of penance were supported by the prayers of the clergy and the congregation).

From the viewpoint of Mark and his readers, it is not surprising that Jesus began his ministry to the paralysed man by declaring that he had been absolved from his sins. We expect Christ, as God's Messiah, to exercise divine authority. But the Jewish men of the law neither recognized Christ's authority, nor indeed did they expect the Messiah to forgive sins when he came. That was the prerogative of God alone. The most a man could do in this life was to plead to God for forgiveness, adopt the signs of penitence—ashes, sackcloth, fasting—and offer the appropriate sacrifices for ritual cleansing, joining in the ceremonies of the Day of Atonement. Divine forgiveness would then be demonstrated in the blessings which God gave him.

5   But Jesus having announced, **my son, your sins are forgiven**, went on boldly to perform a miraculous sign of his authority in healing the
10 man and, in so doing, claimed for himself the title of **Son of Man**. So far in this Gospel he had been called only 'the son of God', 'my Son, my Beloved', 'the Holy One of God'; now he assumed the messianic title in an act which demonstrated more than his other healings the inner meaning of his mission. The result is that the onlookers were astonished and praised God—the reaction of awe and wonder at the mighty work of God.

Most commentators believe that the story was formed by the bringing together (probably before Mark received it) of two incidents, a straightforward healing (verses 1–5a, 11–12) and a dialogue with the lawyers about the forgiveness of sins (5b–10), the phrase **he turned to the paralysed**

10 **man** forming a bridge between the two narratives. The authority of
Christ was linked with the Church's ministry of reconciliation in the
Matthean version of this passage, which ends, 'The people . . . praised
God for granting such authority to men' (9.8).

EIGHTH SUNDAY BEFORE EASTER
Second Sunday before Lent

2 Kings 5. 1–14
One of the stories of the Elisha saga which gives us a vivid impression of
1 the personalities involved. The name **Naaman** is attested from non-
biblical sources as a common Arab name in pre-Islamic times. We notice
in passing that his success as a warrior was accredited to the Lord's
doing—an instance of how the God of Israel was recognized at work
outside his chosen people. The leprosy was not of a kind that debarred
Naaman from society; it was more of an embarrassment than an affliction.
The maid, who plays a role in the story not unlike that of her kind in a
Mozart opera, was presumably a victim of the kidnapping raids by
Aramean gangs along the borders of Syria and Israel, who had been sold
in the market at Damascus. Elisha was brought into the story by the
3 maid, not as 'the man of God', his usual title, but as **the prophet**; he is
not associated here with any school or community as in other stories but
is shown to have his own house in Samaria, where he had the opportunity
of keeping an eye on the affairs of state and interpreting the word of God
6 in the court as required. **This letter is to inform you.** . . . Letters
between kings asking for favours are known from other non-biblical
sources. The letter itself was shortened in the report; the preliminary
greetings were omitted. The request was sent direct to the king, not to the
prophet; evidently the king of Aram regarded Elisha as a servant through
whom the royal virtue of healing was exercised. The king, suspecting
that the king of Aram was picking a quarrel, rent his clothes in anguish.
Elisha intervened, and eventually Naaman came to the prophet's house,
in great pomp and carrying an enormous gift.

But he was humiliated. Elisha did not go out to greet him personally,
and his advice was beneath the general's dignity. Naaman was expecting
a ritual healing, but Elisha put his pride to the test. Man has to be brought

low before God can act. Again, it was a servant who advised Naaman to do as he was told. The number seven is a sign of completion.

2 Corinthians 12. 1–10

In this piece of autobiography Paul described a tremendous religious experience he once had. He said he did not wish to boast about it, but because he wanted to relate what God had done, he referred to himself
2 indirectly as **a Christian man.**

It had been an experience of exultation similar to that described by John in the book of Revelation. He had been caught up into the third
4 heaven (the highest in Jewish mythology) and there **heard words so secret that human lips may not repeat them.** What he had learned had been too deep to communicate to others. It was perhaps these visions and revelations which had given Paul's theology its distinctive and inspired originality.

Reverting to the matter of boasting, the apostle continued that he was prepared to boast about what God had revealed, but he would not do this
6 because **I should not like anyone to form an estimate of me which goes beyond the evidence of his own ears and eyes.** For himself, he was content to be accepted for what he had said and done himself, not for the visions and marks of divine favour. Paul here balanced humbly on that delicate divide which separates a joyful account of what God is doing in us from those forms of personal testimony which verge on self-glorification.

It was on a point of humility that the apostle mentioned an unhealed infirmity, **a sharp physical pain.** The alternative in the NEB footnote,
7 **a thorn, for the flesh,** might mean that his readers knew all about it. The nature of this affliction is not known, though there have been many guesses—epilepsy, malaria, stammering (which could account for his poor showing as a speaker, 1 Cor. 2.1) or an eye weakness (the reference to eyes and poor sight might be inferred from Gal. 4.12–16, 6.11). From this weakness he had three times asked God to deliver him, but the
9 answer had been, **My grace is all you need; power comes to its full strength in weakness** (the same thought is in Isaiah 40.29).

And so Paul had to come to terms with his affliction. God gave him no healing. The weakness had now become a thing of pride and joy, for it was the means through which the divine presence 'rested upon him'. The Greek means 'tabernacle upon me', the phrase chosen to recall the period when the people of Israel in the wilderness brought the tent of meeting with them as the temporary resting-place of God.

Afflictions, then, were things with which Paul could be content. They were means through which God exercised his power. Hence the paradox,
10 when I am weak, then I am strong.

* **Mark 7. 24–end**
24 The two healings were given in Gentile territory. **The territory of Tyre** is the hinterland of the port of the Mediterranean. It was in the Roman province of Syria and its inhabitants were called 'Phoenicians of Syria' to distinguish them from the Phoenician settlers who had founded Carthage. The Ten Towns, the Decapolis, was a league of Greco-Roman cities to the east and south-east of Galilee. Jesus may have spent some time in these areas to escape from his enemies and/or the misguided enthusiasm of his followers.

The interest of the first story is in the dialogue. For the first time in this gospel Jesus is approached by a 'pagan' (that is the meaning of the term 'Gentile' in this passage—not only that the suppliant was a foreigner but also that she was of a different religion). At first Jesus' reaction is
27 cautious: **'Let the children be satisfied first; it is not fair to take the children's bread and throw it to the dogs.'** Indeed, he is definitely off-putting: commentators have tried to soften the implication of the use of the word 'dogs', but the most straightforward interpretation is that our Lord was initially reacting like any orthodox Jew. The belief that the gospel is to be preached first to the Jews and then only after that to the Gentiles emerges through several New Testament passages (e.g. Acts 13.46, 18.6, Rom. 1.16). In their missionary work Paul and his companions preached first to the Jews of the Dispersion in a city. But the Syro-Phoenician woman was not to be rebuffed. Although she addressed
28 him with reverence ('**Sir**' is the NEB's translation of *kurie*, 'Lord') she turned his remark wittily to repeat her request, and her persistence is rewarded. Jesus exorcizes the unclean spirit from a distance. In Matthew's version Christ marvels at the woman's faith (15.28).

The second story is a powerful illustration of the way in which OT prophecies were fulfilled in Christ. 'On that day deaf men shall hear when a book is read' (Isa. 29.18), and 'The tongue of the dumb shall shout aloud' (Isa. 35.6). Those who have been deaf and dumb will both hear and proclaim the Good News. But it is also an illustration of a healing through the use of signs in a manner not uncommon in that age (the emperor Vespasian was said to have healed a blind man through the use of saliva). The touch with the hand, the use of spittle and the word of healing in the original language are all marks of ancient miracle tales.

We find them again in the fourth gospel's account of the healing of the
34 man born blind (John 9.1–7). **Looking up to heaven** was a gesture of
prayer, **sighed** may have been a form of exorcism (exsufflation), and
36 **'Ephphatha'** looks like a version of the Aramaic *ethpattah*. Jesus forbade
them to tell anyone: most commentators think that this is one of a
number of occasions when the evangelist has introduced the theory that
Jesus wanted his identity as the Messiah to be kept secret until just
before his passion and death. Whether this is true or not, both healings
reveal the saving grace of God in Jesus Christ in restoring men and
women (Gentiles as well as Jews) to wholeness in its fullest sense. The
wonder of the crowd is like an act of worship.

SEVENTH SUNDAY BEFORE EASTER
The Sunday next before Lent

Hosea 14. 1–7
The book of the prophet Hosea, which teaches the faithfulness and forgiveness of God in terms of a husband-wife image, ends with a form of
confession and absolution that might be called a rite for a liturgy of
penance. Although no actual service is proposed, it contains the necessary
elements: verses 1–2a, an exhortation to repentance; 2b–3, a form of
confession said by the people; and 4–7, a promise of forgiveness spoken
by the Lord.
2   The people were to approach God: **Come with your words ready.**
Theirs was not an approach through the sacrificial cult. The phrase
with cattle from our pens is better rendered **with fruit from our
lips** (NEB footnote and most commentators). What they renounced was a
3 military alliance with Assyria (**horses to ride** means additional cavalry
and chariotry) and idolatry, which the prophet has often denounced in
his book.
God's forgiveness is expressed in terms of healing, of loving them
4 **freely, of my own bounty,** of turning away anger, and of fertility—the
opposite of those disasters which had been brought on Israel by her sinfulness. The effect of God's love is described by a comparison with
plant life. He is like the dews necessary to bring fruitfulness to vegetation
during the dry summers; his permanence is like the deep roots of the

giant trees of Lebanon; his beauty is like the olive tree, and his scent like the slopes of Lebanon, where the moist atmosphere rises among flowers and shrubs. The picture is changed in verse 7 for one of a forgiven Israel living in God's love like a man dwelling securely under a fig or vine-tree, enjoying the abundance of the harvest, especially the bread and the wine, the corn and the vine.

Philemon 1–16

The punishment due to a runaway slave in the ancient world was severe. He could be executed. The situation in which Paul intervened in this letter, therefore, was an extremely delicate one. Philemon was the head of a household, perhaps in Colossae, who had been converted by Paul (19) and whose dwelling was used as a meeting-place for a Christian congregation consisting of his own relatives (Apphia, his wife?, and Archippus) and his servants and perhaps also people from the neighbourhood. It was a typical arrangement for a local church in the early centuries. One of his slaves, Onesimus ('useful' or 'profitable'), had run away, probably with stolen goods, had met Paul in prison, and had been converted or brought to repentance by the apostle. Paul was now sending him back to his master with a promise to repay any debts outstanding.

8   The apostle might have reminded Philemon that it was his Christian duty to forgive the slave and accept him back, **I might make bold to point out your duty.** But instead he appealed to him as a Christian brother to restore him as one who is more than a slave. There is a gentle

11 pun on Onesimus' name in the phrases **once so little use to you, but now useful indeed.**

Against the background of slavery as an institution in the society within which the Church had to work, there is much in this passage which demonstrates how the relationship between Christians transcends social barriers and institutions. The case of Philemon gave Paul the opportunity to call for a practical demonstration of love between members of the Christian community with profound theological meaning. The act of forgiveness of a master for a slave is a reflection of the forgiveness of God, who saves men from the slavery of sin and accepts them as children, as brothers of his Son, Jesus Christ.

In a letter to the church at Ephesus, written about A.D. 100, Ignatius refers to a bishop at Ephesus called Onesimus, 'a man whose love is beyond words' (Eph. 1.3). If he was once Philemon's slave, then Paul's letter of recommendation and Philemon's act of clemency brought a great blessing on the Church.

* Mark 2. 13–17

The passage links two incidents demonstrating Jesus Christ's friendly relationships with the moral and religious outcasts. The Jewish principle of separation from what was unclean was carried to an extreme degree by the Pharisees, whose name meant 'those who are separated'. Although they are frequently depicted as Christ's enemies, many of them were men of high principle and integrity; Psalm 119 represents the ideal of their party.

The call of Levi was similar to the call of the other disciples in this Gospel; it took place in the same vicinity, by the lake-side, and the man called was busy with his profession. But the power of Christ was such that immediately the man left what he was doing, followed Jesus, and entertained him at his house. It was this that caused the criticism. Table-fellowship was a sign and pledge of intimacy in the ancient world, and it was inconceivable to a Jew that a man of God should take a meal with one who not only was a swindler but also served a foreign authority. Public taxes in the Roman empire were farmed out to contractors who were allowed to make their own profits before they paid the revenue into the state treasury. It was explicitly required that one must avoid such company.

But Jesus' conduct was not determined by the law. He acted because of his unique status as Messiah, as the one sent by God to bring forgiveness to sinners who repent. He did not need to fear the contagion of human sinfulness, and he said as much in his use of the doctor-patient parallel. **It**
17 **is not the healthy that need a doctor, but the sick; I did not come to invite virtuous people but sinners.** The 'virtuous' are not those who are saved (healthy) but those who think they are so free of sin that they have no need of a saviour. The danger of the Pharisaic ideal was that it blinded its followers to their need for salvation so that they were unable to recognize the Messiah in their midst. Christ's use of the word 'invite' suggests that in his mind was the heavenly banquet which, in traditional Jewish imagery, was the destined reward of the righteous.

Matt. 9.9 identifies Levi with one of the Twelve, Matthew, probably because he too was a tax-gatherer. Capernaum, on the northern shore of the Sea of Galilee, was an important station on the route which carried trade from the cities of the Decapolis to the Mediterranean ports. On the frontier between the territories of Herod Antipas and Philip and a centre of the fishing industry on the lake, it was an obvious place for a profitable customs-house.

SEVENTH SUNDAY BEFORE EASTER
The Sunday next before Lent

Numbers 15. 32–36

The origin of the Jewish sabbath (Hebrew *shabbāth*, from the verb *shābath*, 'to desist' or 'to break off') is not known. In the P source (Exod. 31.21–17) God is represented as having instituted the sabbath at the conclusion of his six days of creative acts, as a perpetual covenant with his people. Regulations concerning its observance appear in the Mosaic law, including this passage, which vividly illustrates the severity of its application. Once it is broken there is no way of obtaining God's mercy. The story establishes a precedent. It was not known whether gathering sticks was a deliberate sin 'with a high hand'. But through Moses the divine sentence was pronounced. Even in such a case as this the offender must be taken outside the camp and stoned to rid the community of the contamination of his presence.

Colossians 1. 18–23

For verses 18 to 20 see the commentary on the Ninth Sunday before Christmas Year 1.

Paul applied the message of the primitive Christian hymn to his readers in Colossae. As in the first two chapters of Romans, he reminded them of man's estranged condition from God, and then he drew on the imagery of Israel's sacrificial system to teach how God had reconciled man to himself. Atonement for man's sin had been made by Jesus Christ

22 who, like the sacrificial animals offered in the temple, was **without blemish and innocent in his sight.** It is an imagery which was used with rich and profound variations by a number of NT writers. **Christ's death in his body of flesh and blood** (that is, in his physical, human body) had meant that sinful man could be identified completely with his Saviour and, redeemed by the blood of Christ, was joined with him in a perfect relationship with the Father.

23 **The hope offered in the gospel which you have heard** is presumably both the present assurance that the Christian has in the efficacy of his Saviour's sacrifice and also knowledge that in Jesus he will share in its future consummation. Paul's understanding of what God has done in Christ, is doing, and will do, merges into a vision of continuous saving activity on man's behalf. But he was perhaps lapsing into rhetoric when he wrote **the gospel . . . has been proclaimed in the whole creation**

under heaven. It sounds like a grandiose claim. Yet he sincerely believed that during the course of his own lifetime the kingdom of God would be preached throughout the known world, and he may have had in mind the current idea that the gospel would be known also in the spiritual realms as well ('He who was manifested in the body, vindicated in the spirit, seen by angels'—1 Tim. 3.16).

* John 8. 1–11

Adultery was punishable by death according to the Mosaic law (Lev. 20.10, Deut. 22.22–27) but usually there was no further punishment beyond divorce and social disgrace. In this case, however, where the
4 woman had been caught in the very act, the doctors of the law and the Pharisees were pressing for the full punishment, death by stoning. A difficulty in this detail is that under the Roman administration the Jewish authorities had apparently lost the power to impose the death penalty (John 18.31). Perhaps this group were particularly zealous and were going to kill the woman in spite of this, or perhaps they were on their way to the Roman governor with her. Anyway they brought her to where Jesus was sitting in the temple precincts teaching, to use her as a means of setting a trap. 'In the Law Moses has laid down that such women are to be stoned. What do you say about it?' Similar test questions were put to him in the matter of divorce (Mark 10.2ff = Matt. 19.3ff) and paying tribute to Caesar (Mark 12.13ff and parallels). If Christ had said the law should be enforced, he could be accused of interfering with the Roman administration; if he did not, he could be criticized for not taking the law seriously.

From earliest times Christians have wondered what words Jesus used
6 when he bent down and wrote with his finger on the ground. Jerome said he listed the sins of the woman's accusers. Others have suggested he wrote down some appropriate OT text (e.g. Exod. 23.1, 'You shall not make common cause with a wicked man by giving malicious evidence'). T. W. Manson put forward the view that Jesus was modelling himself on the practice of Roman judges, who wrote down the sentence before they read it aloud. Perhaps he was giving the accusers time to think again. When they persisted with their question, however, he stood
7 up to make his devastating reply, 'That one of you who is faultless shall throw the first stone.' The law required that the witnesses whose evidence had secured the conviction of the accused should take the lead in carrying out the sentence. In effect, Christ had thrown their question back at them in another form. By what right did they presume to usurp

the judgement of God? He did not say that no one should ever be judged. He was exposing their motives by showing that they were not really concerned for justice but were intending to use the law for their own purposes.

They retreated before the truth as it was revealed to them through his
9 question—the eldest first, perhaps, because they realized the implications of what he had said. In the end Jesus was left alone with the woman.
10 When he asked her Has no one condemned you? he used a technical
11 word from the language of the court, *katakrinein*. No more do I. Jesus will not make a judgement, either. Without condoning the past, he demanded right behaviour from the woman in the future. There is no hint of the woman's repentance, but that is not the point of the story. Its purpose is to reveal the divine mercy in the attitude of Jesus—teaching the Church how it, too, must behave when confronted with the sinner.

The passage did not form part of the original gospel. In style it is closer to Luke than to the fourth evangelist. It may have come into the gospel in this position because it fits the theme of judgement in chapter eight. It is generally agreed that, as a text, it is as ancient as most parts of the gospels, and its canonicity has never seriously been questioned.

YEARS I AND 2

ASH WEDNESDAY
See pages 15–20

Isaiah 58. 1–8
The only fast prescribed in the Mosaic Law is that for the Day of Atonement (Lev. 23.26ff), but other fasts were proclaimed at different times, such as in days of national crisis or disaster. The question at issue in this post-exilic oracle of the Third Isaiah is the effectiveness of fasting: why do the people fast if God does not pay any attention to such observances?

The attitude towards the fast shifts in the course of this passage, indicating perhaps different sources (it is thought that although the oracle reached its final form in post-exilic times, it includes some pre-exilic material). Festivals and fasts were announced by trumpet-calls. The prophet, like a trumpet, was to summon people to hear what God says through him about effective fasting. The people were assiduous in wor-
2 ship: they ask counsel of me day by day and say they delight in

knowing my ways. They sought to hold close to God's will, but their fasts were marred because they had pursued their business on a fast day, and made their labourers work for them. Indeed, the fast day had been an occasion for wrangling and quarrelling, presumably in connection with their business affairs. It had even come to acts of violence.

So far the prophet had complained about serious abuses which had happened on fast days. He had not been concerned with the days themselves as religious institutions but with the question whether the turning to God in prayer—and prayer is the most important element in fast days—was genuine and complete. At verse 5, however, there is a change. The
5 attack was directed against the practice of fasting with some scorn. **Is it a fast like this that I require . . . that a man should bow his head like a bulrush and make his bed on sackcloth and ashes?** is intended to be sarcastic. The divergence suggests a separate source for this verse.

From verse 6 onwards we are told what kind of fasting is pleasing to God. Fasting should include justice for the hungry, the poor, the captives, and the oppressed—the classes who are listed in the prophet's commissioning in 61.1ff ('to bring good news to the humble . . .'). Like the gospel that it foreshadowed, the prophecy brought into the notion of penitential acts charitable deeds towards those in need. The outward observance of a fast is no substitute for obedience towards God, especially where other people are involved. The admonition ended with the promise that God would bless them like a dawn light and their wounds would be healed like new skin over old wounds. Their righteousness would go before them in the caravan, and the Lord's glory would be about their trail.

Joel 2. 12–17

Some time about the fourth century B.C. a locust plague left a trail of ravaged crops, and the disaster prompted the prophet Joel to warn the people that the day of the Lord would be an even more terrible experience. They should repent while there was time. The fasting and the weeping and the beating of the breasts were signs of mourning for sin. The scattering of dust on the person and the tearing of the garments were indicative of the worthlessness of sinful man: as a pitiable sight, there was a greater chance that the Lord would have mercy on him (this, it seems, is the primitive intention behind the ritual signs of penitence in the OT). But the prophet knew that the outward signs were not sufficient
13 in themselves. There had to be an inward change as well: **Rend your**

hearts and not your garments. Like the psalmist, he taught that the penitent had to let the Lord work within him: 'Make me a clean heart, O God: and renew a right spirit within me' (Ps. 51.10).

The people could be sure that God would forgive if they repented. **He is gracious and compassionate, long-suffering and ever constant.** These attributes of God are frequently mentioned in the OT. Again, characteristically among the writings of the classical prophets, the Lord 14 is depicted as changing his mind about punishing his sinful people: **It may be that he will turn back and repent and leave a blessing behind him.** The blessing that God will bestow is apparently a bumper harvest, for it will be **enough for grain-offering and drink-offering—** the sacrifices made in the temple to celebrate the success of the harvest.

So an act of ritual penitence was proclaimed for the whole nation with fasting and prayer. The blowing of the trumpet was the normal call to worship. The penitential procession was led by the priests into the temple. All were summoned to participate—elders, children, babes-in-arms, the newly-wed. The prayer, led by the priests, implored the Lord for mercy. And, in a reverent kind of way, it gently pointed out to God that *he* might be dishonoured if he did not listen to the prayer. If disaster struck his 17 people, other nations might ask, **'Where is their God?'**

The distinction between a 'fast' and an 'abstinence' belongs to the later history of the Church.

Amos 5. 6–15

Seeing the idolatry of the northern kingdom in the eighth century B.C., and the exploitation of the people by the capitalists of his day, Amos exhorted them all back to God. He preached repentance, in terms of a summons to a sanctuary, but the prophet realized that the approach to God meant more than an act of worship, and 'to live' meant more than physical survival. It meant an inner conversion of heart and mind.

6   **Resort to the Lord.** God himself is the only sanctuary for man. To ignore him is to invite the divine fire which is the Lord's instrument against his foes. He who is the author of life would become the author of destruction.

At this point a hymn in praise of the Lord as creator appears in the 8 prophecy. Commencing **He who made the Pleiades and Orion,** it is a later addition, and its position in the text has been adjusted in the NEB so that verses 7 and 10 can run together. It praises God as the maker of the stars, the ruler of day and night, and the one who provides rain. The star groups Pleiades and Orion are mentioned in Job 9.9 and 38.31.

158

Then the call for social reform is continued in verse 7 in its new position. The justice administered in the courts has been turned by greed into bitter oppression. The task of the court, which often met in the open square inside the gate of Israelite towns and cities ('in the gate', RSV) was to protect the social order by establishing where wrong lay and correcting it. This was particularly important in the case of the weaker members of society who, without power or influence, could not maintain themselves in the social order without the court's upholding of their rights. The proceedings of the court were not as formally organized as in our own western tradition, nor presided over and directed by professional men. All the adult male citizens of a town, who were not disqualified in some way, were eligible to sit as assessors. Any of them could testify as a witness and offer advice as to which norms applied in a case before the court. The competence of such a court depended on the integrity of the assessors in speaking the truth and upholding what was recognized as right in the community. The ninth commandment (Exod. 20.13) forbade false witness.

10 Therefore to **hate a man who brings the wrongdoer to court and loathe him who speaks the whole truth** is to undermine the system.

Amos accused his hearers of exploiting the weak—they were driving the landed peasantry away from their earlier independence into the condition of serfs; the small farmer no longer owned his own land, but was a tenant of an urban class to whom he must pay rent for the use of his land, a rent that was often a large proportion of the grain which the land produced. Out of the proceeds the exploiters had built themselves houses of stones hewn for the building (contrasted with the more usual practice of using stony rubble available on the site) and planted luxuriant vineyards on fields that belonged to the small farmer. The Lord, speaking through the prophet, knows those who use the courts to maintain this corruption. In verse 13 a comment is added that a prudent man—a figure beloved in the Wisdom sayings (Prov. 10.5, 19, etc.)—will keep quiet, knowing that to raise a complaint or to plead a case in the courts

13 **will be an evil time for him.**

Then our passage ends with an exhortation, followed by a conditional promise. The decision about good and evil is a decision for or against the Lord and is therefore an invocation of his blessing or his judgement. But the Lord's relationship with Israel was his own sovereign concern, and the bestowal of favour and help was in his own will and not what the recipient might expect.

1 Corinthians 9. 24–end

The games in the stadium are used several times in the New Testament as an analogy for Christian living, and in this passage the apostle, using contemporary terminology from the language of athletes, summoned the congregation at Corinth to remember that entering the Church through baptism did not guarantee our final perseverance; the Christian must continue in the way he has begun with all his might—and that involves exercising a mastery over oneself. His metaphor is not quite suitable, for he does not mean to imply that only one Christian in a group will win the prize of eternal life; the force of his argument is that we must not assume that, because we have entered the race, we shall automatically win.

Similarly, the analogy of a champion's crown is used to denote the Christian's prize: it is called 'the unfading garland of glory' in 1 Pet. 5.4, 'the crown of life' in Rev. 2.10. The Isthmian games were held near Corinth and archaeologists have discovered a mosaic in the floor of the office of the director of the games depicting a champion, with a palm in his hand, offering thanks to the goddess of Good Fortune (Tyche) and wearing a crown of withered leaves.

In verse 26 the metaphor shifts from that of discipline in training to controlled effort in the race or boxing match itself. For himself he runs, not in such a way that the onlooker cannot tell where he is going (the Greek phrase has a double negative to emphasize that the Christian's goal is very clear), and not like a boxer dealing ill-directed and ineffectual

26 blows. He treated his body severely. **I bruise my body** could be misleading; the JB translation is clearer, 'I treat my body hard and make it obey me'. This does not mean that a man's body is necessarily evil; rather, it means that Paul recognized that the human body is too easily inclined to what is sinful and disobedient to God and has to be disciplined to serve its right master. In speaking of the Christian's being buried and risen with Jesus Christ in baptism, he told the church in Rome, 'Put yourselves at God's disposal, as dead men raised to life; yield your bodies to him as implements for doing right; for sin shall no longer be your master, because you are no longer under law, but under the grace of God'. (Rom. 6.13–14). To call this *self*-discipline is to miss the point: we are to let God master our bodies, offering ourselves in this race, this contest, with all our will. And Paul placed himself under the same warning by envisaging the possibility that, notwithstanding his work as an apostle, he might himself fall from grace and be rejected.

James 4. 1–10

What James denounced was selfishness run riot, causing divisions within
the congregations to whom he was writing. The use of words like
2 murder, quarrel, and fight suggests that arguments, arising from con-
flicting ambitions and jealousy, have ended in actual blows. This sad
state of affairs made nonsense of his readers' prayers, for their petitions
sprang from unworthy motives and were consequently unanswered.
4 Such prayers cannot be offered in the name of Jesus Christ. You false,
unfaithful creatures is literally 'adulteresses!' in Greek: the imagery of
Israel as an unfaithful wife is traditional in the OT (Hos. 1.2ff) and is
carried over into the Gospel ('this adulterous and sinful generation',
Mark 8.37 RSV); here it is applied to the new Israel (as Paul applied it,
'I betrothed you to Christ, thinking to present you as a chaste virgin to
her true and only husband', 2 Cor. 11.2). The adulterous love of the
world (the term used in the Johannine sense of creation in opposition
to its creator) is apostasy from God.
5   The spirit which God implanted in man turns towards envious
desires is a scripture which now seems to be lost, though it may be based
on Gen. 2.7, when God formed man from the dust of the ground and
breathed into his nostrils the breath of life. There is a real danger that the
spiritual life of man may be turned to evil. Yet resistance to the devil is
effective; the man who humbles himself before God receives all the
8 assistance he needs (quoting Prov. 3.34). Come close to God is a
phrase which normally refers to priests approaching the altar: God never
turns his back on those who draw near to him.

* **Matthew 6. 16–21**

The pericope consists of two sections from the Matthean version of the
Sermon on the Mount, one on fasting and the other on true treasures.

   In addition to the public fasts like the Day of Atonement, private
individuals such as the Pharisees and the followers of John the Baptist
undertook private fasts as a means of religious and moral discipline. The
Pharisee in Jesus' parable of the two men in the temple said he fasted
twice in the week (Luke 18.12). Among the Pharisees Mondays and
Thursdays were kept as fast days. Jesus assumed that fasting would continue among his disciples, at any rate when 'the bridegroom' was taken
from them (Matt. 9.14–15). But he denounced the use of the practice as
a means of displaying one's piety and gaining the reputation of being
a holy person, and therefore he warned his disciples not to use the customary signs of fasting, the unkempt appearance and the strewing of ashes

on the head. On the contrary, Christians who fast must appear to be living normally and joyfully (washed and anointed).

19   Behind the saying about **treasure on earth** is the conviction that the accumulation and hoarding of worldly goods is due to a desire for security, a desire to be rid of anxiety about the future. But Christ argued that, far from removing anxiety, material wealth increases it, because earthly treasures are liable to loss and decay. What his followers should collect is
20 **treasure in heaven.** This heavenly wealth is a permanent possession, freed from the ravages of time and safely out of the reach of thieves. Various sayings of our Lord comment on this—the saying about the pearl of great price, the parable of the rich fool, and the advice to the rich young ruler (Matt. 13.46, Luke 12.16–21, Matt. 19.16–26).

* **Luke 18. 9–14**

The Pharisees, according to Josephus, were 'a body of Jews with the reputation of excelling the rest of their nation in the observances of religion, and as exact exponents of the laws'. Their attitude is reflected in the confession of Paul in Phil. 3.4ff, 'If anyone thinks to base his claims on externals, I could make a stronger case for myself: circumcised on my eighth day, Israelite by race, of the tribe of Benjamin, a Hebrew born and bred; in my attitude to the law, a Pharisee; in pious zeal, a persecutor of the church; in legal rectitude, faultless'. The dangers in this attitude were recognized by the rabbis: Hillel (*c*. 20 B.C.) used to say 'Keep not aloof from the congregation and trust not in thyself until the day of thy death, and judge not thy fellow until thou art come to his place'. It is probable that the parable was directed against the self-righteous section within the party rather than the party as a whole.

The two men in the parable stood for the two extremes in Judaism, the Pharisee representing those whose complete devotion to the law set the supreme standard of Jewish faith and morals, the tax-gatherer representing the lowest moral stratum of Jewish life. Both entered the inner main quadrangle of the temple, perhaps at the time of the morning or the evening sacrifice, when every Jew was expected to pray. Both stood for their prayers—the normal posture. The Pharisee's prayer began as an act of thanksgiving, the best form of prayer. To begin with it was not objectionable. He simply thanked God that he was able to avoid deadly sins and
11 perform many acts of supererogation. **I fast twice a week; I pay tithes on all that I get.** Deut. 14.22 required that only coin, wine, and oil should be tithed, together with beasts, if the man dealt in them. Mondays and Thursdays were fast days for pious Jews. But then in his prayer the

Pharisee went on to compare himself with the tax-gatherer, and here his pride came in. The tax-gatherer, on the other hand, was overwhelmed by his sense of unworthiness (and we must not make the mistake of regarding him as a decent sort of chap: he was a scoundrel—his saving grace was that he had come to realize it). From a distance and with downcast eyes he could only ask God for mercy with a penitential beating of his breast.

Jesus' comment shows that what matters is not a man's personal achievements or past record but his present attitude towards God. The Pharisee was so satisfied with himself that God could do nothing for him. He did not see that he needed a physician. The tax-gatherer knew his need, and in that there was hope.

LENT 1
Sixth Sunday before Easter

Genesis 2. 7–9; 3. 1–7
See Ninth and Eighth Sundays before Christmas Year 2

Hebrews 2. 14–end
The opening verses of this passage finalize the argument that the author has been putting forward at the beginning of this letter; that Jesus Christ was the true Son of God, superior to all the angels, and that he became truly human, sharing in full the human experiences of temptation, suffering, and death, in order to be the High Priest of mankind before God the
14 Father in heaven. Thus he **shared the same flesh and blood,** a common Jewish saying to denote humanity in its frailty and dependence before God.

Fear of death, and of the consequences of death, is seen as a slavery imposed on the whole human race. Speculations about terrible punishments awaiting the soul after death abounded in the ancient world. Man would fall even more into the power of the devil after he had died. The rabbis wrote of the Angel of Death wielding the power of death, and in the Wisdom of Solomon it was held that God did not make death, that man was made for incorruption, and that it was through the devil that death entered into the world (Wisd. 1.13, 2.23–24). Death, then, was the realm of the evil one.

The incarnation, said the author of Hebrews, was to liberate men from this dreadful fate. Precisely how Jesus through death broke the devil's power over death is not explained. Basically the thought seems to be that Jesus, through dying and then rising from the dead, passed in his humanity beyond the power of the devil so that, in his risen life, he was able to crush the effect that that power had over the rest of humanity. This is why the author insisted on the full union of the Son of God with our human nature. The New Testament reflects the tension between the teaching that Christ has already destroyed death (2 Tim. 1.10) and the belief that the complete annihilation of the devil awaits the last day (Rev. 12.9) and the last enemy to be destroyed is death (1 Cor. 15.26). This conquest of Christ over death is pictured in Rev. 1.18: 'Do not be afraid. I am the first and the last, and I am the living one; for I was dead and now I am alive for evermore and I hold the keys of death and Hades.'

16   Christ represents **the sons of Abraham**—not the Jews, but the new
17   Israel. **He had to be made like these brothers of his in every way, so that he might be merciful and faithful as their high priest before God, to expiate the sins of the people.** This is the first mention of our Lord's high priestly office in a letter which elaborates it at length in later chapters. The office of a high priest is to represent men in their relationship to God and to reconcile men to God through the ordered means of the cult. Christ's work is described here in the imagery of sacrifice, using the concept of expiation—making amends for sins. Expiation is one of the underlying motives of sacrifice in the Bible, and it is what the high priest was believed to achieve on the Day of Atonement, when he offered the sacrifice for the sins of the people. Christ as our High Priest could intercede sympathetically for men since he himself knew the temptations to which they are subject. This is another reason why the author emphasized the Son of God's full participation in human nature. Christ is not only the leader and the consecrator of his people: he is their mediator as well. And in strong contrast with the Jewish high priests, he
17   is merciful in that he is compassionate towards men, and he is faithful in his obedience to God the Father.

* **Matthew 4. 1–11**
After his baptism by John, Jesus was led by the Spirit into the desert to be tempted. We cannot tell whether the location, the suggestions put by the devil, and the threefold form of the temptations are a record of what happened or a stylization of a constant battle that Jesus had throughout

his ministry. But this does not matter: neither possibility adds or takes away from the importance of the event in our salvation-history.

Reference to the wilderness is significant. Christ was remaking the journey of the Israelites through the desert where they were tempted. The people succumbed, but Jesus resisted, because he was full of the Spirit. He used three scriptural sayings taken from the story of Israel to counter the temptations (Deut. 8.3, 6.16, 6.13). Deuteronomy was the 'Book of Moses' which gave the scriptural principles on which the chosen people were to occupy the promised land (Deut. 4.1). What sort of a Joshua (Jesus) was Christ to be, as he led the true Israel to the promised land of the Kingdom of God? This was the basic question behind the suggestions put to him by the devil.

3   **If you are the Son of God, tell these stones to become bread.** Israel—and with her all mankind—forgot her task in life and longed to return to the fleshpots of Egypt. Was Christ to appear before the Jewish nations as the benefactor who provides the messianic banquet in material terms, making bread out of stones? He replied that man is to feed on the word of God, a greater manna than that which appeared in the wilderness. It is true that on one, if not two, later occasions he did in fact provide bread in the desert for thousands of people, but this was in a moment of practical necessity, and the fourth Gospel used the miracle as a sign of the Bread of Life (John 6.49–50).

6   **If you are the Son of God, throw yourself down; for Scripture says, 'He will put his angels in charge of you, and they will support you in their arms, for fear you should strike your foot against a stone'** (even the devil can quote scripture, in this case Ps. 91.11–12, for his own purposes!). The parapet of the temple on which they were standing is usually thought to be the south-east corner of the huge wall constructed by Herod the Great round the temple in Jerusalem, from which there was a sheer drop of 150 feet into the Kidron valley below. Was Christ to assume the role of the Messiah of apocalyptic literature, descending from the sky in a miraculous way to draw from the people wonder and awe? Jesus replied that to put God to the test is to fail to trust him. Moses had failed in this way when, in a moment of provocation, he had struck the rock for water at Massah, an act which disqualified him for leadership in the promised land (Exod. 17.2–7, Deut. 32.51). Jesus himself was to be a mightier sign, changing the course of history more than any stunt he might have devised. 'The Jesus we speak of has been raised by God, as we can all bear witness. Exalted thus with God's right hand, he received

the Holy Spirit from the Father, and all that you now see and hear flows from him', said Peter (Acts 2.32–33).

9   All these (kingdoms of the world) I will give you, if you will only fall down and do me homage. Many hill-tops in Judah offer wide views over the Jordan valley and the mountains beyond, which might well be described as a microcosm of the kingdoms of the earth in their glory. These perhaps Jesus saw, as he saw the drop from the parapet of the temple, in his mind's eye during the temptations. Israel had abandoned herself to the worship of worldly idols. Was Jesus to lead his people as a political messiah to a victory over the foreign oppressor, a new David conquering the Philistines of his day? Jesus refused that kind of earthly lordship in exchange for a genuflection, for he was to be given through his death and resurrection a Kingdom greater than any human empire. 'Full authority in heaven and on earth has been committed to me' (Matt. 28.18).

Because Jesus conformed to the will of God, the trials and temptations which were bringing about the downfall of the old dispensation were conquered at the outset of the new, and the truths which underlay the various elements making up the Jewish messianic expectation were more than fulfilled. The messianic hope was transfigured to a promise of salvation for mankind. Already in the baptism and in the temptations evil was trodden underfoot and conquered.

The time that Jesus was in the wilderness has a symbolic significance. Apart from Israel's forty years' wanderings in the desert, Moses spent forty days on mount Sinai (Exod. 24.18) and Elijah fasted for forty days on his way to mount Horeb (1 Kings 19.8). In biblical imagery these were all periods of purification and preparation before a mighty work of God. Fasting too has a purifying effect; men fasted and prayed before undertaking work in answer to God's call.

Jesus was to face temptation again (Matt. 16.22 and 26.36–46) but this preliminary battle in the wilderness was both a sequel to his baptism in the Jordan (temptation is a common experience of mystics and others after a period of high exaltation) and an overture to his ministry. The idea of temptation is not incompatible with Christ's sinlessness. Temptation is not sin; it is a form of testing. Indeed, it is a sign of Christ's total identification of himself with the human condition. 'Ours is not a high priest unable to sympathize with our weaknesses, but one who, because of his likeness to us, has been tested in every way, only without sin' (Heb. 4.15). So he began his ministry without resorting to the world's ways of making friends and influencing people, taking over when John had been

arrested. He proclaimed the gospel of the Kingdom with the summons
16 to repentance, and the people that lived in darkness saw a great light
(verse 16, quoting Isa. 9.2).

LENT 1
Sixth Sunday before Easter

Genesis 4. 1–10   See Eighth Sunday before Christmas Year 1

Hebrews 4. 12–end
'The word of God' is not used in this passage in the Johannine sense of
the divine Logos but, as it is sometimes used in the OT, as God's messenger. God's word is not dead and empty speech; it is dynamic with life,
communicating itself to men. 'The word which comes from my mouth
12 (shall) prevail' (Isa. 55.11). Its effect is that of a **two-edged sword**: it
penetrates beneath the surface. Outward behaviour may be exemplary,
but it is possible underneath to cherish a spirit of rebellion against God.
God's scrutiny penetrates to those depths of the human personality
12 where **life and spirit, joints and marrow, divide**. At the centre is the
heart, and the word of God searches that too.
　　The author contrasted **Christ** as our High Priest with the Levitical high
priest in his cultic office. The high priest in Jerusalem was able only to
step beyond the veil in the temple; Jesus passed through the seven heavens
(of current mythology) to the throne of God above them: the juxtaposition
14 of the name and title **Jesus Son of God** underlines the union of the
human and the divine natures in Christ. This is the faith in which
Christians stand.
　　Anticipating the objection that such an exalted being could not possibly
sympathize with the spiritual, intellectual, and moral frailties of human
nature, the author asserted that Christ can in fact do this because he has
shared in that same nature. He has a real kinship with mankind because
15 he has been **tested every way, as we are** (NEB footnote). The only
difference is that he was not guilty of conscious and deliberate acts of
rebellion against the Father. Christian confidence, then, rests in the
knowledge that the barrier between God and man has been removed by
Jesus; all can approach the throne of God—not just the high priest as in

the Jewish cult—and all can ask for pardon which God in his mercy so freely gives.

* Luke 4. 1–13
The Lucan account of the temptation is substantially but not verbally paralleled in Matthew. There are some slight differences:

Luke heightened the impression given by Matthew (and by Mark) 1 that Jesus went into the desert in a state of Spirit possession: **Full of the Spirit.**

The second temptation in Matthew (on the parapet of the temple) became the third in Luke.

In Luke's second temptation (the kingdoms of the world) the author increased the dramatic effect of the devil's revelation by saying it happened 5 **in a flash.**

There is no reference to the ministry of angels in Luke.

(For further commentary on the subject, see Lent 1 Year 1.)

LENT 2
Fifth Sunday before Easter

Genesis 6. 11–end
The creation of the world involved by implication a covenant between God and man—man's obedience to the will of God as symbolized by the command not to eat of the tree of knowledge of good and evil. This covenant was broken by the fall. One scribal tradition of the Book of Genesis carried the idea of the formal beginnings of a restored covenant back to Noah, and this is a feature of the Jahwist account of the Flood. The story bears some resemblance to Babylonian myths based perhaps on folk memories of the disastrous floods experienced in the valley of the Euphrates and the Tigris. The myth of the flood was enlarged into a widespread, universal destruction. But the myth is only of minor importance to the Jahwist scribes. They saw that the order which had been established by God at the creation of the world was breaking down. Water, the primeval symbol of sin, overwhelmed the world to destroy it.

But in spite of the world's sin God's purpose was not frustrated. In Noah he saw the one blameless man of his time, and with him God made his restored covenant—a sign of God's commitment to those whom he had chosen (later with Abraham, Gen. 15.17, and then with the whole of Israel, Exod. 19.1). A remnant would be saved through the ark. Noah's faith in God was such that he was willing to start constructing this huge floating crate (it was hardly a ship—the Hebrews were not seafarers) on dry land far from any water.

20   Two of every kind of bird, beast, and reptile, shall come to you to be kept alive. Behind this detail in the OT parable is the belief that somehow man's sin affects the whole of creation. In the story of Gen. 2, God had given man responsibility for all the animals in allowing him to choose names for them; now the animals are mysteriously linked with man's destiny.

The NT writers looked back on the flood as a divine judgement which foreshadowed that of the latter days ('As things were in Noah's days, so will they be when the Son of Man comes', Matt. 27.37, Luke 17.26). Noah's salvation was interpreted as a prefiguring of the saving waters of baptism (1 Pet. 3.20–21)—one of the themes of Lent (see p. 15)—and from this the early Fathers taught that the ark was a type or sign of the Church. This is why the Church is referred to as 'the ark of salvation' in ancient baptismal prayers.

1 John 4. 1–6

The passage leads on from the statement in 3.24b: 'This is how we can make sure that he (Jesus Christ) dwells within us: we know it from the Spirit he has given us'. The proof of fellowship with God is the indwelling of the Spirit: 'I will ask the Father, and he will give another to be your Advocate, who will be with you for ever—the Spirit of truth' (John 14.16). Christians are anointed with the Spirit because they are the people of the Anointed One, the Messiah. Christ breathed the Spirit upon the disciples when he appeared in the upper room on the day of resurrection.

1 John was written to counter the influence of those who were creating a division in the Church through heretical teaching. The author warned his readers to test such teachers by their moral obedience to God, by their love of their brethren, and—at this point he applied a third test—to see if they possessed the Spirit of truth. This could be decided if they denied the reality of the incarnation: everyone who possessed the Holy Spirit

2   would say that Jesus Christ has come in the flesh. A distinction is made in the author's mind between the Spirit of God and the spirit of man. The spirit of man is that principle of life in a human being which is infused and directed by the Spirit of God when he or she turns to

Jesus Christ. When not possessed by the Spirit, the spirit of man is controlled by the spirit of Antichrist.

The concept of a conflict between good and evil in 1 and 2 John, then, is described in terms of an encounter within man between the Spirit of God and the spirit of Antichrist. The title is not used elsewhere in the NT, but he is called 'the Enemy' in 2 Thess. 2.4 and 'the Beast' in Rev. 13 and 17. He is in the world, but Christians may have supreme confidence in God, for he has conquered the evil one through Jesus Christ. It can be

4 said of Christians, therefore, that **you have the mastery over these false prophets, because he who inspires you is greater than he who inspires the godless world.**

* Luke 19. 41–end

The evangelist began the gospel by declaring that God had 'visited and redeemed his people' (1.68, RSV), and the long central section of his book is designed to lead up to the day when Jesus announced to his disciples, 'We are now going up to Jerusalem' (18.31)—a key text for succeeding generations of Christians as they embark on the spiritual pilgrimage offered to them each year in the season of Lent. In this passage we read of the day when Jesus came to Jerusalem on a royal visit, only to find

44 that the city was not ready for him—**you did not recognize God's moment when it came** ('you did not know the time of your visitation', RSV). Yet God has visited his people, and if Jerusalem will not receive Jesus Christ as her Saviour then he comes as her Judge.

The road from Bethphage and Bethany leads over a shoulder of the Mount of Olives and still today the traveller sees the most famous picture of the holy city across the Kidron valley. Where the Dome of the Rock now stands Christ would have seen the magnificent buildings of the temple and beyond, on higher ground, the royal palace of Herod. At the

42 sight Jesus uttered a lament, **if only you had known, on this great day, the way that leads to peace!** The name of the city may be connected etymologically with the Hebrew *shalem* and mean 'vision of peace' or 'city of peace'. The lament continues with a prophecy of the destruction of Jerusalem in A.D. 70 drawn from similar warnings and descriptions of sieges in the Old Testament (e.g. Ps. 137.9, Isa. 37.33, and Jer. 52).

In Mark's Gospel the cleansing of the temple took place the day after the triumphal entry and was an independent act of prophetic symbolism. In this passage Luke has given it a slightly different meaning: it has become an illustration of the way in which Jerusalem was unprepared for the visitation. The temple authorities had allowed traders to set up stalls in the Court of the Gentiles where pilgrims could exchange their currency for the half-shekels for the payment of the annual tax and where they could buy animals without blemish (Lev. 1.3) for the sacrificial offerings. Convenient though this may have been, Christ condemned it as a scandal of greed and dishonesty within the sacred precincts. His words were made up of two prophetic texts, 'My house shall be called a house of prayer for all nations' (Isa. 56.7) and 'Do you think that this house, this house which bears my name, is a robbers' cave?' (Jer. 7.11).

47   Although he challenged the authorities in this way so that **the chief priests and lawyers were bent on making an end of him**, Jesus was supported by the people sufficiently to be able to teach for several days in the temple. Not everyone in Jerusalem rejected God's visitation— which made the ultimate fate of the city all the more tragic.

LENT 2
Fifth Sunday before Easter

Genesis 7. 17–23

This passage is from the Priestly source of the book of Genesis and sees the flood as a catastrophe involving the whole universe. The waters over the heavens poured down on to the earth below and the waters under the earth gushed out, and there was a destruction of the biblical cosmos on a scale greater than that from a rainstorm. The two halves of the chaotic primeval sea, which had been separated—one above the heavens, the other below the earth—by God's creative power, were united. Creation sank back into chaos. The catastrophe was not only the concern of men and animals, as in the Yahwist tradition (see the commentary on 6.11–22

19 Year 1) but also of all that God had made. **More and more the waters increased over the earth until they covered all the high mountains**

21 **under heaven**: the effect of the flood was absolute. **Everything died that had the breath of the spirit of life in its nostrils** (NEB footnote): an early expression bringing together 'breath', 'spirit', and 'life', later to assume great significance in the thought of the NT writers. Forty is one of the Bible's sacred numbers.

1 John 3. 1–10

The author was writing to refute erroneous ideas about the possibility of a Christian's falling into sin and about the working of God's grace. Among his readers there were some who were saying that the Christian could not sin, whatever he did, or that it did not matter if a Christian did sin, for this only gave a greater opportunity for more grace (the teaching Paul countered in Rom. 6). The author had to affirm the truth that Christ, because he has conquered sin, drives out the sin of the Christian in whom he dwells, but that the Christian is still in the process of becoming what Christ has made him.

1 The disciples of Jesus were called **God's children**—Christ taught us to address the Father with him as 'Our Father' and declared that whoever did the will of God was his brother, sister, mother (Mark 3.35). This is what the Christian is in reality. Repentance and faith, baptism and the receiving of the Holy Spirit bring the Christian into the family of God, the Church, where he is no longer a slave but a son of God.

The footnote references in the NEB to verse 2 indicate the various ways of reading it, but they do not alter the meaning of the passage. Verses 1 to 3 say this: We can hope that we shall be like Christ, both now and at the
2 end of time, **when he appears** (NEB footnote), because we know that we are God's children; this means that we must be purified, because Christ is pure, and it also means that we must not expect the world to recognize us as God's children, for it did not even recognize Christ himself when he came—indeed, we should not be surprised if it hates us (3.13). But we know that when the reality of our status as God's children
3 is made manifest at the second coming, **we shall be like him**, because we have lived in purity.

The argument is amplified in the rest of the reading. Sin is deliberate
4 disobedience to God—**God's law** is synonymous with the will of God as revealed in Jesus Christ. **Christ appeared, as you know, to do away with sins, and there is no sin in him.** The sinlessness of Christ is affirmed throughout the New Testament, though sinlessness does not
6 mean he was freed from temptation. **No man . . . who dwells in him is a sinner; the sinner has not seen him and does not know him.** To sin is to be blind to God.

Righteousness is always expressed in what a man says and does:
7 **it is the man who does right who is righteous.** It is never independent of conduct. This is how the Christian becomes what God has made him
8 in Christ. **The devil has been a sinner from the first** could mean either from the start of history, if he is a fallen angel, or from the time that

172

sin entered the world. The work of Jesus Christ is seen in terms of doing battle against the devil in this world and conquering him.

9   A child of God does not commit sin. Not a warning but an affirmation. Because the divine seed has been implanted in the Christian (seed here may mean either the principle of the new life which is implanted when a man is born again unto the family of God, or the seed which is the word of God as in the parable of the sower (Mark 4.14): the exact meaning does not matter, for the result is the same) he is prevented from sinning. God's child does not sin. The finality of this statement is startling. We are aware of our failings (or some of them!). Does their existence mean that we are

10 children of the devil? No, for John was not a perfectionist. He recognized the recurrence of sin within the Christian fellowship, for in 1.9 he wrote, 'If we confess our sins, he is just and may be trusted to forgive our sins and to cleanse us from every kind of wrong.' What he meant was that there is in the heart and mind and will of the child of God a continuous renunciation of sin, which began when he was baptized. This renunciation is so radical that the intention of sinning is never accepted; and sin, when it occurs, is immediately repented, confessed, and rejected as utterly alien to the Christian life.

* **Matthew 12. 22–32**
    The exorcism of the blind mute—the completeness of the cure is stressed

22 by the detail that both speech and sight were restored—raised the question in people's minds: Can this Jesus be the expected Messiah? It was popularly believed that God would inaugurate a new age by means of a divinely appointed person, an Anointed One, who would be David's

23 successor—that is the meaning of Son of David—as leader of the nation. Some believed that this Messiah was already among them and would reveal his identity when the appropriate moment came. This was a hope on which the fanatical opponents of the Roman regime flourished.

But the Pharisees made the accusation that Jesus could only control demons in other people because he was himself possessed by Satan. The

24 meaning of Beelzebub is uncertain: it is usually interpreted 'lord of flies' or 'lord of dung', but it may mean 'lord of the dwelling', a more suitable derivation in the light of verses 25 and 29, which would then contain a play on the meaning of the word. In this saying Beelzebub is identified with Satan or one of his vassals.

Our Lord in replying exposed the fallacy of the Pharisees' accusation: If it is Satan who casts out Satan, Satan is divided against himself; how then can his kingdom stand? The casting out of the demon was

an assault on Satan's kingdom; he would hardly drive out one of his own
27 vassals. **And if it is by Beelzebub that I cast out devils, by whom do
your own people drive them out?** The Jews had their own exorcists
(presumably like the sons of Sceva, the chief priest at Ephesus, Acts
19.13ff). Would they say that their own men drove out devils through the
power of Satan? This leads Christ to speak of the real source of his
28 authority: **If it is by the Spirit of God that I drive out devils, then be
sure the kingdom of God has already come upon you.**

In Luke's version of the saying (Luke 11.20) Christ uses the phrase,
'the finger of God'. This associated his power with Moses. When the
plague of maggots appeared in Egypt as a result of Moses' striking the
dust with his staff, Pharaoh's magicians attributed the wonder to 'the
finger of God' (Exod. 8.19). Furthermore, the words on the tablets of
stone on mount Sinai were written with the finger of God. God was able
to perform the greatest works with what in human terms would be the
smallest possible effort—the touch of a finger.

The binding of the strong man—a phrase used among the early
Fathers to describe the overpowering of the devil—is, then, only possible
29 by the Spirit of God. In describing a **strong man's house** Christ may
have imagined a local prince, such as one of the sons of Herod; many of
their palaces were heavily fortified against insurgents or raiders.

30   **He who is not with me is against me, and he who does not gather
with me scatters.** There is no neutrality in the warfare against the
incursions of evil. One is either for God or against him. To sit still and do
nothing is to promote the cause of Beelzebub.

31   The passage goes on to include the warning that **slander spoken
against the Spirit,** the ultimate refusal to recognize the manifest work
of God, is unforgivable. The gravest aspect of the incident, from Jesus'
point of view, was the spiritual condition which his opponents' accusation
revealed: they were unable to seek the forgiveness of God because they
saw no need for forgiveness. The deliberate misrepresentation of a good
deed, performed in the power of the Holy Spirit, is the work of the devil.
By their charge the Pharisees have condemned themselves, not Jesus.

The distinction between speaking **against the Son of Man** and
32 speaking **against the Holy Spirit** is not easy to understand. Its most
probable meaning is that during the ministry of Jesus (as 'Son of man')
it was understandable and excusable not to recognize Jesus as the Messiah,
but after Pentecost the ultimate rejection of the recognized and understandable work of the Holy Spirit places a man outside the scope of God's
grace.

LENT 3
Fourth Sunday before Easter

Genesis 22. 1–13   See Second Sunday before Christmas Year 2

Colossians 1. 24–end
This passage contains one of the most daring of Paul's assertions—
namely, that in his own body he is 'making up all that has still to be
undergone by Christ for the sake of his body, the Church' (JB). It is daring
because the NT is clear that Christ suffered once and for all and that his
self-surrender was unique and complete, the fountainhead of all reconciliation and a free gift to us that cannot be earned.

Yet Christians have to suffer in this world, in varying and often, it
appears, in unfair degrees. What Paul did, by his profound insight into
the nature of Christ's union with his people in the Church, was to realize
that what we suffer in this world is a means of being united with Christ
in his suffering. Baptism is a once-for-all sacramental participation in the
death and resurrection of Christ. If we are risen with Christ (3.1), we live
a life transformed by the power of Christ's saving acts. This does not
protect us from the ravages of life which afflict us; yet because Christ
triumphed over the suffering and death with which he was afflicted, we
too shall triumph over them. The things we suffer can, in a sense, be the
means by which the Body of Christ fulfils her part in Jesus' saving acts.
This is creative suffering, suffering accepted to effect an ultimate good.

24   Paul did not usually speak of **his** (Christ's) **body which is the church**
in a universal sense. Nor was it usual for him to designate the Church as
Christ's body; it is *Christians* who are the body of Christ in the Pauline
letters. Here, then, is something more than a mere metaphor. **His body
which is the church** expresses the solidarity which Christians have with
Christ and with one another. Paul saw himself as the Church's servant
(*diakonos*, 'a minister') for the benefit of the Colossian Christians; his
task (*oikonomian*, 'a stewardship', a household word) was the 'mystery'
(RSV) of God's secret purpose, now divulged to his people. Its content
27   was **Christ in you, the hope of glory to come**, so that the character of
Jesus is reproduced in believers through the Holy Spirit individually
and corporately to manifest Christ present **among** them (NEB footnote).
The thing had happened which it was impossible for most Jews ever to
conceive: the Gentiles have a Messiah! Paul's purpose was that they should
grow in Christ. This they would never do if they followed the false

teaching which he has had to combat among them; they would only mature if they grasped the wisdom of God in which he had instructed them. The favourite image of the athlete appears in the final sentence as Paul described how he toiled in the power of Christ to this end.

* Luke 9. 18–27

Jesus' first direct instruction about his destiny is set in the context of prayer. He was praying before he asked his disciples whom they thought
19 he was. **Some say John the Baptist, others Elijah . . .**; the various answers revealed, among other things, that there was some substance to Herod's fear that Jesus would continue the Baptist's movement. It was
20 Peter who confessed Jesus to be **God's Messiah.** The charge not to divulge this to anyone has the atmosphere of the messianic secret—the identity of God's Anointed One in Jewish expectation was known only to God until he chose to reveal him—but it is probably due to the practical fact that Jesus did not at that time wish to be known. To be hailed as a Messiah of that kind would involve political complications which might prevent the proclamation of the gospel.
22   **The Son of man has to undergo great sufferings.** The title in the synoptic Gospels is confined to Jesus' own utterances; it seems to have been the name by which he chose to designate himself, in contrast to his hesitation in accepting the name of Messiah. And he used it here to show that the Jewish concept of messiahship must undergo a radical change before it could be applied to him. His rejection and death was not what the Messiah was supposed to undergo. The association of the idea of the suffering Servant of God with the Anointed one was one that was made by Jesus himself.
23   Some commentators have suggested that the expression, **he must take up his cross,** belongs to the post-resurrection era, since it could hardly have had the meaning of total self-denial before Christ's own crucifixion. Death by nailing to a cross was the Roman method of dealing with rebels. If Jesus had used these words to his disciples, they would probably have misunderstood him as meaning that they must risk their lives in acts of open rebellion against the Roman occupation forces. Whether this is correct or not, Christ's invitation has a vital spiritual application. The Christian disciple is called to die daily to himself and to live in the risen
26 Lord. A man's response determines his fate before the **Son of Man** on the last day. The original Christian conception of the coming judgement is one which included God active within it and in which he would send his angels to gather his elect from the four corners of the world. It was

founded on God's promise to gather his own together (Zech. 2.6 LXX).
The Son of Man is an addition to this scene and is associated with it
in later Jewish apocalyptic. Compared with the other synoptic writers,
Luke slightly modifies the massive drama of the scene in a few words.

27   I tell you this: there are some of those standing here who will
not taste of death before they have seen the kingdom of God also
causes commentators difficulties. It could mean that Jesus, within the
limitations of his human knowledge, expected the establishment of the
Kingdom in the near future. Or it could mean that Jesus foretold that
some would see the power of the Kingdom in the resurrection, the
ascension, the gift of the Spirit, and the mission of the Church.

LENT 3
Fourth Sunday before Easter

Genesis 12. 1–9
The beginning of the saga of Abraham, son of Terah, from southern
Mesopotamia. It is a saga which was important to the Jews, but it was
even more important to the Christian Church, as we shall see when we
examine today's epistle.

Although Abraham is probably a historical figure—his character comes
over strongly in the stories about him—it is difficult to fit him in with the
ancient history of Babylon. Probably he was one of those who revolted
against contemporary polytheism and sought a new home where he could
worship his God in peace. The main feature of Abraham's life is that
he was willing to answer God's call and to believe in God's promise
5 about the future, and to set out with his childless wife, Sarah, and all
the dependants they had acquired in Harran, together with Lot,
for the unknown land. It was this act of faith which led to the raising
up by God of a people of faith, the nation of God's choice through
Abraham.

'Abram' and 'Abraham' were two forms of the same name, the difference
being due to varying dialects. The name meant 'High Father' or 'He is
great because of his noble descent'. But because of its similarity with the
Heb. ab haman, it was interpreted as 'Father of a multitude' or 'Father
of a host of nations' (Gen. 17.5 NEB footnote).

3   The formula, **All the families on earth will pray to be blessed as you are blessed,** is repeated four times in the Book of Genesis and in the NT. Another translation is, 'The nations shall say to each other: may you be blessed as Abraham was', but in the LXX and NT this becomes, 'In you all the nations shall be blessed'.

Two background features are worthy of note. The first is that to leave home and to break ancestral bonds was to expect of ancient men almost the impossible. The attachment to one's family district in a largely static society was exceptionally strong, and one moved only in drastic circumstances, such as famine or warfare. The second is that although the story tells an actual fact about Israel's beginnings, it is doubtful whether the narrator's interest here and in what follows is solely in the representation of past events. In this call Israel saw not only an event in her earliest history, but also a basic characteristic of her life under God. Taken from the community of nations and never really rooted in Canaan (she considered herself even there a stranger, Lev. 25.23, Ps. 39.12), Israel saw herself being led on a special road whose plan and goal were in the Lord's hand. God's people are always a pilgrim people.

1 Peter 2. 19–end

This passage on the sufferings of Christ arose out of the author's admonition to Christian slaves who found themselves unjustly punished by their masters—a situation that was not uncommon in the ancient world, where a slave was regarded as the personal possession of his master and subject
20 to his changing whims. The admonition, **What credit is there in fortitude when you have done wrong and are beaten for it?** is akin to Christ's own saying, 'If you love only those who love you, what credit is that to you? Even sinners love those who love them. . . . But you must love your enemies. . . .' (Luke 6.32–35). There is nothing extraordinary in bearing patiently a punishment which one deserves—many would boast about the toughness with which they endured it! But to bear undeserved suffering patiently, that is extraordinary conduct and characteristic of a Christian.

The author then moved on to Christ's passion as an example. Christ himself, though innocent, suffered treatment that was totally unjust, and the vocation of a Christian is to imitate him in this—a theme which runs strongly through the NT (1 Thess. 1.6, 'You . . . followed the example set by us and by the Lord', is perhaps one of the earliest expressions of it). He seems to have used a liturgical or credal text—perhaps a hymn— as a means of elaborating his meditation on the passion of Christ, adding a few of his own words to it as a means of applying it to the people he is writing to. This citation is discernible in verses 21–25 in the short rhythmic phrases which are based on quotations or references to the fourth Servant Song, Isa. 52.13–53.12—another NT theme. The slaves were reminded that their Lord Christ, who had been no less blameless than they were, suffered unjustly as the prophet had foretold. If they were 23 tempted to protest their innocence, they were to remember his silence. **He did not retort with abuse . . . but committed his cause to the One who judges justly**: he preferred to leave the vindication of his righteousness to God the Father rather than to take action himself against his enemies.

24   Commentators are not agreed on the exegesis of **he carried our sins to the gibbet**: 'gibbet' translates an archaic Greek word, *xulon*, which literally means 'wood' and was used of a cross. It was therefore associated with the punishment of malefactors. If the preposition 'to' is retained, then the cross becomes an altar on which Christ made the sacrifice for our sins (though there is no other parallel of the cross being considered as an altar in this particular sense in the NT); but if the preposition 'on' (NEB footnote) is read, then Christ becomes the sacrificial scapegoat on whom the high priest laid the sins of the people in the ritual of the Day of Atonement (though the scapegoat was not slaughtered but driven into the desert). But generally what the verses do is to draw together various ideas from the sacrificial system of the OT to teach that, as in the Servant Song, 'bearing sins' means taking the blame for sins, accepting the 24 punishment due for them, and so achieving their putting away. **In his own person** is literally 'in his body': what Christ did he did as man, sharing our human nature. His sufferings and death were vicarious; as our representative, he endured the penalties which our sins merited.

The purpose of his death was that we might abandon sin; his saving act challenges us to renew our lives in righteousness. So by his 'bruise' (NEB's **wounds** obscures the implication that Christ's wounds were more terrible than the bruise a slave might receive when he was ill-treated) we are healed—restored to health from the hurt that our sins have inflicted on us.

The picture of God shepherding his people is found in all parts of the OT, just as the metaphor of scattered or shepherdless sheep is regularly applied to Israel when misguided, discomfited, or leaderless. In the prophets the image of the shepherd begins to take on a messianic character (Ezek. 34.22–23: 'I will save my flock, and they shall be ravaged no more; I will judge between one sheep and another. Then I will set over them one

shepherd to take care of them, my servant David; he shall care for them
and become their shepherd.') This title passes to Jesus Christ in the NT,
though not directly, only by implication, in the Gospels. It was a favourite
subject in early Christian art in the paintings in the Roman catacombs,
25 mosaics and sculptures. Christ's function as **Shepherd** includes ruling,
so he is **Guardian** of his people. The noun *episkopos*, 'guardian', became
the technical name for the Church's chief minister, the bishop, and it was
already in use as such in some of Paul's communities. But here it has no
ecclesiastical overtones; it retains its original connotation, 'one who in-
spects, watches over, protects'. **Souls** means 'yourselves'.

* **Matthew 16. 13–end**
In the fourth Gospel the disciples knew from the beginning that Jesus
was the Son of God and the Christ (John 1.34,41), but in the synoptic
Gospels Peter's confession of faith was the turning-point. It opened the
way to Christ's teaching about the nature of his messiahship; it led into
the prediction of the cross; it was the basis on which instruction about the
Christian community was given.

Caesarea Philippi was twenty miles north of the Sea of Galilee in a
13 pagan (non-Jewish) district. Asked by Jesus, **Who do men say that the
Son of man is?** the disciples reply that Jesus was identified with the
prophets, John the Baptist restored to life, Elijah who was expected to
return before the final day of judgement, or Jeremiah. But when asked,
15 **Who do you say that I am?** it was Simon Peter (given his two names to
mark the solemnity of the occasion) who answered: **You are the Messiah, the Son of the Living God.** 'Son of the living God' is only in
Matthew and is thought to be a later addition. The title marks Jesus'
unique nature and filial relation to the Father, demonstrating that his
messiahship was something far greater than and radically different from
Jewish expectation.

Israel had not responded to Jesus' proclamation of the Kingdom of
God, but Peter's confession revealed that the disciples were beginning to
form that core which Christ needed for the carrying forward of the gospel
after his death, resurrection, and ascension; and so Peter's act of faith
was the foundation on which the Church could be built. It gave Peter a
place of distinction among the band of disciples: his name proclaimed his
18 office, he was *Petros* (Greek), *Cephas* (Aramaic), **the Rock.** The congregation (here and in Matt. 18.17 called *ekklesia* a 'church') within Israel
would not be conquered by the power of death; Christ gave the keys, a
figurative expression denoting the trust put in a steward by a master of

the house, to the apostles to exercise authority within the Church.
19 'Bind' and 'loose', translated in the NEB as **forbid** and **allow**, are rabbinic
terms for disciplinary procedures in being bound (sentenced) to excom-
munication and in being loosed (absolved) from it. The injunction to
secrecy was common sense. Until Jesus could establish by teaching and
suffering what it meant to be the anointed one, and what this meant for
the faith and life of his disciples, to tell people that he was the Messiah
would arouse false hopes among nationalist Jews and cause trouble.
21   **From that time** indicates the turning-point we have just mentioned.
Jesus had been proclaiming the Kingdom of heaven to the people. Now
he began to prepare his disciples for what they would see him undergo on
the cross in terms of the suffering Servant of God from the Second Isaiah.
But he also prophesied his resurrection. This prediction of the passion
and resurrection of Christ in compact phrases suggests that they became
the summary of the apostolic Church's message; they occur three times
in this gospel (16.21, 17.22f, 20.18f). Peter's reaction was that of a Jew
caught up in the more conventional kind of messianic expectation in
which it was unthinkable that the Christ should suffer. The intensity of
23 Jesus' reply, **Away with you, Satan,** indicates the courage it took to face
death. Peter momentarily played the devil's role, placing **a stumbling-
block** of disobedience in front of Christ.
     Jesus invited his followers to be ready for self-sacrifice, even to death.
25 **Whoever cares for his own safety is lost; but if a man will let
himself be lost for my sake, he will find his true self.** This is the
death and resurrection as it applies to the Christian. Using the apocalyptic
vision of the coming of the Son of Man from Daniel 10, Christ then applied
the advent of that mysterious figure both to the final judgement and to the
28 saving events which **some of those standing here** would see—the
resurrection, the ascension, the gift of the Spirit, the mission of the
Church.

LENT 4
Third Sunday before Easter

Exodus 34. 29–end
Behind the narratives of the transfiguration of Christ in the Gospels is a

conscious parallelism with the theophany on mount Sinai when Moses
received the covenant from God. Part of the story of this theophany forms
the OT reading for today. Aaron and the people saw Moses coming down
from the mountain with the two tablets on which the words of the coven-
29 ant had been written, and **the skin of his face shone** because he had been
talking with God. The miracle of this encounter, as far as Jewish theology
was concerned, was that Moses had been able to see God and speak to
him without perishing in the process, for it was thought that the glory of
God was such that no man could see God and live. The Hebrew word 'to
radiate', *qaran*, is derived from *qeren*, a horn, and this gave rise in later
art forms to a depicting of Moses with horns to simulate the glory of God
shining from his face. The radiation frightened the people, so Moses had
to put a veil or a priest's mask over his face. The task of Moses in speaking
with God and conveying the divine commands to the people expresses
exactly the offices of priest and prophet, both of which merge in the life
of the great patriarch.

Verses 29–33 and 34–35 belong to separate Priestly traditions. The
latter is part of the story of Moses' going into the tent of meeting to
commune with God, but it has been transferred to the encounter on
Sinai.

The Exodus story also describes the tabernacle and the tent which
sheltered it. The divine presence, the *shekinah*, descended as a pillar of
cloud upon this tent, and Moses spoke with God there. It is probable that
the story was influenced by the Jewish traditions surrounding the celebration of the feast of Tabernacles, the last of the three great annual pilgrimage festivals—the other two being Passover and Pentecost. The feast
of Tabernacles arose out of the custom of erecting tents in the vineyards at
harvest-time in order that the work of gathering the fruit could be
continued from dawn to dusk without interruption. The law was cere-
monially read aloud by the Levitical priesthood to the people during these
celebrations (Deut. 31.9–13). Later, the giving of the law on mount Sinai
was associated with the feast of Pentecost, but its connection with the
feast of Tabernacles was never wholly lost. The erection of tents in the
vineyards and the gathering in of the harvest prompted Jews to look
forward to the end of time, when they would be encamped with the Lord
for ever, surrounded by the fruits of his goodness. Then God would be
enthroned as ruler of all his people (Isa. 32.15–18, Ezek. 47.12, Hos.
12.9–10, etc.).

2 Corinthians 3. 4–end

Paul's critics at Corinth challenged his authority. By what right did he claim to be an apostle? Where were his credentials (3.1)? In reply, Paul pointed out that the very existence of the Corinthian Church was proof of the authenticity of his apostleship. His readers would not have responded to the gospel he preached if God had not called them. They were themselves, therefore, like a visible 'letter of introduction' written by the Holy Spirit. At this point—and it is where our passage begins—the apostle's mind followed the imagery on a related subject and said that the Spirit's work was fulfilling a prophecy that under the new covenant God's law would be written in men's hearts. He quoted two illustrations.

The first of these is that of the law, 'written not with ink but with the Spirit of the living God, written not on stone tablets but on the pages of the human heart' (verse 3 comes just before our passage, but it is taken up again in verse 6). Behind this sentence are the words of Jeremiah about God writing his law in the inward parts of his people (Jer. 31.33) and those of Ezekiel about God giving his people hearts of flesh instead of hearts of stone (Ezek. 11.19). These concepts are contrasted with the law of Moses inscribed on tablets of stone (Exod. 31.18). The apostle could write with complete confidence because his 'qualification' was found not
6 in himself but in God: **it is he who has qualified us to dispense his new covenant—a covenant expressed not in a written document, but in a spiritual bond.** This was what made Paul a minister of the new covenant which, being in the Spirit and not in a document, gives life instead of death.

For his second illustration Paul turned to the story in Exod. 34.29–35, which described how Moses had to put a veil over his face after he had been communing with God because, when he came near to the people of Israel, the divine glory was reflected in it. Moses was a foreshadowing, or a type, of Christ. Just as the Israelites saw the glory of God reflected in Moses' face, so Christians possessing the Holy Spirit see the divine glory reflected in Jesus Christ. But how much greater is the glory of the new covenant, since it works for the salvation of man instead of his condemna-
11 tion, as the old dispensation did. **For if that which was soon to fade had its moment of splendour, how much greater is the splendour of that which endures!** There is no need for the Christian to hide from
12 that splendour, as Moses had to by putting a veil over his face. **With such a hope as this we speak out boldly.**

With the reference to the veil, Paul's thought switched to the Jews of

his time and he saw their lack of response to the gospel as the result of
14 another kind of veil being dropped over their minds. **When the lesson is read from the old covenant** (he was referring to the reading of the OT in the synagogue services) they failed to recognize that the old covenant with its binding law had been abrogated in Christ. Quoting Isa. 61.1–2, he reminded the readers of his letter that it is in repentance that this kind of blockage is removed. It is possible that Paul believed that wherever the OT referred to 'Lord' it meant Christ and that it was Christ whom Moses encountered in the tent of meeting. But Christ is the Spirit—the apostle does not seem to distinguish between the two here—and the Spirit gives the true interpretation of the OT.

18 **We all reflect as in a mirror the splendour of the Lord; thus we are transfigured into his likeness, from splendour to splendour.** Because Christians have the Spirit they can, unlike the Jews, behold the glory of God, and they reflect that glory as a mirror reflects the sunlight. Consequently, they are themselves changed by their beholding.

* **Luke 9. 28–36**
The gospel continues last Sunday's reading.
For a general discussion of the meaning of the transfiguration, see pp. 187–8.

28 The differences in Luke's account are as follows: Luke has **about eight days** after the previous discourse, while Mark and Matthew have six days.

The order of the names of the second and third disciples are changed round so that Peter and John come together, as in the early chapters of Acts.

29 **The appearance of his face changed and his clothes became dazzling white.** Luke avoided using the verb 'transfigured' (Greek *metemorphothe* Mark 9.2), perhaps because for his Hellenistic readers it might have had associations with pagan cults.

30 He described Moses and Elijah as **two men** before mentioning their names, thus enabling him to link the two witnesses with the two men at the resurrection (24.4) and the ascension (Acts 1.10).

31 **Moses and Elijah spoke of Jesus' departure, the destiny he was to fulfil in Jerusalem.** *Exodus* means 'departure' but is also a euphemism for 'death'. Furthermore, Luke must have had in mind the exodus which Moses had led from Egypt and during which he had died. The transfiguration thus pointed forward to the paschal death and resurrection of Christ.

32   The disciples **had been in a deep sleep**, following the Biblical tradition of sleep before a vision.

33   Peter's suggestion about making **three shelters** is rationalized by the explanation that the figures were moving away.

34   The disciples **were afraid as they entered the cloud**, Luke suggesting that their awe was due, not to the enveloping of the cloud, but to consciousness of the divine presence.

35   Luke added **my Chosen** to identify Jesus more clearly as the new Moses of God, from Ps. 106.23, 'Moses his chosen'.

LENT 4
Third Sunday before Easter

Exodus 3. 1–6
Moses, driven out of Egypt for championing his own race, was reduced from being a royal prince to a wandering shepherd. The passage tells of the call of Moses just before he was given his apostolic commission by God, thus beginning the great saga of the Exodus (see Sixth Sunday before Christmas Year 1).

At the beginning of the summer, when the grass on the lower slopes begins to burn up, the Bedouin go up the mountain slopes. The location of Horeb is uncertain; it was probably one of the peaks in the Sinai group in the Arabian peninsula. Mountains were regarded in ancient times as dwelling-places for the gods, and throughout the OT and NT a mountain was a favourite rendezvous for an encounter with God.

2   **The angel of the Lord appeared to him in the flame of a burning bush.** Yahweh revealed himself as an angel in the midst of the fire. The theophany was described in this way because it was believed that God's majesty was so glorious that no man could gaze directly at him and live.

5   **Take off your sandals**—the removal of the shoes is still a mark of respect for sacred ground among Muslims.

6   **I am the God of your forefathers, the God of Abraham, the God of Isaac, the God of Jacob.** The announcement establishes the fact that there is a continuity in God's dealings with his people. God was still faithful to the covenant that he had made with Abraham, and his people would yet again experience his saving power.

2 Peter 1. 16–19

This passage represents the main part of 2 Peter, claiming that the apostolic teaching is firmly founded on a historical revelation which in itself confirms what earlier prophecy had foretold. The author, a Jewish Christian familiar with Hellenistic cults, represented himself as the apostle Simon Peter and appealed to the experience of the transfiguration in support of his case.

16 The **tales artfully spun** were the legendary stories about the gods current in Hellenistic mythology. Christianity is based not on similar mythology but on truths which are supported by tangible and objective evidence. **The power of Jesus** is the divine might which he possessed as risen Lord; **his coming** is the appearance at the transfiguration which, for this writer, looked forward to the final advent of the Son of God at the end of the world. (*Parousia* was a word taken from Hellenistic cults to describe the epiphany of the gods; it entered Christian vocabulary via

16 Hellenistic Judaism.) Behind the phrase **we saw him with our own eyes in majesty** are two words (*epoptes*, eye-witnesses; *megaleiotes*, majesty) also from Hellenist cults: the former denoted those initiated into sacred mysteries; the second the revelation of divine power. On the other hand, the writer showed a typical Hebrew reserve about using the

17 divine name and referred to **the sublime Presence**; the synoptic Gospels, we note, make no mention of God in their accounts of the transfiguration and represent the voice as coming from the cloud. **This is my Son, my Beloved, on whom my favour rests** has been affected in the manuscripts by parallels in the Gospels. (See NEB footnote.) It

17 comes close to Matthew's version, but differs from it by adding **on**
18 **whom my favour rests**. The mount of transfiguration is now **the sacred mountain**, a specific spot hallowed by the religious memory of the Church.

The transfiguration disclosed Christ's divine nature and ratified it by the heavenly voice, confirming his power and future coming. The writer

19 saw it as confirming also **the message of the prophets**, meaning here not just the prophetic books but the whole of the OT, which he assumed looked forward to the glorious coming of the Messiah and his subsequent establishment of his Kingdom. 'God's word', he said, is truly 'a lantern unto my feet, and a light unto my path' (Ps. 119.105), and Christ is the morning star (Num. 24.17), illuminating men's minds, until the day of the Lord comes.

* **Matthew 17. 1–13**

The transfiguration is one of the events in the Gospel which reveals Jesus as the Messiah of God and the bringer of salvation. Moses and Elijah, representing the law and the prophets, stand by him as witness to the truth that in Christ the promises of God made in the OT have been fulfilled. The details of the event recall the apocalyptic vision of a man clothed in white linen which Daniel received after keeping a fast for three weeks (in the Bible a fast is, among other things, a means by which men prepare themselves to receive a revelation from God). 'The wise leaders shall shine like the bright vault of heaven, and those who have guided the people in the true path shall be like stars for ever and ever' (Dan. 10.5, 12.3). The whiteness of the garments, the charge to keep the messianic secret, the conversation with Moses and Elijah (one dead, the other ascended into heaven), the metamorphosis of Christ (*metamorphomai*, 'to be transformed'): all these emphasize the eschatological nature of the event. For a moment, eternal reality had broken through into the present order.

1 **Six days later Jesus took Peter, James, and John the brother of James, and led them up a high mountain.** The detail of the time after the confession of Peter at Caesarea Philippi is unusual. It may be a historical reminiscence, or it may be due to Exod. 24.16–18. 'The glory of the Lord rested upon Mount Sinai, and the cloud covered the mountain for six days; and on the seventh day he called to Moses out of the cloud. The glory of the Lord looked to the Israelites like a devouring fire on the mountain-top. Moses entered the cloud and went up the mountain; there he stayed forty days and forty nights.' The feast of Tabernacles lasted seven days. Peter, James, and John also shared the agony in the garden with Christ (26.37). The mountain is the place where God traditionally reveals himself to men in the OT (Elijah as well as Moses, 1 Kings 19.1–12, see Fifth Sunday before Christmas Year 1).

4 **If you wish, I will make three shelters here, one for you, one for Moses, one for Elijah.** Peter's offer could mean that he wanted to make permanent a vision which could only be temporary, the purpose of all shrines. Or it could be a distant echo of the celebrations of the feast of Tabernacles, where the tents were erected for harvesting and where it was believed God would come and 'tabernacle' with his people (*skene*, a 'tent' or 'tabernacle').

5 **A voice called from the cloud, 'This is my Son, my Beloved, on whom my favour rests; listen to him'.** The cloud is a sign of the divine presence, the *shekinah*, in the story of the Exodus, and it was from

it that God spoke at the transfiguration. The voice was heard on two other occasions, at the baptism (3.17) and at the beginning of the passion (John 12.28, see Lent 5 Year 1). Like the baptism, the transfiguration was an epiphany in which the veil which separates the invisible from the visible and the future from the present is removed for a moment and the truth revealed. The voice may have been quoting Deut. 18.15, 'The Lord your God will raise up a prophet from among you like myself (Moses), and you shall listen to him'. The disciples fall on their faces as Daniel had done before the vision of the heavenly man and, also like Daniel, they were touched by Jesus who told them to stand up.

The parallelism between mount Sinai and the transfiguration is underlined more strongly by Matthew than the other evangelists. Only Matthew
2 notes that Christ's face, like the face of Moses, **shone like the sun**, a detail used by Paul immediately before today's epistle (2 Cor. 3.7), and only Matthew adds the phrase from Isa. 42.1, **on whom my favour rests, thus linking the event with the song of the Servant of God. For** this writer, Jesus Christ is the second Moses, the Servant of God who through obedience and suffering was able to offer himself for the salvation of man. It is these implications, together with the rich eschatological content of the narrative, which have led some commentators to believe that behind this story is the memory of one of the resurrection appearances of our Lord.

Further details indicate that Matthew was presenting Jesus as the new
10 Moses. The scene is followed by a question about Elijah: **Why then do our teachers say that Elijah must come first?** The teachers are the doctors of the law whose traditional interpretation of Mal. 4.5, 'I will send you the prophet Elijah before the great and terrible day of the Lord comes', had been to give Elijah a mighty role as the one who would
11 **come and set everything right.** Jesus' reply was that Elijah had already come. John the Baptist had fulfilled Elijah's task; so the implication is
12 that he (Jesus) was to fulfil Moses'. **The Son of Man is to suffer at their hands,** a prophecy that his own fate would be the same as John's as well.

LENT 5
Second Sunday before Easter

Exodus 6. 2–13 See Sixth Sunday before Christmas Year 2
But when Moses repeated God's words to the people, they refused to hear because of their lack of faith and difficult conditions. From the beginning their failure to respond to God's spokesmen jeopardized Israel's future.

Colossians 2. 8–15
In early Christian history the Colossian Church had a reputation for dabbling in wild theological speculations—a reputation which it acquired from its foundations, judging by Paul's letter. Its members mixed mythical ideas with beliefs about the angelic powers who were supposed to
8 control the universe. **Elemental spirits,** *stoicheia*, could mean simple forms of doctrine (**elementary ideas,** NEB footnote). It was against such deviations from Christian teaching that Paul uttered the warning in this passage.

He began by asserting the divinity of Christ in the sense that God's power is fully integrated in him and not dissipated over other spiritual
9 beings. **It is in Christ that the complete being of the Godhead dwells embodied.** This has an incarnational meaning, but it also has the sense of 'dwelling in the body of Christ, the Church' (**corporately,** NEB footnote). One sense leads to another in Paul's theology, and the double reference could explain the use of the present tense in the verb 'dwells', as in 1 Cor. 15.12ff. Every power and authority in the universe is subject to Christ as Head, even the elemental spirits of the world.

11   **In him also you were circumcised, not in a physical sense, but by being divested of the lower nature; this is Christ's way of circumcision.** Paul saw the act of circumcision as a tiny analogy of the crucifixion; as the body of a Jewish baby boy was offered for the surgical act in obedience to the law, so the human body of Christ was offered for the sacrificial act of crucifixion in obedience to the will of God. This perfect obedience was the climax and implementation of Christ's own baptism in the Jordan and led, through Calvary and death, to resurrection and life. The passion of Christ, commemorated on this Passion Sunday, is a consequence of this 'circumcision'.

Through baptism each Christian is brought into this 'circumcision'.

Earlier in this epistle Paul had spoken of this union in terms of Christ as
the Head and the Church as his body (1.18) and of his own sufferings as
a share in the sufferings of Christ (1.24). Now he underlined the way in
which the Colossian Christians were joined to Christ, not through bap-
12 tism as a mechanical ritual act, but **through faith in the active power
of God, who raised (Jesus) from the dead** and who appointed baptism as the sacramental sign by which men and women in penitence and
faith are united with Christ.

The 'deadness' of the Colossians was evident in two ways: first, they
13 were **morally uncircumcised** in that they were outside the covenant of
Israel; and, secondly, they were in the grip of their sins. It was only in
Christ that, in spite of this, they were now part of the true Israel of God.
14 **For Christ has cancelled the bond which pledged us to the decrees
of the law.** The image is that of an I.O.U., an undertaking to obey the
law of God imposed by a man's conscience. The law, disobeyed by man,
stands as his accuser to God. This incriminating document Christ has
destroyed by letting himself be nailed to the cross (did Paul know of the
notice put on the cross proclaiming Jesus as King of the Jews?).

The passage ends with a picture of Christ, like a triumphant warrior,
leading in a victory procession the hostile powers of the spiritual universe
as a parade of the captives—a common feature of parades in the ancient
world which marked the successful conclusion of a campaign.

* John 12. 20–32

After the entry into Jerusalem (12.2-19) a group of Greeks who went up
to worship at the festival approached Philip, presumably because they
thought that, being the disciple with a Greek name and a Gentile background, they could count on his sympathy. They were Gentiles who were
sufficiently attracted to the religion of Israel to attend the synagogues of
the dispersion and to adopt some of the practices of Judaism, including
the making of pilgrimages to the holy city for the feasts. Like the Gentiles
at Colossae to whom Paul wrote, they were seeking Christ but were still
some distance from him. Philip went to tell his fellow-townsman Andrew,
and they both went to Jesus.

We hear no more of these Greeks, for at that moment John inserted
23 into his Gospel Jesus' declaration, **The hour has come for the Son of
Man to be glorified.** Hitherto in this Gospel Christ had said that his
hour had not yet come. Perhaps the homage of the Greeks foreshadowed
the worldwide homage that was to be given to our Lord, and this was a
sign that the climax of his ministry was at hand. He explained the mean-

ing of his passion and death in terms of a grain of wheat which, falling into the ground and dying, bears a rich harvest of new life. The disciples
25 had to learn that the way to life is through renunciation: **the man who loves himself is lost, but he who hates himself in this world will be kept safe for eternal life.** It is the Johannine parallel to Mark 8.34, 'Anyone who wishes to be a follower of mine must leave self behind; he must take up his cross and come with me'; except that in the fourth Gospel there is a further saying that the disciple who shares in Christ's suffering will also share in the honour which the Father gives him.

There is no agony in the garden in John. In its place comes the incident in verses 27–32. Christ wondered whether to ask that the cup of suffering
27 might be taken from him, **Father, save me from this hour**; but no sooner had the thought entered his mind than he banished it with a fresh surrender of his will to the Father ('Not what I will, but what thou wilt', Mark 14.36). Instead, he glorified God and experienced a theophany,
28 **a voice sounded from heaven: 'I have glorified it, and I will glorify it again.'** (This is the third time the Father addresses the Son from heaven; the first time was at the baptism, the second at the transfiguration.) God had already glorified his name through the ministry of Jesus, and he would glorify it again in his death. Thunder is recognized as the voice of God in the OT (Exod. 19.19, Ps. 24.3). The voice spoke, said Jesus, for the benefit of the crowd.
31 Jesus continued his discourse, the repetition of **Now** giving it a certain emphasis, and declared that his death was the moment of crisis for the world (*crisis*, 'judgement') whereby the power of evil would be broken. By rejecting Jesus, men condemn themselves, but by the providence of God this very rejection is made the means of salvation. Though Jesus trod 'the winepress of the wrath and retribution of God' (Rev. 19.15) in the sense that he bore the effect of sin in dying on the cross, yet when he was lifted up, in the glory of the cross and in the ascension, he would draw all men to himself. Behind this saying is the image of the serpent whom Moses lifted up in the wilderness for the healing of the people.

LENT 5
Second Sunday before Eastter

Jeremiah 31. 31–34

As the Jews came to recognize that God demands moral obedience rather than a formal obedience in rituals, they came to see that the performance of a ritual sacrifice was an empty and hypocritical gesture without the proper disposition of the heart in the worshippers. The sacrifices in their various forms—peace offerings, burnt offerings and especially sin and guilt offerings—must express true repentance and obedience in the lives of the people. The sacrifice of bulls which Moses celebrated to inaugurate the covenant between God and his people on mount Sinai was only valid as a ritual if the people kept their promise, 'We will do all that the Lord has told us'. The blood of the covenant was merely a seal on the act of obedience which they had already made (Exod. 24.3ff).

With the failure of the old covenant, Jeremiah was one of the prophets who came to see that what men needed was a new heart and a new spirit before they could be obedient to the law of God. So the prophet looked
31 forward to the time when God would **make a new covenant with Israel and Judah.** In this new covenant the desire to obey him would be set so deeply within their hearts that there would be no question of their
34 wishing to disobey. **All of them, high and low alike, shall know me, says the Lord;** and in this sentence to know the Lord means that they would have a 'knowledge' which is akin to what the Christian means by 'faith'. In these circumstances the new covenant would be superior to the
33 old, for the sins of the people would be forgiven, and **I will become their God and they shall become my people.** Prophecies of this new and eternal covenant appear also in Ezek. 36.25–28 and Isa. 55.3, etc.

Hebrews 9. 11–14

The author interpreted the work of Jesus Christ in terms of the sacrificial ritual of the temple in Jerusalem, which had probably ended by the time this letter was written. In this ritual Christ is high priest. The variants,
11 **high priest of good things already in being,** or **high priest of good things which are to be** (NEB footnote), make the difference between saying that the perfect relationship with God, which is the aim of the Christian life, is wholly an other-worldly experience, and claiming that to some extent at least we are able to enter into that relationship here and now.

11   The tent of his priesthood is a greater and more perfect one; the NEB identifies the 'tent' as the sanctuary within which Christ exercises his high priestly office, namely, the heavenly sanctuary. (JB translates, 'He has passed through the greater, the more perfect tent'.) Made by men's hands was probably a phrase used by Jewish writers in the Hellenistic world to describe idols, and in the NT is used by Jesus and by his followers of the temple at Jerusalem (Mark 14.58, Acts 7.48). Jesus did not offer blood in order to gain access to this heavenly sanctuary;
12   he gained it through the sacrifice of his own blood. Thus he has entered the sanctuary once and for all and secured an eternal deliverance.

But how is Christ's sacrifice effective for all times? Starting with the ritual sacrifices of the old covenant, the author acknowledged that these
13   were partially effective, at least in matters of external purity. The blood of bulls and goats was used in the sacrifices on the Day of Atonement; the sprinkled ashes of a heifer were used for making 'water of impurity' for the cleansing of persons and vessels and clothes ritually polluted by contact with a dead body (Lev. 16.14f., Num. 19).

If these are effective in rituals, he said, how much greater is the
14   power of the blood of Christ; he offered himself without blemish to God, a spiritual and eternal sacrifice. He who in self-sacrifice offered himself to God in his full and perfect humanity, was himself eternal by nature. Because of this, the salvation which he procured for us by his blood is everlasting. As the external sacrifices were effective for ritual cleansing, so the personal self-sacrifice of one who is eternal will cleanse us spiritually and fit us for the service of the living God. The original words suggest a sacred ministry of a liturgical kind, though of course the author sees the whole of a Christian's life embraced within this phrase.

* Mark 10. 32–45
32   The road, going up to Jerusalem, may well have been crowded with pilgrims on their way to celebrate the Passover. Jesus and his disciples were about to enter Jericho, and they would see beyond that town the road ascending up towards the mount of Olives many miles away and nearly four thousand feet higher. In the eyes of this evangelist, Jerusalem was the centre of hostility to Christ and also the goal of his journey. Our Lord was determined to fulfil his work—Luke recorded that he 'set his face resolutely towards Jerusalem' (9.51)—and the disciples seem to have understood something of what was involved, so that

32 **they were filled with awe; while those who followed behind were afraid.**

The third prediction of the passion is more detailed than the previous two (8.31, 9.31). Some have said that it was a piece of the Church's 33– teaching after the event: **The Son of Man will be given up (betrayed)** 34 **. . . condemned . . . handed over to the foreign power . . . mocked, spat upon and flogged . . . killed . . . rise again.** Certainly it reads like the programme of Good Friday and Easter Day. But we need not suppose that Christ, even within the limitations of his humanity, had no idea what his fate might be when he reached the city.

33   The disciples had not understood what the title **Son of Man** meant. Perhaps they still thought in terms of an earthly kingdom, to be established when Jesus reached Jerusalem. It was from this hope that James 37 and John made their request, **to sit in state with you.** They wanted to be Christ's chief courtiers. But Jesus challenged them first about facing 38 suffering, allegorized in terms of a **cup** and a **baptism**. The former was used in the OT as a symbol for suffering and for the stern judgement of God; the latter as a metaphor for being dipped beneath a wave of afflictions. The link with the Eucharist and Christian initiation may well be behind the record of Christ's challenge. Perhaps in the circumstances in which Mark wrote, to accept baptism and become a communicant was to accept the danger that one might be called on to suffer and die for one's faith. The disciples accepted the challenge, but Jesus then told them that 40 **to sit at my right or left is not for me to grant; it is for those to whom it has already been assigned by my Father** (NEB footnote). Later tradition assumed that the two places of honour were not assigned to the brothers because Peter and James 'the Lord's brother' emerged as the leaders of the Church.

43   **Whoever wants to be great must be your servant.** This had already been said (9.35), but had to be repeated when Jesus saw signs of ambition among his followers. He called for humility and self-giving within the Christian community on the pattern of his own life as a servant. 45 For him, that service led to the surrender of his life **as a ransom for many.** God had ransomed his people in OT times—saved them from the effects of their disobedience and sin. The Son of Man in Daniel 7.14 was exalted to a position where he would be served by all peoples. But for Jesus that lay in the future. On his way up to Jerusalem, he knew that his destiny involved suffering; and since he is the representative of his disciples, in all succeeding generations each Christian must learn first to 44 **be the willing slave of all.** The idea of vicarious suffering was current

in contemporary Judaism as a result of the martyrdoms experienced at
the time of the Maccabees some two centuries previously (2 Macc.
7.37–38), and in Isa. 53.12 there is a phrase which suggests that the
Servant of God 'bore the sin of many'.

PALM SUNDAY
The Sunday next before Easter

See pages 9–14

Isaiah 50. 4–9a

Although the third of the songs of the Servant of the Lord is technically
a lament, it breathes entire confidence that prayer will be answered. He
4 had been given **the tongue of a teacher** and other charisms for ministry
among the people of Israel, **the weary**; he had been given an insight
4 into the divine mind as revealed in prophecy and fulfilled in event. And
he did not disobey what God told him to do and to say, even though
obedience entailed suffering. He accepted the consequences of his work
7 in the knowledge that **the Lord God stands by to help me.** It was
in this complete confidence in God that he was enabled to see his suffer-
7 ings as the fulfilment of the divine will. So he could say, **I have set my
face like flint, for I know that I shall not be put to shame, because
one who will clear my name is on my side.** In the thought of Israel
the shame which suffering brought to the sufferer—because it was regarded as a punishment for sin—was almost as hard to bear as the pain
itself.

      This confidence was then expressed by the prophet in terms taken from
8 legal processes. **Who dares argue against me?** . . . The Servant
summoned those who opposed him and persecuted him to stand on trial
with him, for he was convinced that God would justify him and that no
one could condemn him.

Zechariah 9. 9–12

The second part of the book of Zechariah (9.1 to 14.21) consists of a collection of oracles of uncertain date but much later than the earlier part.
It is possible that they come from the Greek period, following the con-

quests of Alexander the Great (336–323 B.C.). This passage is part of a prophecy that the Messiah will come in an even greater conquest than that of Alexander—Aramean, Phoenician, and Philistine cities are mentioned in the first half of the chapter—but he will come in humility, demonstrated by the ass on which he will be riding. (The poetic parallelism in the Hebrew text caused Matthew to understand that there were two animals.)

10   **He shall banish chariots from Ephraim** means that the northern tribes will be reunited with Judah when the messianic kingdom is established. The Messiah's victory is a humble one; his cause is won by the power of God, not by the force of arms. Yet his kingdom will embrace lands greater than the empire of David, **from sea to sea** (Mediterranean to the Dead Sea—or the Arabian Sea?—and **from the River**, the Euphrates, to the far south.) The ancient custom of riding on a donkey was not always significant of humility; it could also be a sign of dignity.

Philippians 2. 5–11   See Pentecost 10 Year 1

1 Corinthians 1. 18–25
The contrast between the mind of God and the mind of man is nowhere demonstrated more vividly than in the teaching (*logos* is translated 'word' RSV, 'doctrine' NEB, 'language' JB) of the cross of Christ, the historic act of Christ's crucifixion and all that stemmed from it. The apostle
18   saw it in terms of the end of man: for **those on their way to ruin** (the present tense suggests that the end of a person may be anticipated by their reactions to the gospel now) the effect is the opposite to these **who are on the way to salvation.** The two ways, going in opposite directions, manifest the contrast between the mind of God and the mind of man. Paul reinforced this by quoting the OT (Isa. 29.44 LXX); the prophet had predicted the overthrowing of the world's wisdom—the wisdom of those who sought the meaning of life in religious-philosophical ideas of a human origin. Salvation, deliverance on the last day, is not gained by gnosticism of this kind; it comes by faith, the 'folly' of accepting the teaching of the cross as presented by Paul and his companions.

The whole passage has a rhetorical polish which suggests that the apostle was using material which he had worked over before. In the traditions of contemporary schools of rhetoric, he asked a series of
19   questions in the style of a diatribe, **Where . . .?** to underline how narrow and foolish, contrasted with the wisdom of God, is the mind of man as exemplified by the wise man, the scholar, the disputant.

Paul was not deprecating human wisdom as such, for he said elsewhere: 'All that may be known of God by men lies plain before their eyes; indeed, God himself has disclosed it to them. His invisible attributes, that is to say his everlasting power and deity, have been visible, ever since the world began, to the eye of reason, in the things he has made' (Rom. 1.19–20). God reveals himself through creation. What Paul was saying is that even with the reason that God had given man when he created him, man did not recognize God. So when God acted to save man, he exposed what the world considers wisdom as the folly it truly is.

Nor did the apostle criticize the Jews for seeking signs or the Gentiles (the word is used in the sense of non-Jews, foreigners in general) for seeking the meaning of life. Jesus Christ performed miracles which pointed to the reality of his mission and explained the meaning of life. What Paul condemned was that attitude which refuses to recognize the way God wants things done. The Jew saw the will of God epitomized in the law; the Greek saw the highest form of wisdom in human speculations; but the wisdom of God is in the proclamation of the cross of Christ—the total salvation event in Christ from the passion to Pentecost—through which divine power flows into the world as never before.

23 The cross was a **stumbling block to Jews** because it was an offence to their understanding of the law of God; it was **folly to Greeks** because, from the human viewpoint, it appeared a senseless waste of a good life. Yet although it was in direct contradiction of human ideas of wisdom and power, it achieved what human wisdom and power could never achieve. It made the gospel more than a theological system; it made it the power of God in the world, so that our proclamation of the good news of salvation in Jesus Christ must be expressed as much by what we are and what we do as by what we say.

* **Mark 14. 1—15. 41**
1 **The festival of Passover and Unleavened Bread** was the junction, long before NT times, of two ancient celebrations. The Passover was a springtime festival at which the slaughter of the lambs within the temple precincts and the eating of them in household groups in homes, lodgings, and tents around the city was understood as a symbolic enactment of the Exodus from Egypt (Exod. 12). The festival of Unleavened Bread, on the other hand, seems to have originated as a kind of New Year celebration, in which old leaven was removed from the house and only leavened bread was eaten for the following week, as a sign of renewal. The preparations were made on the 14th day of the month Nisan, which fell during March

and April in the present calendar. As the Jewish calendar was a lunar one, the date had to be constantly adjusted. On that day all leaven was removed from the house and destroyed. In the afternoon the lambs were slaughtered before the great altar in the temple. After sunset which, according to the Jewish way of reckoning, was the beginning of the next day, i.e. the 15th Nisan, the people assembled in their families or groups of friends to make a solemn meal of the roasted lamb, the meat having been brought from the temple by a member of the family or the group. Since the festival of Unleavened Bread was combined with this meal, unleavened bread and cakes were eaten, and the celebrations continued for one week during which all the bread was prepared without leaven.

There are problems concerning the dating of the events of the passion in the synoptic Gospels and in John. The differences between the Jewish reckoning of a day (from the previous evening) and the Roman one (from midnight to midnight), and the custom of including in any numbering of the days the actual day from which the count was made (so that two days off means Wednesday–Thursday, not Tuesday–Wednesday–Thursday, as we would calculate today), solves some of the problems, but not all of them. Suffice it to say that in 14.1–11 the evangelist is telling us what happened on the Wednesday before the crucifixion, and in 14.12–72 what happened on the Thursday.

3   During these days Jesus was staying **at Bethany, in the house of Simon the leper,** evidently well known in the evangelist's circle, for he made no further attempt to identify him. The **small bottle of very costly perfume, oil of pure nard,** was a long-necked container full of an unguent made from a rare Indian plant much prized in the ancient world. The breaking open of the bottle indicated the woman's extrava-

5 gance. **300 denarii** (NEB footnote) equalled a year's wages for a working man. **The ointment was poured over Jesus' head.** Perhaps the woman was an enthusiast, who hoped that Jesus would rule over the nation, for the anointing of the head was part of the coronation ceremony of a king (1 Kings 1.38–40). Christ's rebuke of those who criticized her was not an expression of indifference to the needs of the poor; he saw that the woman's act was a spontaneous gesture of her sense of the honour due to

8 him. **She is beforehand with anointing my body for burial.** Christ accepted the gesture and made it a prophetic sign. The Messiah ('the anointed one') was to die. There·would be no time to anoint his body after the crucifixion. In the midst of the Jews' rejection of him and their

9 intrigue, there were those who recognized his messiahship. **Wherever in all the world the Gospel is proclaimed, what she has done will be**

told as her memorial. If this is a later addition, as most commentators believe, it is nevertheless true. The anointing at Bethany has become part of the passion narrative.

10   **Judas Iscariot, one of the Twelve, went to the chief priests to betray him to them.** What was Judas' motive? It could hardly have been financial. Was he disillusioned with Jesus when he saw his Master rejecting an earthly messiahship? Was he trying to force God to reveal his purpose in Christ by a miracle? Or was he tricked into believing that the chief priests wanted to protect Jesus from his enemies?

Whether or not the Last Supper was a Passover meal has been debated by scholars for a long time. We have already noted the problems of dating the events of the passion. In the synoptic Gospels the Supper is a Passover celebration, but in the fourth Gospel it is eaten on the day before the Passover. For our purposes, the matter is academic. No one disputes the paschal nature of the Last Supper, set as it is within the festival of the Jews' liberation from slavery (to become for Christians the greater festival of liberation from sin and death).

13   **Two of his disciples** (Peter and John in Luke 22.8) were given a rendezvous with a man carrying a jar of water. Identification would not be difficult, as women rather than men carried jars in the East, though the large stone water-jars were carried by men (John 2.7). Was the room used by Jesus in the house that which belonged to the mother of John Mark (cf. Acts 12.12)? If it was a proper Passover meal the disciples would have had to prepare the lamb, the unleavened bread, bitter herbs, a sauce called *charoseth*, and cups of wine. If it was a *kiddush*—a social-religious gathering of the kind held by groups of pious Jews in preparation for festivals such as the Passover—the preliminaries would have been less elaborate.

Jesus presided over the meal as leader of the group. At the Passover the father of the household was at the head of the table. The ritual involved blessings, wine drunk at four different intervals, explanations over the elements of the meal, and the singing of the Hillel psalms (Pss. 113–118). The unleavened bread symbolized the past misery (the 'bread of affliction'), the bitter herbs symbolized past slavery, and the lamb recalled God's 'passing over' Egypt, and so on. Even if the Last Supper was not a Passover meal, there would be nothing unusual in Jesus' giving explanations of its elements. The room would probably be furnished with rugs and cushions and a low table, at which the guests would recline.

21   **The Son of Man is going the way appointed for him in the**

scriptures. No scriptural text is quoted, but the words are a reminder that God's purpose is behind the tragic events. They are part of 'the deliberate will and plan of God' (Acts 2.23).

The account of the institution of the Eucharist is brief and simple. Interest is focused on its religious significance, not on historical details. Early liturgical traditions in the Church may have preserved and shaped some of the phrases we find in this and in other accounts in the NT

22, (Matt. 22.26–29; Luke 22.17–19; 1 Corinthians 11.23–26). **Take this;**
24 **this is my body. . . . This is my blood, the blood of the covenant, shed for many.** Jesus was soon to leave his disciples and the visible union between them was to be broken until the kingdom of God comes in its fulness. He therefore provided an outward and visible sign of an inward and invisible union by associating the broken bread and the shared wine with his body and blood. Those who partake of the loaf and the cup participate in the atoning sacrifice of his death through which he inaugurated the new covenant, and are brought into union with him and with each other. Questions about the mode of Christ's presence in the bread and wine did not arise. The ancient world was familiar with symbols which effected, or helped to effect, that which they symbolized.

The words used by Jesus when he prayed over the bread and wine were probably something like these:

'Blessed art thou, O Lord, God, king of the world, who hast brought forth bread from the earth.'

'Blessed art thou, O Lord our God, king of the world, who hast created the fruit of the vine.'

23 *Eucharistesas*, **offer thanks**, is the origin of the word 'Eucharist'. The prayers of thanksgiving said by the celebrant over the bread and wine in the Church's Eucharist are thought by many scholars to have developed out of the Jewish table blessings such as those used by our Lord at the Last Supper. The OT passages which supply the background to the phrase, 'blood of the covenant', are Exod. 24.4–8, the covenant on Sinai with its inaugural sacrifice of blood, and Jer. 31.31–34, the prophecy of a new covenant.

25 **I tell you this: never again shall I drink from the fruit of the vine until that day when I drink it new in the kingdom of God.** New (*kainos*) means new in quality, not in time. The kingdom of God was often described as a heavenly banquet presided over by the Messiah. A prophecy of Christ's death is expanded by a saying rich with biblical ideas, making the Last Supper a foretaste of a future reality (just as the Jewish Passover meal was interpreted as an anticipation of the coming

redemption which God had promised his people). Jesus supported his
prediction of the disciples' desertion by a quotation from Zech. 13.7.

28 Appearances of the risen Lord in **Galilee** are recorded in Matt. 28.16–20
and in John 21, but it may be that Jesus was using the name as a symbol
of the whole world. In the OT Galilee meant 'land of the heathen' (as in
Matt. 4.15)—after his resurrection Jesus would go before his disciples
into all the world. Peter's protest, characteristic of him, was answered by

30 another prophecy, **Before the cock crows twice, you yourself will
disown me three times.** Cock-crow in the east is between midnight
and one or two in the morning.

32   **Gethsemane**—the name probably means 'oil-press' or 'olive grove'—
is on the slopes of the mount of Olives facing the eastern wall of Jerusalem.

34 **My heart is ready to break with grief,** Jesus told the three leading
disciples. The story of the passion is at this point in great contrast to the
version in John, where Jesus faced the future with calmness and assurance

36 (12.27). **Abba, Father:** did Jesus actually say this prayer (the only
witnesses were asleep)? The intimate Aramaic word, Abba, had been used
by Jesus when he taught his disciples to pray, and **Not what I will, but
what thou wilt,** is almost the same as the Lord's Prayer. 'He offered up
prayers and petitions, with loud cries and tears, to God who was able to
deliver him from the grave', wrote the author of Hebrews (5.7). Christ's
petitions to the Father in the midst of his horror and dismay must have
been much like this, asking God for deliverance from death but accepting
in obedience whatever was to happen. Then, after the third repetition of

41 the prayer, he announced, **The hour has come. The Son of Man is
betrayed to sinful men.** There is a hidden irony in the statement. The
last thing that was expected of the Messiah was that he should be
betrayed and made to suffer.

41   Judas has arranged a **signal** to distinguish Jesus among the small group
in the dim light under the trees. A kiss on the head or on the hand was a
normal form of greeting between a rabbi and his pupil. The incident of

53 **the young man** is a mystery. It could have been a piece of autobiography
slipped in by Mark himself, though there is nothing to support this
popular assumption.

The evangelist described three stages in the condemnation of Jesus.
First, he was interrogated before the Sanhedrin at night, shortly after his
arrest. It met under the chairmanship of Joseph Caiaphas, who was
High Priest from A.D. 18 to 35. Second, the Sanhedrin reconvened
briefly at daybreak to finalize its plans for its appeal to Pilate. Third, Jesus
was brought before the Roman governor.

The hearing before the Sanhedrin followed the normal Jewish legal procedure. Witnesses were called (a charge could only be sustained if two witnesses gave evidence independently of one another) but what they said was not apparently sufficiently reliable. Even the accusation that 58 Jesus had said **I will throw down this temple, made with human hands, and in three days I will build another, not made with hands** was not substantiated (though if it had been, it would have been enough to charge Jesus with blasphemy). The High Priest's first question, an attempt to get Jesus to incriminate himself, was unanswered, but the second question evoked Christ's unequivocal claim to be the Messiah: 61– **'Are you the Messiah, the Son of the Blessed One?'** Jesus said, **'I** 62 **am; and you will see the Son of Man seated on the right hand of God and coming with the clouds of heaven.'** Two great OT texts were drawn together in this affirmation: Daniel's vision of the last judgement and the coming of the Son of Man ('I saw one like a son of man coming with the clouds of heaven; he approached the Ancient of Years and was presented to him'—7.13), and Psalm 110 which was then interpreted as a prophecy of the One who was to come and who would be given supremacy next only to God ('The Lord says . . . sit at my right hand'). This claim was sufficient to charge Jesus with blasphemy, punishable by death (Lev. 24.16).

Since the Sanhedrin did not have authority to impose the death penalty, they had to bring Jesus before the Roman governor for his permission to execute the prisoner. The governor conducted his affairs early in the morning, and while they were waiting Jesus was maltreated. The house of the High Priest, traditionally located in the upper, western part of the old city, near Sion Church and the Coenaculum, was probably a substantial building round a courtyard with one gate leading into the street. The interrogation of Jesus presumably took place in one of the large rooms on the first floor. Peter had got into the courtyard, with the bystanders who had been attracted to the house by the unusual nocturnal events, and it was there that his denials were made. The story may have come from the apostle himself. It is a remarkable illustration of the way in which the Gospels do not attempt to whitewash the reputations of the first leaders of the Church.

Pontius Pilate was procurator of the imperial province of Judah from about A.D. 26 to 36. He showed little tact in his administering of an unusually difficult province—various riots occurred during his time in office because of his blunders—though he could not have been a complete failure, for Tiberius kept him in office for ten years. But there is nothing

in Mark's narrative to suggest that he acted irregularly in condemning Jesus. It may have been for political motives rather than concern for justice that he allowed Jesus to be executed—Tiberius would not have
5.12 been pleased if he had released **the man you call king of the Jews**. The silence of Jesus, both before the Sanhedrin and before Pilate, is notable. It fulfilled the OT picture of the 'suffering servant':

> He was afflicted, he submitted to be struck down and did not open his
> mouth;
> he was led like a sheep to the slaughter,
> like a ewe that is dumb before the shearers,
> and he would not open his mouth   (Isa. 53.7).

Up until this time the crowd had been on Jesus' side. Why did they
13,14 now cry **Crucify him!** when Pilate attempted to use the Passover custom of releasing a prisoner to free Jesus? Perhaps the chief priests had brought together a body of their supporters to make a demonstration.

When the Roman governor came to Jerusalem from his capital (the
16 port of Caesarea), he brought with him his own **company** of troops (the word used is the Greek name for a cohort of up to six hundred men) and
18 it was these men who mocked Jesus. The salute, **Hail! King of the Jews** was a parody of **Ave, Caesar, victor, imperator!** The fortress on the north-west corner of the temple which has been located by archaeologists, the Antonia, is believed to have contained the *praetorium* (NEB footnote).

The cruel form of execution known as crucifixion was a common sight in Palestine under the Roman administration since it was the punishment
27 for those who committed violence and insurrection. **Bandits** (armed rebels) were typical victims. The same punishment was considered
26 appropriate for Jesus because he had claimed to be **The King of the Jews**, as the inscription pointed out. Executions took place outside the city walls, beside the highways, so that people would see them on their way in and out of the gates. Stakes were driven into the ground, or suitable trees were trimmed, and the victim was forced to carry the *patibulum*, or cross-beam, which was then fixed to the upright support. The traditional site of Jesus' crucifixion was the spot where in the fourth century Constantine built his great church with its associated shrines. A rocky mound (which still exists in the present Church of the Holy Sepulchre) could
22 have been **Golgotha, which means 'Place of a skull'** ('Calvary', *Calvarium*, is the traditional Latin translation). The drugged wine was an anaesthetic, offered by the women of Jerusalem as an act of mercy for condemned men. 'Give strong drink to him who is perishing, and wine to

those in bitter distress' (Prov. 31.6). The executioners had a customary right to the clothes of the victim. The psalm, which speaks of a man who suffered at the hands of his enemies, includes the verse,

> They share out my garments among them
> And cast lots for my clothes   (Ps. 22.18).

29 **The passers-by hurled abuse at him.** The mocking looks back at earlier events in the gospel—the saying about rebuilding the temple (14.58), the healing ('saving') of the sick, and the messianic claim (14.62). The text echoes various OT passages—'All those who pass by . . . hiss and wag their heads at you' (Lam. 2.15), 'All who see me jeer at me, make mouths at me, and wag their heads' (Ps. 22.7); 'I have become the victim of their taunts; when they see me, they toss their heads' (Ps.
34 109.25). **Eli, Eli, lema sabachthani?** Jesus cried the first verse of Psalm 22 in Aramaic. With these words he shared in the dereliction of our humanity, but it should be noted that the psalm ends with an act of
35 faith and hope in God. **He is calling Elijah.** The prophet was looked on as a protector of distressed Jews.

The curtain of the temple was probably the veil in front of the Holy of Holies. The tearing of this veil symbolized to Christians the complete and uninterrupted access to God that men now have through the death of Jesus (Eph. 2.14–18; Heb. 9.1–12; 10.19–25). The officer who was in charge of the execution squad—a centurion commanded a detachment of about a hundred men (he was roughly equivalent to a non-commissioned officer in a modern army)—marvelled that Jesus died with a triumphant
39 cry (John 19.20). **Truly this man was a son of God:** to the Greek-speaking citizen of his day the phrase referred to one who seemed endowed with exceptional powers or who was blessed with divine favour, but to the Christian it has, of course, a more profound significance (as Mark indicated, for he used the phrase in the first verse of the gospel).
40 **Mary of Magdala** (Magdala is on the north-west shore of the Lake of Galilee) was, according to Luke 8.3, delivered of seven demons. **Mary the mother of James the younger and of Joseph** could have been the mother of Jesus, if it is accepted that Jesus had brothers with these common names, but it is a strange way of identifying her. Matt. 27.56 speaks of these two women but not of **Salome.**

* **Matthew 21. 1–13**
The Mount of Olives, rising from the deep narrow cleft of the Kidron valley opposite the eastern wall of the city of Jerusalem, is featured in

Jewish eschatology, both as a place where the Messiah would appear, and as the place of the general resurrection. On it the prophets were supposed to be buried, and around it are hundreds of tombs and sepulchres. When this evangelist reported that many of God's people arose from sleep after the resurrection and entered the holy city (27.53), we can assume he meant they came from these slopes. Bethphage and Bethany are on the other side of the Mount of Olives from Jerusalem, just off the road from Jericho. Bethany was an obvious place for a pause on Jesus' pilgrimage
2 from Jericho, and the village opposite was Bethphage, about a mile away. The arrangements for borrowing the donkey may have been made beforehand, as were the later arrangements for using the upper room (26.18), but Matthew narrated the incident as if it were an act of fore-
5 knowledge. Characteristically, he added, This was to fulfil the prophecy, and then quoted Zech. 9.9.

The quotation of Zechariah is taken from the Hebrew text where there is a poetic parallelism. Matthew took this to mean two animals, as the RSV and JB translations indicate. The NEB adjusts Matthew's mistake by
5 translating, Here is your king, who comes to you in gentleness, riding on an ass, riding on the foal of a beast of burden. Mark and Luke refer only to one animal.

In describing the messianic king's humble mode of entering the city, Zechariah had in mind the unpretentious and unwarlike nature of his rule. Jesus, by performing this action, deliberately associated himself with that prophecy and gave it a profounder meaning. The details of the triumphal entry into Jerusalem are capable of a more prosaic explanation —that for some reason Jesus needed a lift to reach Jerusalem, and that happy pilgrims on the road cheered his progress—but there seems little doubt that in fact it was a gesture staged by him to demonstrate that he was the Messiah.

The shouts of the crowd came from Psalm 118, one of the Hallel Psalms (113—118) sung at Passovertide. 'Save us, we beseech thee (*Hosanna*), O Lord . . . Blessed be he that cometh in the name of the Lord' (verses 25–26). *Hosanna* had become a liturgical acclamation of joy. The use of branches from trees was common in festival pilgrimage processions. The
9 welcome they gave to Jesus as Son of David indicated that they recognized him as the Messiah. (Matthew was particularly careful to base Christ's claim to messiahship on his ancestry from king David.) But when the people from the city came out to see what the excitement was about,
11 the crowd simply said that This is the prophet Jesus, from Nazareth in Galilee, as if Matthew wanted to draw attention away from the

political implications of Jesus' messiahship to the imminence of the Kingdom in his teaching.

Christ's first act on entering the city was highly significant: he cited Isa. 56.7 and Jer. 7.11 in denouncing those who bought and sold in the Court of the Gentiles in the temple. The temple was a sacred place and must be respected. The confusion of business and the haggling over prices ruined its atmosphere as a place of worship, and the greed for
13 profit made it a robbers' cave. Despite its humble pose, then, the entry into Jerusalem by Jesus and his subsequent action (in the synoptic Gospels) in cleansing the temple threw a challenge before the Jewish authorities which they could not ignore.

MAUNDY THURSDAY

Exodus 12. 1–14

The Priestly account of the institution of the Passover. An ancient nomadic spring festival was reinterpreted as a memorial of the Lord's deliverance of his people given, according to the scheme of the book of
2 Exodus, in Egypt. This month is for you the first of months introduces what was to be a new way of calculating the beginning of the new year. The month of Passover, called in other sources 'the month Abib' (Babylonian 'Nisan') is our March–April.

The whole community of Israel is the Hebrew *'edah*, the basic meaning of which is 'to appoint'. With *qahal* it is used to describe the assembly of the people, and it was rendered in the LXX by *ekklesia*, 'church.' Why the head of the household should select the lamb without blemish, a male
3 one year old, on the tenth day of this month is not apparent. Like the third and the seventh days, it may have had some ritual significance. The
6 animal was to be slaughtered between the two evenings (NEB footnote), that is, between sunset and the sight of the first star. The smearing of the
7 blood on the two door-posts and on the lintel of every house in which they shall eat the lamb had the practical purpose during the Exodus of indicating which houses in Egypt were occupied by the Israelites. The ritual manipulation of blood had a highly religious significance and was the prerogative of the priests in later Israel. In the

Passover ritual this priestly function was performed by the head of the household—a 'lay celebration' which went back into antiquity before the establishment of a priestly monopoly in sacred things.

The Passover was a nocturnal feast. To bake without leaven means speedy cooking before a hurried departure, as on the last night in Egypt. Bitter herbs are lettuce or chicory, to be dried and carried on the journey. The meat had to be cooked sufficiently to prevent the eating of any blood —probably roasted on a spit so that the fat would drop into the fire. Any

11 remains were to be burned to preserve ritual purity. **It is the Lord's Passover,** Hebrew *Pesah*, Greek *Pascha*. The meaning of the word is uncertain; it could mean 'protect', 'save', 'be lame', 'placate', etc. 'Pass', 'pass over', and 'share' are suggested by the contexts in which it is used.

14 **You shall keep this day as a day of remembrance, and make it a pilgrim-feast, a festival of the Lord.** The Hebrew *zikkaron* is one of the words translated as *mnemosunon* in LXX, implying that a ritual act of remembrance brings into the present something of the reality of what is celebrated—an *anamnesis*.

For Christians the Jewish Passover became a prophetic sign of the great Passover in which Christ, the Lamb of God, was sacrificed on the cross during the paschal celebrations in Jerusalem to bring salvation to men in a new Exodus. The Eucharist, in which Christians offer a prayer of thanksgiving over bread and wine and consume the elements in a sacramental communion with God and with each other, is the Church's means of celebrating the new Passover of the Lord.

1 Corinthians 11. 23–29

In dealing with the disorders which took place in the Christian assembly at Corinth, Paul reminded his readers of Jesus' acts and words at the Last

23 Supper. **The tradition came to Paul from the Lord himself:** this can mean either that the story came to the apostle directly from God by revelation, such as that which brought about his conversion on the Damascus road, or (more probably) that the narrative was handed down to Paul through the teaching processes of the Church. Hellenism as well as Judaism had its collections of **tradition** which were passed down by word of mouth until they were committed to writing—that is how the Gospels themselves came to be written—and it would be within the scope of Paul's belief about the people of God and their union in Christ to say that a tradition handed on by them to him would be as 'from the Lord himself'.

The narrative of the institution of the Eucharist in this letter is the oldest written account of the event in the NT; it is nearer to the narrative in Luke than those in Mark and Matthew. In the manner of a prophet, Christ identified the bread over which he had said the blessing and which 24 he had broken as his body: **This is my body, which is for you; do this as a memorial of me.** The lamb eaten at the Passover meal was called the 'body of the Passover lamb' in Jewish teaching, and Jesus at the Last Supper seems to have applied this concept to the meal he was sharing with his disciples and his own sacrificial self-offering on the cross. The Jews at Passover time celebrated their deliverance from Egypt: the Passover Haggadah declared, 'He brought us out from slavery to liberty, from sorrow to joy, from darkness to great light, from servitude to redemption'. Christ similarly delivered the new Israel from the servitude of sin; and the Eucharist was their means of both celebrating that redemption and 24 participating in it. That is why Christ said it is for you.

25   The command to do this is linked with the idea of memorial. *Anamnesis* has a meaning far deeper than the English understanding of an act of remembrance. What Israel remembered at Passover time was what God had done for them, his mighty acts of deliverance from Egypt, his guidance through the wilderness into the promised land; but the events commemorated were made present in the people's celebration of them. Similarly, the Christian celebration of 'Christ our Passover' made real among the worshippers the mighty acts of God in Christ which were associated with the Last Supper itself. Christ had given himself on behalf of his people, and they shared in the benefits of his passion in eating a loaf at a meal held in his memory.

The cup of blessing was passed round in a Jewish meal for the final prayer, and it was at this point that Christ said, **This cup is the new 25 covenant sealed by my blood. Whenever you drink it, do this as a memorial of me.** The direct identification of the wine itself with the blood of Christ was made in the Marcan-Matthean tradition (Matt. 26.27; Mark 14.24). Perhaps the tradition which Paul here quoted came from a strongly Jewish-Christian source, where any idea of partaking of blood, even as a sacramental sign, would have been avoided; the change to a direct identification in Matthew and Mark may have been due to a later modification in the tradition of the Last Supper when the saying over the loaf influenced the form of the saying over the cup.

Behind the saying over the cup are the OT passages Exod. 24.8 and Jer. 31.31–34. To drink the cup is to enter into the new covenant established in Christ's blood. When the covenant on Sinai was made, Moses sprinkled the people with the blood of the sacrificial victims, saying, 'Behold the blood of the covenant which the Lord has made with you';

and Jeremiah, after the failure of the old covenant, foretold the establishment of a new covenant between God and man, which would include the
forgiveness of sins and personal union with God himself. So the shedding
of Christ's blood marked the inauguration of a new covenant in which
men's sins are forgiven and union with God is re-established. The Passover background to the Last Supper provides a way of interpreting the
Supper and the cross from Israel's salvation-history.

The command to 'Do this' is repeated, and the apostle went on to assert
that the celebration of the Supper is a proclamation of Christ's death—
and all the benefits which accrue to it for the Church—until the return of
Christ to judge the world. Paul expected this to be in his own time; the
Supper linked men and women across time and space with the saving
grace of God in Christ until the Second Coming.

The passage concludes with a warning about worthy reception—or
29 rather, reception after penitential self-examination. He does not discern
the Body has at least two interpretations (the use of the capital letter in
the NEB acknowledges this): it can mean Christ's Body in the sacramental
sign, and/or his Body in the assembled Christian community. The
precise meaning is not easy to define, but it implies a separation from Christ
and his Church for those who are guilty of desecrating the sacrament.

* **John 13. 1–15**
The public proclamation of the gospel by Jesus had ended. His hour had
come—the hour for which he had come into the world, and which was
through suffering, death, and resurrection, to manifest the glory which he
shared with the Father. It was also the hour when he was to leave his
disciples in the world (always seen as transitory and unsatisfying, even
hostile, by this evangelist) where they, too, would experience suffering
and death. So he gave them a sign to show them that, following in his path
of love and humility, they also might share in his resurrection and glory.

To wash the feet of guests was the normal duty of servants before a
meal; it was unusual for the host to perform the task while a meal was
being eaten. Perhaps Jesus only thought of it after they had commenced
the Last Supper. He may have discerned the way in which Satan was
taking possession of Judas' mind and wanted, in one final gesture of love,
to save him from falling into sin. We can assume that, even though Judas'
betrayal fitted in with Christ's destiny, the disciple still had the free will
to be loyal if he had wished to be. Anyway, Jesus enacted a parable of
self-sacrifice for others. The sign is all the more striking because the evan-

gelist recorded that as he was enacting it, Jesus was conscious of his divine authority and of the way of glory which was his from God.

6   Peter's character comes through clearly in the dialogue. **You, Lord, washing my feet?** As in Matt. 16.22, when he rejected the suggestion offered, he could not be in fellowship with him. Peter's impetuosity brought him into conflict with his leader. Jesus firmly pointed out that unless Peter had the humility to accept the service which his Saviour offered, he could not be in fellowship with him. Peter's impetuosity
9 swung in the opposite direction. **Then, Lord, not my feet only; wash my hands and head as well!**—the hands and head are the other *foci* of man's thought and action. But the bathing which Jesus offers—his
10 sacrifice for sin—is complete. **A man who has bathed needs no further washing.** The NEB footnote alternative **needs only to wash his feet,** can be interpreted as a reference to the sacramental sign which Jesus offers in the feet-washing. The sacrifice of the cross cleanses a man; he needs only to appropriate it through the washing which Jesus institutes.

The feet-washing becomes therefore a type of Christian baptism. The laying aside and taking up of Christ's garments have been interpreted over the centuries as an analogy of the laying aside and the taking up of his human nature in his death and resurrection; the feet-washing is a sacramental sign of participation in that death and resurrection without which we cannot have fellowship with him; it is also the baptismal sign which we need because through Christ we have been made clean. The words of institution are not included in the Johannine account of the Last Supper; they are implicit throughout the Gospel through the discourse of chapter 6 (the feeding of the five thousand and the 'bread from heaven' discourse, see Easter 1 Year 2). But in their place is this incident which can be interpreted as an institution of baptism, without which a man may not share in the Lord's fellowship and the Lord's table.

The concluding words of the passage charge the disciples, and through them the Christian Church, to continue the ministry of love and service to one another (a Johannine characteristic is that a Christian's duty is
13 first to other members of the Church). **You call me 'Master' and 'Lord', and rightly so, for that is what I am.** The Jewish pupil never addressed his master by his name but always as *Rabbi umari*, 'my teacher and my lord'. The title is uniquely suitable for Jesus Christ since he was the
14– disciples' Teacher and Lord par excellence. **Then if I, your Lord and**
15 **Master, have washed your feet, you also ought to wash one another's feet. I have set you an example: you are to do as I have done for you.**

The Christian duty of love and service is echoed in Phil. 2.5 ('Let your bearing towards one another arise out of your life in Christ Jesus') and 1 Pet. 2.21 ('Christ suffered on your behalf, and thereby left you an example'). 'Washing the feet of God's people' (1 Tim. 5.10) was one of the qualifications for being a widow in the true sense of support from the Christian community; it was a mark of service and hospitality.

GOOD FRIDAY

Isaiah 52. 13–53. end

The last of the four songs of the Servant of God in Isaiah has been an important source for the Church's understanding of the sacrifice of Jesus Christ, not only because its concepts were used to interpret what Christ achieved through the cross, but also because Jesus himself seems consciously to have identified himself with the Servant in pursuing his mission. Through this song the prophet explored the mystery of vicarious suffering—the righteous Servant who shared in afflictions to such an extent that in so doing he carried the cause of that suffering, the sin of the people. The identity of this Servant is unknown; it is best not to limit that identification to one individual or to the corporate personality of Israel, but to include both.

The passage reports what the people said, 53.1–11a, within a framework of something God said, 52.13ff and 53.11b–12 (or perhaps 53.11–12, following the capital letter in the NEB).

God introduced the work of his Servant with the word **Behold**, a word used by this prophet when introducing a vision. The misfortunes of the Servant were to be reversed; he would share in the glory of God 13 himself, **he shall be lifted up, exalted to the heights.** What God does for him would have consequences throughout the world: just as the rulers of the nations had recoiled at the sight of him, so they would be 15 amazed, **For they see what they had never been told and things unheard before fill their thoughts.**

The picture of the Servant of God which is drawn in 53.1–11 is of one who was so disfigured by suffering that others rejected him and then despised him. He experienced that involuntary yet cruel retreat of men 2 from one of their number who is so disfigured that to them he lost all the likeness of a man—he ceased to resemble a human being. In the OT the beauty of a person is a sign that God blessed them; there was nothing beautiful about the Servant, so it was assumed he was a man without a blessing.

4   Yet on himself he bore our sufferings, is the confession of men who had changed their opinion of the Servant. The rhythmic interplay of the words 'he' and 'we' is noteworthy. They had never dreamed that the one
5 who suffered was pierced for our transgressions, tortured for our iniquities. Thus, the healing gained for others by his stripes included also the forgiveness of their sins and the removal of their punishment. The Servant's exaltation brought them to realize this.

The report, interrupted by this confession (verses 4-6), continues with the details of the Servant's sufferings, but this time they are the result of physical violence, not disease. His silence in the midst of suffering,
7 he did not open his mouth, and his complete isolation, cut off from
8 the world of living men, are poignant details which increase the horror of the passion. The report then goes on to tell of the Servant's death and burial, either as a result of illness or violence. Shame followed him to his grave, for he was buried with malefactors.
10   Finally, verses 10-12 report his deliverance. The Servant who made himself a sacrifice for sin—the word is used for a guilt offering (NEB footnote) was restored by God to be vindicated and rewarded by prosperity, a long life, children and grandchildren. How this would come about is not explained. But at the end of the song came the words which were to find their way into Christian teaching on the cross of Christ,
12 he bore the sin of many.

Hebrews 10. 1–25

Law is used by the author of Hebrews in this passage in the sense of the cult of Judaism, not of the moral code which Paul referred to in his epistles (though obviously both cult and code are but different sections of the same law). These ritual practices, said the author, were only a dim reflection of the good things which were to come when the promises were fulfilled. Levitical sacrifices cleansed only ritual offences; they never succeeded in removing the real sins which formed a barrier between God and his people. If they had been effective in removing that barrier, it would not have been necessary for the priests to repeat them year after year—they would have done that once and for all. The cult, on the contrary, only succeeded in making men remember their sinful state (the
3 word for brought to mind is *anamnesis*, the same word Christ used at

the Last Supper when he spoke of the Eucharist as a 'remembrance' (Luke 22.19); it implies something vividly and consciously made present again.) Sins cannot be removed by animal sacrifices—the author may
4 have in mind the ritual of the Day of Atonement, though **the blood of bulls and goats** suggests the whole complex of ritual oblations made in the former temple at Jerusalem (assuming the author wrote after A.D. 70).

He next quoted Ps. 40.8–10, as the words of Christ before his incarnation, spoken to the Father, giving the reason for his coming into the world. They underline the Son's obedience in carrying out the human task which the Father had destined for him. The author's quotation is made more striking by a difference in the Hebrew and Greek versions of verse 8 of this psalm. The Hebrew version reads, 'But mine ears hast thou opened' (Revised Psalter), but the Greek version of the LXX reads,
5 **Thou hast prepared a body for me.** The LXX text enabled the author of Hebrews to show how the OT teaches God's rejection of the ritual sacrifices, his preparation of a human body for the speaker in the psalm (the Son), and the promise of obedience to God's will on the part of the speaker. All kinds of expiatory sacrifices were rejected. The speaker in the psalm also quotes an earlier scripture, Deut. 6.5 or Jer. 15.16. Instead of sacrifices, the coming Messiah should offer to God the body which was to be given to him. The author commented on this to show how the cult is now cancelled with the sacrifice of Christ. Verse 10 asserts that the unique and completed sacrifice of Christ, the offering of his human life in
10 obedience to the will of God, has **consecrated** (made holy, belonging to God) the Christian community.

The priests of the temple in Jerusalem were occupied each day in offering sacrifices, standing before the altar; but Jesus Christ, our one High Priest, made one offering of himself on the cross, and this single sacrifice is effective for the remission of sins—which the former oblations could never be. Ps. 110, used earlier in this letter, was quoted again: Jesus **took his seat at the right hand of God, where he waits henceforth until**
12– **his enemies are made his footstool.** The session of Christ, contrasted
13 with the standing attitude of the priests, denotes not only Jesus' divine status but also the completion of his work. His enemies are the forces of evil still active in the world. By that single offering Christ has achieved 'the eternal perfection of all whom he is sanctifying' (JB); the sentence embraces the work of Christ in its completion and also in its continual process in the lives of Christians.

The fact that God's forgiveness has been obtained by Christ's sacrifice is proved by quotations from Jeremiah's prophecy of the new covenant,

already used earlier in the letter. The new covenant promised by God is
17 established and the past forgotten as well as forgiven—**their sins and
wicked deeds I will remember no more at all.**

We are admitted into the sanctuary through the sacrifice of Jesus
20 Christ **by the new, living way which he has opened for us through
the curtain, the way of his flesh.** The way is new because Jesus
inaugurated it; it is living because it was inaugurated through the death
and resurrection of the living Lord ('I am the way; I am the truth and I
am life; no one comes to the Father except by me', John 14.6) The way
of his flesh is a difficult phrase to interpret. JB has 'through the curtain,
that is to say, his body'. Perhaps the most satisfactory solution is to understand it as referring to Jesus' flesh *and* blood, which he shared with us
as humans and which he offered in sacrifice. It is this sacrifice which is
the curtain through which we are admitted into the sanctuary.

The rest of the passage works out the consequences of this offering in
22 Christian living. We approach the sanctuary **in sincerity of heart and
full assurance of faith,** through our baptism, we are firm **in the**
23 **confession of our hope,** and we study **how each of us may best
rouse others to love and active goodness** within the Christian com-
25 munity, spurred on **because you see the Day drawing near.** Faith,
hope, and love—the primary virtues—are the three bases on which this
exhortation stands.

Hebrews 4. 14–16, 5. 7–9

The ritual function of the high priest on the Day of Atonement (*Yom
Kippur*) was an important one. The day was kept by the people on the
tenth of the seventh month (*Tishri*, September–October) with fasting
and penitence to seek God's mercy for their sins.

The ceremonies were laid down in Leviticus 16. Discarding his normal
vestments, the high priest bathed and put on a linen robe. In the temple
precincts he killed a bullock as a sin-offering for himself and his assistants,
and entered alone into the holy of holies to sprinkle blood round the
Mercy-seat. Then he returned to the people, who presented him with
two goats. One of these he selected as a sacrifice and killed it, sprinkling
the blood in the holy of holies and on the altar where the daily oblations
were made; on the other he laid his hands, confessed over it the sins
Israel had committed in the past year, and prayed for forgiveness. This
animal, the scapegoat, was then taken into the wilderness—the abode
of evil—and destroyed. The significance of the first sacrifice was that the
life-blood of the goat was supposed to unite God and his people in the

transaction; the significance of the second was that the animal carried away the people's sins to the place where sin belonged.

The faults confessed by the high priest were the sins of ignorance committed unwittingly by himself and the people—a healthy recognition that in a religion of law men can still sin, even when they have obeyed every precept. Wilful transgressions such as murder, adultery, sabbath-breaking, and suchlike had to be dealt with under the ordinary provisions of the law; the sacrificial system itself could not effect atonement for them.

The author of Hebrews expounds Jesus Christ's ministry and sacrifice in terms of this cult. The death, resurrection, and ascension of Christ were the means whereby he entered the holy of holies—heaven itself. His people, unlike the Jews, are able to enter the holy of holies with him:

4.16 **we may boldly approach the throne of our gracious God, where we may receive mercy and in his grace find timely help.**

But a high priest must be able to sympathize with the human condition since his task is to plead to God on man's behalf—his petitions would be less sincere if he was not involved with the people in their plight. Christ, says the author, did not share in man's sin like the Jewish

4.15 high priests, but he had been **tested in** every way and was able to sympathize with human suffering more perfectly than the high priests

5.8 because he had **learned obedience in the school of suffering.** Through pain of body and anguish of mind he had paid the price of obedience to God. Since that had been accomplished, Christ was now perfected as the one high priest who is able to secure the forgiveness of sins and salvation for men. What the Jewish high priest had attempted to obtain on the Day of Atonement, Christ had successfully won.

The author assumes that his readers were familiar with the story of the

5.7 agony in the garden of Gethsemane, when Jesus **offered up prayers and petition, with loud cries and tears, to God who was able to deliver him from the grave. Because of his humble submission his prayer was heard** and God raised him from the dead.

* John 18. 1—19. 37
Only points of special interest in the Johannine narrative of the passion will be noted here. For a further commentary on the passion see pages 197–204.

6   **When he said, 'I am he', they drew back and fell to the ground.** Linked with the 'I am' sayings of the fourth Gospel, this incident under-

9 lines the divine authority of Christ. **This was to make good his words, 'I have not lost one of those whom thou gavest me.'** Here and in

verse 32 the author uses a 'fulfilment saying' not in order to refer to an OT text but to point out the accuracy of a prophecy made by Christ himself. Here the reference is to the sentence in the prayer of Christ 17.12 ('When I was with them, I protected by the power of thy name those whom thou has given me.'). In verse 32 the references are to the 'Son of man being lifted up' sayings (3.14; 8.28; and 12.32), indicating that he would be executed by the Romans' method of crucifixion rather than by the Jews' method of stoning.

11   **This is the cup my Father has given me; shall I not drink it?** This is a suggestive variation of the prayer which Jesus offered in Gethsemane, according to the synoptic narratives. Only John calls Gethsemane 'a garden'.

13   **They took him first to Annas.** Matthew and Mark reported that Jesus was brought before a specially convened meeting of the Sanhedrin on the night of his arrest; Luke said that Jesus was held in Caiaphas' house during the night. Annas had been relieved of the office of High Priest in A.D. 15, but he still remained influential in Jerusalem, for five of his sons held the office, including Caiaphas, who was High Priest from A.D. 18 to 36. According to the fourth Gospel, Peter's denial also took place here. The variations in the details are not incompatible. The special meeting of the Sanhedrin could have been summoned to meet near Annas' house, and Jesus taken to Caiaphas' house afterwards.

28   **The Jews stayed outside the headquarters.** According to the fourth Gospel's chronology, the crucifixion took place on the eve of the Passover, at the time the paschal lambs were being slaughtered in the temple.

29   **What charge do you bring against this man?** John did not mention the morning interrogation of Jesus by the Sanhedrin, but he indicated that the Jews brought Christ to Pilate because they were not allowed to put anyone to death. They were evasive about the charge, however; the synoptic Gospels are clear that the Jews' initial complaint against Jesus was that he had blasphemed. In John's account Pilate questioned the Jews outside the building and Jesus inside.

32   **The fulfilment of the words by which Jesus had indicated the manner of his death.** See comment on verse 9 above.

38   **Pilate said, 'What is truth?'** He showed by this question that he was not on the side of truth. However, he admitted Jesus' innocence and attempted to secure his release.

19.12   **If you let this man go, you are no friend of Caesar.** Every Roman administrator aspired to be *amicus Caesaris*, to have influence in the

imperial court. The Jews' threat ended Pilate's attempt to save Jesus, and
he formally handed him over in the public tribunal outside the governor's
residence. John timed the crucifixion a day earlier than the synoptic
Gospels, when the lambs were being slaughtered, and at a later hour,
noon instead of nine o'clock in the morning (to coincide with the killing
of the lambs?).

26   **Mother, there is your son.** Only John reported that Jesus' mother
was at the cross. Christ's words to her, and to the disciple whom he loved,
have been interpreted by the Church as addressed to all Christians, Mary
herself symbolizing the community of the redeemed.

28   **I thirst.** The incident of giving drugged wine to Jesus was characteristically given deeper significance by John. The true meaning of this word
from the cross is to be found in Ps. 63.1, 'O God, thou art my God, I seek
thee, my soul thirsts for thee'.

30   **It is accomplished!** In the fourth Gospel Jesus' life and work were
seen moving towards an appointed destiny. The last word from the cross
drew these threads together in fulfilment.

YEARS I AND 2

EASTER DAY
See pages 7–9

Exodus 14. 15–22
The passage tells of the most critical moment in the history of Israel. The
flight from Egypt had been halted at the Red Sea (JB uses the alternative
name, 'Sea of Reeds'). Behind them was the pursuing army of Pharaoh.
'We would rather be slaves to the Egyptians than die here in the wilderness', they said (14.13). In the crisis the Lord spoke directly to Moses.

The various traditions which go to make up the Pentateuch contribute
to the details of the story. The oldest, the Jahwist source, says that the
Lord sent a strong east wind to drive back the waters of the Red Sea; the
Elohist source says that the angel of God and Moses' rod were the means
for the expression of God's power; the Priestly source says the gesture
of Moses' hand made the waters as a wall on either side of the Israelites.
But whatever each tradition contributed, the event was regarded in the
OT as the mighty act of God on behalf of his people and was constantly
referred to by prophet and psalmist. It takes the same focal importance
in the OT as the resurrection of Jesus Christ takes in the New. And it

provides the interpretation of the resurrection as the new exodus, an escape from death and slavery through the waters of baptism—the free gift of God's faithfulness and love.

Isaiah 12

The prophet had announced a new exodus for the people of God (11.12ff), and since Moses and the Israelites sang to the Lord after their deliverance from the Egyptians at the Red Sea (Exod. 15.1ff) the prophet provided two short psalms as a response to the announcement of the new exodus. Israel would praise God again for removing his anger from them and showing them his strength, for delivering them from great danger and setting himself over them as their defence. The provision of water from the rock in the wilderness during the first exodus is recalled in verse 3:

3 You shall draw water with joy from the springs of deliverance.

The second psalm (verses 4–6) includes all the elements of the people's
4 response to God—proclaiming his word (make his deeds known), praying and praising him, and giving thanks to him, because of the assurance of his presence in majesty.

On this day the psalms become a hymn for the risen Christ to sing to his people.

Isaiah 43. 16–21

A proclamation of salvation given by the prophet in the Lord's name to the people exiled in Babylon. The God who spoke was the God who
16 opened a way in the sea and a path through mighty waters—who made the exodus from Egypt possible for the Israelities. This exodus made up the early confession of faith for the Jews. As in a creed, they identified their God as the one who had brought them out of Egypt, and this mighty act was frequently celebrated in the psalms. Yet the Lord now tells them to do an astonishing thing. They are to set aside the
18 memory of this early exodus: Cease to dwell on days gone by and to brood over past history. Why? Because Yahweh is going to do a tremendous and wonderful new thing that will completely overshadow the former mighty work.

What God is going to do is to lead his people through a new exodus, not
19 through the Red Sea, but through the wilderness which separates Babylon from Jerusalem. Once more he is to be the redeemer and liberator of Israel. The new exodus, like the old, would be marked by
20 miraculous events—the provision of water in the desert. And it would lead to the fulfilment of God's purposes. He has created the people for

218

himself in order that they might praise him by telling of his salvation to an ever-widening circle of adherents.

Revelation 1. 10–18

Part of the introduction to John's letters to the seven churches. **It was on the Lord's day, and I was caught up in the Spirit**: an early reference to Sunday, the first day of the week, the day of resurrection; and a description of pure worship in the Spirit. The seven lamps, familiar to anyone who saw a seven-branched candlestick in a Jewish synagogue, represent the seven churches to whom the letter was addressed. Standing

13 among them is **one like a son of man** (lit. 'a man', i.e. a human being), Jesus Christ in his risen humanity vested with the glory of deity. This is depicted in terms of the robe and girdle of the high priest (Exod. 28.4), the white hair of the Ancient of Days (Dan. 7.9), the flaming eyes of divine knowledge (eyes that pierce the hearts of men), the feet of burnished brass like Ezekiel's cherubim (Ezek. 1.7), and the voice like the sound of rushing waters, from the same prophet (Ezek. 43.2), demonstrating his strength and inspiring fear at his majesty. The seven stars are the seven angels, the heavenly counterpart of the seven churches (the imagery is perhaps taken from the seven known planets of the time), hanging like a necklace of jewels in the right hand of the figure.

It is, however, not helpful to analyse too closely the details of John's vision. Based on the angel of Daniel (10.5–6), it gathered together divine manifestations from various parts of the OT and put them together to give readers a picture of the risen Christ in order to call forth from the readers the same response of awe and wonder which the prophet himself experienced in his trance.

It was believed that no one could see God and live. John fell on his feet at the vision (as the women fell at the feet of the risen Christ), but

18 the figure lifted him up: **Do not be afraid. I am the first and the last, and I am the living one; for I was dead and now I am alive for evermore, and I hold the keys of Death and Death's domain.** Christ has not only resumed his eternal life which he had with the Father before the world began; he has also through his resurrection entered upon a new and victorious life in which death itself is conquered. Hades, *Sheol*, was the place of departed souls in Jewish mythology.

1 Corinthians 15. 12–20

Four of the epistles in Eastertide are taken from this chapter of 1 Corinthians, in which the apostle taught about life after death. Easter 3 Year 1

(1 Cor. 15.1–11) affirms as in a creed the Christian faith in the resurrection
of Jesus. This passage deals with the resurrection of Christians.

Belief in our own resurrection, said the apostle, is rooted in faith in
Christ's resurrection. Arguing against some who attempted to set limits
to the resurrection of Christians or who did not believe that it was possible,
he pointed out that, if what they said was true, then the Christian had
nothing to preach and nothing to believe. **Our gospel is null and void,**
14 **and so is your faith.** The apostles would then be shown to be lying
against God, because they had said of him that he had raised Jesus from
the dead. Faith would be a delusion, sins would not have been forgiven,
19 believers who had died would be lost for ever, and **we of all men are
most to be pitied** because, believing that in the risen Christ we had
everything, in the dead Christ we would have nothing.

But in fact Christ has been raised from the dead. Furthermore, he is
the first instalment of that crop which promises the ultimate offering of
the whole: since he has been raised, the rest of mankind can also be
raised in him.

20 The image of the **firstfruits of the harvest of the dead** may have
been in Paul's mind because of references to the Passover which he had
made in this letter. A feature of the Passover celebrations was the presentation of the sheaf from the first cutting of the corn in the fields as a promise of a greater harvest to come.

Colossians 3. 1–11

To be risen with Christ is the Pauline equivalent to being born again in
baptism: 'When we were baptized into union with Christ Jesus we were
baptized into his death. . . . In Christ Jesus the life-giving law of the
Spirit has set you free from the law of sin and death' (Rom. 6.3, 8.2).
The baptized, therefore, must no longer be concerned with the trivial
matters of this life but must direct their attention to the important matters
1 of heaven; for it is there that Christ is, risen and **seated at the right
hand of God.** The right hand of God is the symbol for God's activity
in power among men, and the ascension to the right hand of God was
the early Church's symbolic way of describing how Christ shared in the
sovereignty of God and yet remained distinct as a person. The Church
was being led towards the formation of the doctrine of the Trinity.

In a true sense, through repentance, faith, baptism, and the receiving
of the Holy Spirit, we have already shared in Christ's resurrection; and
the Christian lives, not just in imitation of Christ, but motivated and
guided by the resurrection life of Christ within him by virtue of his

spiritual union with God in the power of the Spirit. Just as Christ's once-for-all death and resurrection in history foreshadowed the future baptismal death-and-resurrection of Christians, so it also foreshadows the future resurrection of the whole personality of the Christian beyond his natural death. The Christian's baptism, therefore, looks forward to 3 the fulfilment of that resurrection beyond the grave: You died; and now your life lies hidden with Christ in God.

Paul based on this teaching his insistence that the moral conduct of the Christian would demonstrate this risen life of Christ within him. God's dreadful judgement (*orge*, wrath, the reaction of a personal God 6 against sin and evil) is impending. Paul's list of sins and his injunctions may be a form of catechetical instruction given to converts before their baptism. Expressions such as 'putting to death', 'laying aside', 'discarding' and 'putting on' originated in this kind of teaching and were ritualized in the putting on of the white robe of the chrism in the later Christian rites of initiation. The apostle teaches in this passage that through baptism man is renewed in that image of his Creator which was his in the beginning, but which has been spoilt by disobedience and sin. Paul 10 conceived of this as a continuous process (is being constantly renewed). With that restored image the social distinctions between men and the sexual distinctions between men and women disappear, as all are one in Christ.

* **Matthew 28. 1–10**

Matthew based his account of the resurrection on Mark 16.1–8 (see Easter Day Year 1), but with alterations and additions. In Mark the women approach the tomb to complete the work of anointing the body of Jesus, which remained to be done after the hasty burial before the sabbath began. On arrival they find the stone which sealed the tomb already removed and they see inside a young man in white who tells them that the resurrection had already occurred before sending them off with the message for the disciples. In Matthew there is no mention of the anointing; 1 the women came to look at the grave. But what they see is a terrifying accompaniment of the resurrection, an earthquake and the descent of the angel to roll away the stone and sit on it. The guards who had been placed over the tomb collapse with fear.

The Marcan narrative is resumed in verse 5 when the angel announces the resurrection which Jesus had foretold (12.40, 16.21, etc.), and that the disciples are to meet him in Galilee. Then in verse 8 Matthew used his own sources to tell of an encounter with the risen Christ which the women had on their errand. When Jesus greets them, they fall prostrate—the position of adoration, but also of fear in the presence of deity—and he repeats the message about meeting him in Galilee. Matthew was not so much concerned to explain how the resurrection happened as to describe the event in terms of an OT theophany. The God of Israel, as of old, was now bringing deliverance with his mighty hand and outstretched arm.

1 The other Mary was Mary the mother of James (Mark 16.1).

* John 20. 1–10 (11–18)
1 While it was still dark would be somewhere between 3 and 6 a.m. Although only Mary of Magdala is mentioned, the 'we' of verse 2 suggests that there were others with her, as in the Synoptic accounts. The stone covering the entrance of the small cave-tomb, a natural rock formation or artificially constructed as a sepulchre, had been removed, and she suspected a grave robbery. She ran to tell Peter and the other disciple,
2 the one whom Jesus loved, traditionally recognized as John.

The visit of the two disciples to the tomb confirmed the discovery. More than that, it demonstrated that the disappearance of the body was
5 not the result of a robbery but of a supernatural act: the linen wrappings, which would have been disturbed or taken away if there had been a theft of the corpse, were lying in such a way as to suggest that the spiritual and glorified body of Christ had passed through them without disturbing them. Only the cloth which had wrapped round the corpse's head appeared to have been removed to some distance. This cloth would in any case have been separate from the winding-sheet, and John's words may mean no more than that it was observed to be still in this separate position. As a result of seeing the empty tomb and the grave clothes, John came to a faith in the resurrection which Peter apparently had not reached at that time. But the teaching of the OT as interpreted by the early Church, an interpretation initiated by Jesus Christ himself and guided by the Holy Spirit, about the resurrection now took on a meaning for them.
12 The two angels play a less important role in the fourth Gospel than the figure(s) in the tomb in the synoptic Gospels. They merely provide Mary of Magdala with an opportunity to explain why she is weeping. It was to her that the risen Christ appeared first. She did not recognize him at once; she thought he was the gardener. In an allegorical sense he was 'the gardener' who came to reopen the garden of Eden for sinful man. The Fathers expounded the incident in this way, though it is not obvious that the evangelist thought of it so. Then, when Mary did
16 recognize him, she used the term Rabbuni, the word for the divine Lord,

a stronger term than Rabbi—recognizing him in an act of faith like that
of Thomas later that day (20.28. See Easter 1 Year 1).

The fourth Gospel does not picture the ascension as a separate event,
though the words of Christ to Mary as she clung to him indicate that the
completion of Christ's glorification took place when he returned to his
Father's side. The way is prepared for the Johannine Pentecost (20.22.
See Easter 1 Year 1). Although Jesus Christ accepted the disciples as
17 my brothers, he still made a distinction between his relationship to the
Father and theirs by mentioning the Father twice as 'my' and 'your'.
The unique relationship of 'God's only Son, he who is nearest to the
Father's heart' (1.18) remained.

The fourth Gospel's presentation of the resurrection is in striking
contrast to that of the Synoptics, especially Matthew. There is no mighty
act in which the hosts of evil are routed and the power of God vindicated.
Rather, the resurrection takes place quietly and irresistibly, like the rising
of the sun at dawn, when the shadows of the night are slowly removed
and the freshness of the garden sweetens the beginning of a new day.

* Mark 16. 1–8

The resurrection of Christ is the centre of salvation-history, the dramatic
event prepared for and promised by God for thousands of years. With
great simplicity Mark told the first effect it had on some of Jesus' followers.
It was not the disciples who discovered the empty tomb but the women
who, practically unnoticed throughout his Gospel, had followed Jesus to
his crucifixion and watched from afar. The spices had been brought after
sundown on the sabbath in preparation for the embalming of the body.
A visit to the grave for the purpose would be entirely natural. The stone
across the sepulchre would keep out marauders and animals.

The great moments of the Gospels are often marked by angelic activity,
though the evangelist did not stress the supernatural nature of the figure
5 seated at the tomb. He is a youth wearing a white robe. Some commentators have suggested that it was Mark himself, who had arrived
earlier at the tomb and realized the fulfilment of Christ's sayings that
he would rise from the dead. The young man's only function was to
explain that Jesus had been raised up and to send a message to the
disciples through the women. Jesus had promised to meet his disciples in
Galilee, the scene of much of his earthly ministry. The special mention of
Peter among the disciples is a feature of this Gospel.

The fear and awe of the women is the fear and awe of humanity in the
presence of a mighty act of God; eventually they recovered from their

tongue-tied terror sufficiently to tell the disciples what had happened,
but if the evangelist ended his Gospel at the words, **They said nothing**
8 **to anybody, for they were afraid,** he left this to be understood in the
continuous teaching of the Church down to his own day. The real evidence
of the resurrection for his readers was the presence of the Christian
community to which they belonged and the knowledge of the risen Lord
in their own lives.

THE RESURRECTION APPEARANCES

When the narratives of the resurrection given by the four evangelists are
compared, it can be seen that they display far more differences than do the
narratives of the passion. From this, biblical scholarship has deduced
that the stories in question were given a stereotyped form at a later stage
than the passion narratives. The passion was a single event, the core of the
apostolic preaching; the resurrection appearances were many. ('He
showed himself to these men after his death, and gave ample proof that
he was alive: over a period of forty days he appeared to them and taught
them about the kingdom of God' Acts 1.3.) Neither Paul nor any of the
evangelists attempted to give all the events. They made their choice, no
wider than was necessary to proclaim fittingly the one great message. Under
these circumstances a fixed form of narrative about the resurrection was
not established so quickly, and several lines of tradition were formed with
divergences in detail. These divergences go back to the first Easter morning when the women went to the tomb.

We need not elaborate on the divergences here, but we should note that
the four accounts agree on the main themes: the empty tomb, the
appearance of an angelic messenger, and the message—the Lord is risen
and is alive. And behind the narrative is the awareness that we are in
touch with events beyond this world, events which can only be grasped
by men with a vivid faith in the living God, who works with power to
fulfil his holy and gracious purposes. The gospel of the resurrection can
only be interpreted within this faith; then the rise and power of the early
Church can be explained.